The old song belongs to our old selves, the new song is proper to persons made new. The old covenant sings an old song, the new covenant demands a new song. Under the old covenant the promises dealt with temporal, earthly benefits, and therefore anyone who is in love with earthly goods is still singing the old song, but anyone who wants to sing a new song must love the things of eternity. Such love is itself new and eternal; it is always new because it never grows old. . . . And this song is of peace, a song of charity.

St. Augustine

Hark! the glad celestial hymn
angel choirs above are raising;
cherubim and seraphim,
in unceasing chorus praising,
fill the heavens with sweet accord:
"Holy, holy, holy Lord!"

Lo, the apostolic train
joins your sacred name to hallow;
prophets swell the glad refrain,
and the white-robed martyrs follow;
and from morn to set of sun,
through the church the song goes on.

from the *Te Deum*
(vers. Ignaz Franz,
trans. Clarence A. Walworth)

The CALVIN INSTITUTE OF CHRISTIAN WORSHIP LITURGICAL STUDIES Series, edited by John D. Witvliet, is designed to promote reflection on the history, theology, and practice of Christian worship and to stimulate worship renewal in Christian congregations. Contributions include writings by pastoral worship leaders from a wide range of communities and scholars from a wide range of disciplines. The ultimate goal of these contributions is to nurture worship practices that are spiritually vital and theologically rooted.

Published

Gather into One: Praying and Singing Globally
C. Michael Hawn

The Substance of Things Seen: Art, Faith, and the Christian Community
Robin M. Jensen

*Wonderful Words of Life: Hymns in American
Protestant History and Theology*
Richard J. Mouw and Mark A Noll, Editors

*Discerning the Spirits:
A Guide to Thinking about Christian Worship Today*
Cornelius Plantinga Jr. and Sue A. Rozeboom

Voicing God's Psalms
Calvin Seerveld

*My Only Comfort: Death, Deliverance,
and Discipleship in the Music of Bach*
Calvin R. Stapert

A New Song for an Old World:
Musical Thought in the Early Church
Calvin R. Stapert

An Architecture of Immanence
Mark A. Torgerson

A More Profound Alleluia: Theology and Worship in Harmony
Leanne Van Dyk, Editor

Christian Worship in Reformed Churches Past and Present
Lukas Vischer, Editor

A NEW SONG *for an* OLD WORLD

Musical Thought in the Early Church

Calvin R. Stapert

WILLIAM B. EERDMANS PUBLISHING COMPANY

GRAND RAPIDS, MICHIGAN

Published 2007 by

Wm. B. Eerdmans Publishing Co.

Grand Rapids, Michigan

Library of Congress Cataloging-in-Publication Data

Stapert, Calvin, 1942-

A new song for an old world: musical thought in the early church / Calvin R. Stapert.

p.   cm.

ISBN 978-0-8028-3219-1 (pbk.: alk. paper)

1. Music — Religious aspects — Christianity.   2. Church music.

3. Music — Philosophy and aesthetics.   4. Public worship.

5. Bible. O.T. Psalms — Criticism, interpretation, etc.   I. Title.

BV290.S82 2007

264′.209015 — dc22

2006028677

www.eerdmans.com

Dedicated to the memory of my mother

Jessie Broekema Stapert

who sang psalms while she worked around the house

Contents

Foreword

The Recovery of Ancient Christianity

This volume represents many years of Calvin Stapert's reflections and learning about the earliest centuries of the church. As a student and now a colleague of Dr. Stapert, I know that a nearly finished manuscript of this volume has been marinating in his computer hard-drive for some time. It is an honor to mark its publication in this brief foreword.

Despite its lengthy gestation, this volume could hardly be appearing at a more propitious time. Interest in the early church appears to be near an all-time high. The "emergent," or "emerging," church movement, the rise of postmodernism, and the explosion of Christianity in the global South and East have all fueled interest in the recovery of the spirit and practice of the early church, an interest sometimes branded as "Ancient Future" Christianity.

The significant question for us now is *how* we will return to the early church. Will we simply look there for the kinds of things we are already predisposed to like? Will we refer to the early church simply to buttress arguments for ideas or practices that we are proposing as innovations? Or will we let these early Christian witnesses interrogate, challenge, and instruct us? Indeed, many discussions of the early or ancient church have a kind of romanticized mystical glow about them. We like the feel of "mystery." We long for a unity in the body of Christ that seems impossible to achieve in an era with so many denominations and splinter groups. We long for a world that is not polarized by red and blue state religious rhetoric. We sense the poverty of individualism and commercialism that has come into our contemporary faith. And we project all of these hopes into what we choose to remember from the ancients.

The good news in this is that we are returning to some remarkably fine sources, to communities and leaders who struggled mightily to practice vital and faithful Christianity, to texts that bear witness to epic struggles of faith and probe deeply the meaning of the gospel for the Christian life. Even when our "use" of the early church is not always well considered, the target of our reference ends up being a very rich source for learning. The challenge for us is to draw on this recent interest in the early church and to channel it toward disciplined historical encounters. One of the best antidotes to simplistic summaries of this or any period is simply taking the time to digest the now readily available documents that come to us from that ancient period.

This is what Calvin Stapert does so well. As a teacher, Dr. Stapert always asked those of us who studied with him never to remain content with textbook summaries, but to deal with the ancients in their own words. As a writer, he continues the practice, exposing us to texts that have gone largely unread in contemporary discussions about musical practice. The result is a volume that shows us that the wisdom of the early church is much more nuanced than we might have guessed. We learn about lofty Trinitarian hymns but also nitty-gritty disputes about the decaying effects of pagan musical practices. We sense the grandeur of metaphysical theories of music but also the down-to-earth economic and socio-cultural realities that demanded a Christian response.

May all of us who read the pages of this book not only find inspiration for ideas we already like, but also find ourselves challenged by weighty themes that we are tempted to ignore or downplay.

The Development of Western Music

This volume also has much to contribute to an entirely different conversation, one more at home in the music departments of research universities and liberal arts colleges than church ministry conferences.

Standard music history and appreciation courses in many public and private colleges and universities include units of study on ancient practices of music, both Western and non-Western. They must do so, by and large, without having ancient musical scores, remnants of ancient instruments, or other clues about daily musical practices. Especially for music in the West, this study is shaped through encounters with ancient philosophical texts, most often of Plato and Boethius, with an occasional reference to Augustine. Less well known, but certainly significant in the history of Western music, is the testimony of the ancient Christian writers analyzed in this volume. Thanks to the work of James MacKinnon and other scholars, frequently cited in this volume, we now have ready access to these texts. This volume represents a major step forward in distilling this material for a wide audience.

One particular challenge in standard music histories is to keep the church in view as the communal context for the reflections of writers such as Clement, Tertullian, Ambrose, Chrysostom, and Augustine. Modernist and secularist historiography tends to find little of interest in communal religious life, and thus musical textbooks have often ignored many of the themes probed in this volume. The rise of pluralist and postmodern sensibilities, however, once again offer opportunities for taking seriously the explicitly religious and communal practices that form the context for intellectual history.

Though this volume is explicitly designed to contribute to contemporary discussions about faithful Christian practice, its care with the primary sources and its awareness of the ecclesial context for these sources commend it as a useful resource for musicologists and social, cultural, and intellectual historians in a wide variety of settings.

JOHN D. WITVLIET
Calvin Institute of Christian Worship
Calvin College and Calvin Theological Seminary
Grand Rapids, Michigan

Preface

Footnotes for primary sources first locate the quotation by section numbers (e.g., V, ix, 12) in the originals; these are then followed by page numbers that refer to the translations from which the quotations were taken. Quotations from older translations of the church fathers and other ancient writers have sometimes been slightly modernized. All quotations from the Bible, except those embedded in other quotations, are taken from the English Standard Version.

The debt I owe to an enormous company of translators and other scholars — a company far exceeding the number represented in the notes — is incalculable. Here I can only offer my thanks to them as a group for all they have taught me, and apologize for where I have been a poor learner. And beyond my gratitude for what I have personally learned from them, I am grateful for all their labors that have enabled the contemporary church to keep in touch with the early Christians.

I want to single out two colleagues and friends for special acknowledgment. John Witvliet and Sue Rozeboom showed interest and gave encouragement all along the way. Near the completion, they both read the entire manuscript and made several helpful suggestions. It goes without saying (though I'm saying it) that all the defects that remain are my responsibility.

CHAPTER 1

Prelude: Honor Father and Mother

Remember the days of old; consider the years of many generations.

Deuteronomy 32:7

Are we at liberty to ignore the past? Do the great teachers of the Church . . . not possess a — certainly not heavenly — but, even so, earthly, human "authority"? We should not be too ready to say, No. To my mind the whole question of tradition falls under the Fifth Commandment: Honour father and mother! Certainly that is a limited authority; we have to obey God more than father and mother. But we have also to obey father and mother. . . . There is no question of bondage and constraint. It is merely that in the Church the same kind of obedience as, I hope, you pay to your father and mother, is demanded of you towards the Church's past, towards the "elders" of the Church.

Karl Barth

The title of F. F. Bruce's history of the early church, *The Spreading Flame,* evokes an image of the miraculous spread of the newly established church in the first few centuries of her existence. The title recalls the origin of the church at Pentecost, when the Holy Spirit descended on the apostles in tongues of fire. From a small band of Christ's followers, largely uneducated and without the political and economic power the world thinks necessary for success, Christianity spread until it permeated the entire Mediterranean world and eventually all of Europe.

The flame of Christianity spread to the accompaniment of a "new song," which meant, of course, far more than audible music. In various contexts, "new song" referred to Christ, the Word of God, or to the Christian life. Clement of Alexandria wrote:

> [I]nasmuch as the Word was from the first, He was and is the source of all things; but inasmuch as He has now assumed the name Christ, consecrated of old, and worthy of power, he has been called by me the New Song. . . .
>
> This is the "new song," the manifestation of the Word that was in the beginning, and before the beginning.[1]

Regarding Psalm 40:3, St. Augustine said:

> He put a new song into my mouth. What new song? A hymn to our God. Possibly you were accustomed to sing hymns to other gods, old hymns; it was the old person who sang them, not the new person. Let the new person come to birth and sing a new song; let the renewed person love what has made him or her new. What is more ancient than God, who exists before all things, with no end and no beginning? Yet when you come back to him he is new for you. When you went away from him you grew old. . . .

Commenting on Psalm 149:1, he added:

> The old song belongs to our old selves, the new song is proper to persons made new. The old covenant sings an old song, the new covenant demands a new song. Under the old covenant the promises dealt with temporal, earthly benefits, and therefore anyone who is in love with earthly goods is still singing the old song. But anyone who wants to sing a new song must love the things of eternity. Such love is itself new and eternal; it is always new because it never grows old. . . .
>
> And this song is of peace, a song of charity.

And on Psalm 147:1:

---

1. *Exhortation to the Heathen* I; p. 173.

Do you want to sing and play psalms? Then not only must your voice sing God's praises but your actions must keep in tune with your voice. After you have been singing with your voice you will have to be quiet for a while, but sing with your life in such a way that you never fall silent. . . .

Sing with your voice, then, to edify and encourage yourself and others by the sounds that appeal to the ears, but do not let your heart be dumb or your life be silent. . . .[2]

Although "new song" was typically used in an allegorical sense in early Christian writings, it was not devoid of literal meaning. The early Christian writers insisted that the songs of one's voice and the song of one's life both be in harmony with the "new song." Unfortunately, the sounds of the songs of the early Christians have vanished irretrievably beyond the range of our ears. The music of the early Christians, like nearly all the music of their time, was transmitted orally and never written down. The Greeks had developed a system of musical notation, but only a few fragments of notated music from that period remain, and only one of those fragments has a Christian text.[3] There is no way for us to recover reliable sound images of some five centuries of music from an area that was geographically vast and culturally diverse.

Even though the sounds of the music of the early Christian era have vanished, we can learn something about early Christian musical thought from the writings of the time. Although those writings are numerous, only two are completely devoted to music: St. Augustine's *On Music* (*De musica*, five highly technical books on metrics and one difficult philosophical book) and a sermon by Niceta of Remensiana. Otherwise, the remains of early Christian writing about music are scattered through diverse genres on diverse subjects, usually in brief references.[4] We may lament this situation, but there is a bright side. The lack of systematic discussion and the variety of contexts in which the musical references appear point to something important: music was not something early Christians thought about in isolation. It was involved in their thinking on everything, from the cosmos to the details of daily living. In their speculative thought they looked

2. *Expositions of the Psalms* II, p. 199; VI, pp. 492, 421.

3. That is the so-called Oxyrhyncus Hymn; see below, p. 170.

4. For a convenient and ample sampling of representative early Christian references to music, see *Music in Early Christian Literature*, ed. James McKinnon.

at "the cosmos musically, and at music cosmically."[5] And when they discussed life's activities of work and play, eating and drinking, worship, civic ceremonies, social events, and the like, they often referred to music.

I have written this book as an attempt to help the church get in touch with early Christian thought about music. The overriding reason why I did this is expressed in the quotation from Karl Barth at the head of this chapter. In obedience to the fifth commandment, Christians now — no less than at any other time — need to recall the words of their parents. Forgetting or ignoring what they said is no way to show them the honor that our Lord commands.

The church today, influenced as it is by a "now" generation, is especially in need of Barth's admonition. Unfortunately, an indifferent attitude toward the past is all too prevalent in today's church. Although the recent surge of interest in early Christianity is heartening, it is too early to say that the problem Robert E. Webber pointed out several years ago has gone away. In *Common Roots* he pointed to a tendency among evangelical Protestants to leap "from the New Testament to the present." He went on to say: "Certainly the substance of Christian teaching is found in the New Testament, but to ignore the development of Christian truth in history is a grave mistake."[6] By ignoring her past, the church, in the words of D. H. Williams, is attempting "to stand tall without the deep roots of its history." He quotes Loren Mead regarding the danger of the "tyranny of the new": "When the new way is considered the only way, there is no continuity, fads become the new gospel and in Paul's words, the church is 'blown to and fro by every wind of doctrine.'"[7] Christians need to listen again to earlier voices; listening to them can enrich, broaden, and correct our thinking.

In saying this, I am not claiming that earlier generations got everything right. They were, of course, as prone to error as we are. But we are not likely to be susceptible to the errors they committed, and whatever truth they got a hold of is likely to be truth that we have long since forgotten. "Every age," says C. S. Lewis, "has its own outlook."

It is specially good at seeing certain truths and specially liable to make certain mistakes. We all, therefore, need the books that will cor-

5. Joscelyn Godwin, "The Revival of Speculative Music," p. 373.
6. Webber, *Common Roots*, p. 8.
7. Williams, *Retrieving the Tradition*, pp. 7, 11.

rect the characteristic mistakes of our own period. And that means the old books. All contemporary writers share to some extent the contemporary outlook. . . . Nothing strikes me more when I read the controversies of past ages than the fact that both sides were usually assuming without question a good deal which we should now absolutely deny. They thought that they were as completely opposed as two sides could be, but in fact they were all the time secretly united — united with each other and against earlier and later ages — by a great mass of common assumptions. We may be sure that the characteristic blindness of the twentieth century — the blindness about which posterity will ask, "But how could they have thought that?" — lies where we have never suspected it. . . . None of us can fully escape this blindness, but we shall certainly increase it, and weaken our guard against it, if we read only modern books. Where they are true they will give us truths which we half knew already. Where they are false they will aggravate the error with which we are already dangerously ill. The only palliative is to keep the clean sea breeze of the centuries blowing through our minds. . . .[8]

I think this is true, in particular, with regard to pre-Enlightenment periods. For a long time now, Christian thinkers have recognized that much of the illness in Western civilization — and in the church as well — can be traced to the Enlightenment and its Romantic offspring. Abraham Kuyper saw it as "the expulsion of God from practical and theoretical life."[9]

Voltaire's mad cry, "Down with the scoundrel," was aimed at Christ himself, but this cry was merely the expression of the most hidden thought from which the French Revolution sprang. The fanatic outcry of another philosopher, "We no more need a God," and the odious shibboleth, "No God, no Master," of the Convention; — these were the sacrilegious watchwords which at that time heralded the liberation of man as an emancipation from all Divine Authority.[10]

Many contemporary Christian historians agree with Kuyper that "the French Revolution at the close of the last [eighteenth] century, and in Ger-

8. Lewis, Introduction to *St. Athanasius on the Incarnation,* pp. 4-5.
9. Kuyper, *Lectures on Calvinism,* pp. 23-24.
10. Kuyper, *Lectures on Calvinism,* p. 10.

5

man philosophy in the course of the present [nineteenth] century, form together a life-system which is diametrically opposed to that of our fathers." Ronald Wells, for example, warns:

> It is important for Christians to realize, in a way that many Christians since the eighteenth century have not realized, that they must not be on the defensive on behalf of religion against irreligion. The Enlightenment faith is a religion. . . . But the difficult point for Christians in our time to recognize is that traditional Christianity, both Protestant and Catholic, while continuing and flourishing, became increasingly marginal in a world whose institutions were based on the religious faith of the Enlightenment. . . . The main contours of developments in Western civilization were increasingly founded on the alternate faith presented by the Enlightenment.[11]

This applies to the "main contours of developments" in music as well as to any other area of human activity. Yet Christians today live in a society whose musical thought is based on post-Enlightenment presuppositions, and the music we typically identify with as "ours" — whether we have "classical" or "popular" inclinations — is also overwhelmingly post-Enlightenment. Our musical thought and practice have largely bought into the ideas and practices that came out of the Enlightenment and Romanticism.

I don't mean to suggest that all post-Enlightenment music is unhealthy or that all of its musical thought is erroneous. Far from it. I think that Christians can affirm much of it. But I do suggest that our thinking about music is truncated and twisted because we are the unwitting heirs of musical thought that has its roots in secular, naturalistic Enlightenment and post-Enlightenment thought, which was usually indifferent to — and often hostile toward — Christian thought.

This situation is not unique to music. Christian thought on the other arts has had the same affliction. In his foreword to *Literature Through the Eyes of Faith* by Susan Gallagher and Roger Lundin, Nicholas Wolterstorff says: "Most Christian reflections on literature, over the last century, have been, in a rough-and-ready way, Romantic."[12] The same can be said of music. But the problem runs deeper in music. Pre-Enlightenment litera-

---

11. Wells, *History Through the Eyes of Faith*, p. 137.
12. Gallagher and Lundin, *Literature Through the Eyes of Faith*, p. x.

ture — Christian and non-Christian alike — has far more currency than does pre-Enlightenment music. We have never seen a time when Homer, Sophocles, Virgil, Augustine, Dante, Chaucer, and Milton were not read. And literary theory, though it has often found much to disagree with in Aristotle, Horace, and Sidney, for example, has at least recognized their existence. There is no parallel situation in music. Although the last few decades have seen an enormous growth of interest in "early music," its impact on the overall musical scene is still relatively small. And, more to the point of this book, pre-Enlightenment musical thought has all but vanished. Some music students are still required to read a few bits of pre-Enlightenment musical thought; but even for most music students, let alone the general populace, the musical ideas of Plato or St. Augustine, of John Calvin or Andreas Werckmeister, are largely unknown. Furthermore, the little that is known is considered nothing more than an outdated, irrelevant curiosity.

According to Gallagher and Lundin, "a Christian understanding of literature is grounded in beliefs derived from the Scriptures and developed through the course of Christian history."[13] The same can be said of a Christian understanding of music. But we have ignored all but the latest installments of a conversation about music that has been going on for centuries. The part that influences our thinking most pays little heed either to Scripture or Christian history. So I say, again, that Christians need to listen to earlier voices in the conversation — especially those coming from the first few centuries of the Christian era.

There are two reasons why I believe that, of all our ancestral voices, those of the early church are the most important for us to retrieve. First, they are the least heard today, at least in the area of music; in fact, I would say that for all practical purposes they are lost to the church today. Early Christian musical thought has been vanishing from the church's mind for centuries. If it is not extinct, it certainly is an endangered species, especially in Protestant branches of the church. The musical thought of sixteenth-century reformers such as Luther and Calvin was still heavily indebted to the early church fathers; but those vestiges of the church fathers' thought were quite effectively scrubbed away by the Enlightenment.

A second reason for going back specifically to the early Christians is that I believe their thought on music has particular relevance for us today.

13. Gallagher and Lundin, *Literature Through the Eyes of Faith*, p. 3.

Admittedly, when I read them, I am at times painfully aware of the truth in Peter Brown's observation that we are "dealing with a Christianity whose back is firmly turned toward us, untroubled by our own most urgent, and legitimate, questions."[14] In spite of this, I am convinced that they have a peculiar relevance for us because in some ways their time and ours are similar, and their response to their time was firmly based on God's ever-relevant Word.

Many thinkers of the last half of the twentieth century have noted the similarities between our age and the early Christian era. For example, in 1949 historian Herbert Butterfield wrote: "We are back for the first time in something like the earliest centuries of Christianity, and those early centuries afford some relevant clues of the kind of attitude to adopt."[15] A few years later Daniel D. Williams wrote:

> The temper of our own times and the form of our own problems bear a clear kinship to those of the age in which he [Augustine] wrote. One of our astute political analysts [Hannah Arendt] calls him "the one great thinker who lived in a period which in some respects resembled our own more than any other period in recorded history." His thought was hammered out amid the shattering of a great civilization. Ours, too, is a time of world-shaking struggle, of revolutionary forces set loose.[16]

The similarities did not lessen as the twentieth century moved on. More recently another historian, John Van Dyk, drew the parallel as follows:

> In the Roman Empire the body of Christ stood antithetically over against the pagan spirit of *Romanitas* and orientalism in all its dimensions and in all its expressions. In our contemporary world new spirits have arisen, in some ways parallel to those of the ancient Roman world, and surely as powerful and pervasive. Just as *Romanitas* represented the official state-promoted life style, so a secular materialistic spirit of economism grips our western culture and is promoted by government and consumer alike. And as the oriental religions consti-

14. Brown, *The Body and Society,* p. xvii.
15. Butterfield, *Christianity and History,* p. 135.
16. Williams, "The Significance of St. Augustine Today," p. 4. The quotation from Hannah Arendt is from "Understanding and Politics," *The Partisan Review* (July-Aug. 1953): 390.

tuted an undercurrent to *Romanitas,* so the contemporary search for the security of drugs, astrology, mysticism, or eastern religions underlies western industrial society.[17]

Not to belabor the point, but to make it from a different perspective, I quote the novelist Madeleine L'Engle:

> When I am looking for theologians to stimulate my creativity, theologians who are contemporary enough to speak to these last years of our troubled century, I turn to the Byzantine and Cappadocian Fathers of the early years of the Christian era, because their world was . . . like ours. . . . In the first few centuries A.D., Rome was breaking up; civilization was changing as radically as is our own. . . . Such people as St. Chrysostom, Basil the Great, Gregory of Nyssa and his brilliant sister, Macrina, were facing the same kind of change and challenge that we are, and from them I get great courage.[18]

All this testimony, of course, does not prove that the musical thought of the early Christians has relevance today, but it strongly suggests the possibility. I do not know when it was or what it was that first directed me to suspect that early Christians might have something to teach us about music; but it was a long time ago, and it was a suspicion and a direction in my thinking that has never left me. And more than merely staying with me, that suspicion grew and became a conviction, a conviction strong enough to produce the pages that lie ahead. My conviction, in fact, became strong enough to overcome more than the usual difficulties of writing a book; it overcame my fear that I had no business attempting such a project. To say that the field of early Christian studies is vast is to be guilty of understatement. The times were complex, and the amount of material that has survived is staggering (yet, obviously, very fragmentary and fraught with all kinds of difficulties of interpretation). And the amount of secondary literature on even one major figure — St. Augustine, say — is overwhelming. Only scholars working full time in this field can claim any degree of mastery of it. I cannot make such a claim. Whatever scholarly expertise I have is in other areas of music, and my teaching assignments have offered me few opportunities to spend extended portions of time in the early Chris-

---

17. Van Dyk, "Church and World in Early Christianity," p. 7.
18. L'Engle, *Walking on Water,* p. 88.

tian era. So, though I do have some scholarly and musical qualifications, I must confess that I am very much an amateur in the field of early Christian studies. But since no one better qualified has seemed to be forthcoming with the book I thought needed writing, I have cautiously ventured forward where those more qualified have feared to tread. I hope that what I have written here will not do a disservice to the early Christian thinkers, whom I admire deeply; and whatever its faults, I hope it will be of service to the church I love deeply.

What kind of service might that be? Can what an amateur writes on a subject be of use? C. S. Lewis must have felt the weight of such questions when he wrote *Reflections on the Psalms,* for at the beginning he announces: "This is not a work of scholarship. . . . I write for the unlearned about things in which I am unlearned myself." Then he goes on to explain in what way such a book could still be useful.

> It often happens that two schoolboys can solve difficulties in their work for one another better than the master can. . . . The fellow-pupil can help more than the master because he knows less. The difficulty we want him to explain is one he has recently met. The expert met it so long ago that he has forgotten. He sees the whole subject, by now, in such a different light that he cannot conceive what is really troubling the pupil; he sees a dozen other difficulties which ought to be troubling him but aren't.
>
> In this book, then, I write as one amateur to another. . . . I am "comparing notes," not presuming to instruct.[19]

I suspect, however, that I do not have exactly the same relationship to my readers that Lewis did to his. Most of his had probably read and heard the Psalms many times; I assume that most of mine have read little of what early Christians wrote. So my task is not so much "comparing notes" as it is showing my notes to others, hoping that doing so will encourage them to turn for instruction to some particularly good teachers, the early Christian writers themselves.

The plan of this book is simple. After a foundational chapter on music in the New Testament, there is a chapter sketching the main events and developments during the second and early third centuries, along with some of

19. Lewis, *Reflections on the Psalms,* pp. 1-2.

the main themes in Christian musical thought of the time. After this general and broad sketch, there are two chapters that each present a second-third-century church father and his musical thought. I have chosen Clement of Alexandria and Tertullian because the quantity of their references to music is relatively large and because they were quite different from each other in many ways. Clement was Greek-speaking and kindly disposed toward Greek philosophy; Tertullian was Latin-speaking and vehemently opposed to the church's appropriation of anything pagan, including Greek philosophy.

Chapters 6-8 follow the pattern established in chapters 3-5: a general introduction to the period — in this case the late third century through the early fifth century — is followed by two chapters devoted to individual fathers. Again, I chose Saints Ambrose and John Chrysostom to be representative here partly on the basis of the quantity of musical references in their writings. As with the first pair, Ambrose is Latin-speaking and John Chrysostom is Greek-speaking; but apart from the linguistic difference, the contrast between the two is not as stark as between Clement and Tertullian. I chose these two for this period because they best represent the key strands of early Christian thought on music. In addition, I must admit that some personal favoritism entered into my choice of Chrysostom, and Ambrose seemed a logical choice because, of all the fathers, he is the one who still carries some associations with music based on his hymns and the ancient music repertory known as Ambrosian Chant.

Chapters 3-8 contain a sizable proportion of historical and biographical information; even so, it is still very sketchy. Nevertheless, I hope that there is enough material to give the reader some sense of the circumstances that gave rise to the various, scattered, and usually brief statements about music found in early Christian literature. By the end of chapter 8, if not before, it should be clear that the church fathers, despite their differences, show a remarkable consistency in their views on music, regarding both what music they rejected and denounced and what they affirmed and promoted. Chapters 9 and 10, then, take a closer look at what they rejected and what they affirmed.

Chapter 11 is somewhat *sui generis:* it deals with St. Augustine's thought on music, but unlike the other four chapters devoted to specific fathers, this chapter is not broad in its treatment. If it were, it would be largely another rehearsal of familiar themes. It is valuable to recognize that a mind of the magnitude of Augustine's was in harmony with the other fathers and that his thought supported the main features of early Christian musical thought in general. But it is more important to investigate the broader dimension and greater depth that he adds to it. So Chapter 11 focuses on one remarkable passage, from Book X of the *Confessions,* in which Augustine wrestles with the problem of sensual pleasures, including the pleasures of the ears. Augustine's recognition of the problem is not unique among the fathers, but his treatment of it has no rivals in depth and intensity. Indeed, one would be hard-pressed to find its parallel anywhere.

The book concludes with a chapter that makes some suggestions regarding the relevance of early Christian musical thought for our own time.

CHAPTER 2

The Song of the Church
in the New Testament

Christ Jesus lay in death's strong bonds,
for our offenses given;
but now at God's right hand he stands
and brings us life from heaven.
Therefore let us joyful be,
and sing to God right thankfully
loud songs of alleluia!
Alleluia!

Martin Luther

Therefore in the Gospel you will first find Zachary, father of the great
John, who "prophesied" in the form of a hymn after his long silence.
Nor did Elizabeth, so long barren, fail to "magnify" God from her soul
when her promised son had been born. And when Christ was born on
earth, the army of angels sounded a song of praise, saying: "Glory to
God on high," and proclaiming "peace on earth to men of good will."
. . . And not to prolong this discourse, the Lord himself, a teacher in
words and master in deeds, went out to the Mount of Olives with the
disciples after singing a hymn. . . .

The Apostles also are known to have done likewise when even in
prison they did not cease to sing. And Paul, in turn, admonishes the
prophets of the Church: "When you come together," he says, "each one
of you has a hymn, a teaching, a revelation; let all things be done for

edification." And again in another place: "I will sing with the spirit,"
he says, "I will sing with the mind also." And James puts it like this in
his epistle: "Is anyone among you sad? Let him pray. Is any cheerful?
Let him sing." And John reports in Revelation that, as the Spirit re-
vealed to him, he saw and heard the voice of the heavenly army "like
the sound of many waters and the sound of mighty thunderpeals, cry-
ing, Alleluia!"

Niceta of Remesiana

The New Testament begins and ends with outbursts of song. The birth of Jesus brought about the first outburst — four songs recorded in the first two chapters of Luke. Mary sang the *Magnificat* (1:46-55), Zechariah the *Benedictus* (1:68-79), Simeon the *Nunc dimittis* (2:29-32), and the angels sang, "Glory to God in the highest, and on earth peace among those with whom he is pleased" (2:14). The second outburst occurs in Revelation: there the song to the Lamb is picked up in ever-widening circles until the whole cosmos has joined in.

[T]he four living creatures and the twenty-four elders fell down before the Lamb, each holding a harp and golden bowls full of incense, which are the prayers of the saints. And they sang a new song, saying,

> "Worthy are you to take the scroll
> and to open its seals,
> for you were slain, and by your blood you ransomed
> people for God
> from every tribe and language and people and nation,
> and you have made them a kingdom and priests to our God,
> and they shall reign on the earth."

Then I looked, and I heard around the throne and the living creatures and the elders the voice of many angels, numbering myriads of myriads and thousands of thousands, saying with a loud voice, "Worthy is the Lamb, who was slain, to receive power and wealth and wisdom and might and honor and glory and blessing!" And I heard every creature in heaven and on earth and under the earth and on the sea, and all that is in them, saying, "To him who sits on the throne and to the Lamb be blessing and honor and glory and might forever and ever!" (Rev. 5:8-13)

Participation in this cosmic chorus is not something for which the redeemed on earth have to wait. To be sure, there is a "not yet" aspect to their life on earth: Revelation records the urgent cries of "come, Lord Jesus," and "how long?" Nevertheless, salvation is accomplished, redemption has taken place, and God's people on earth can join the song.

Between Luke and Revelation, however, the New Testament does not say much about music. Only a few key verses reveal the foundation of Christian song. One such verse is Philippians 4:4: "Rejoice in the Lord always; again I will say, Rejoice." At first, this verse might not seem to be about music; certainly, it is about much more than music. But it is also very much about music, because music and rejoicing are so closely linked. Where there is joy, there is music. So close is that link that Roger Bacon, a thirteenth-century philosopher, put the word "rejoice" at the top of his list of musical terms contained in the Bible. The link is clear in James 5:13: "Is anyone cheerful? Let him sing praise." At the creation, when there was great joy over the splendor of God's handiwork, "the morning stars sang together" (Job 38:7). And as I have already noted, in Luke and Revelation the joy of the Incarnation and the joy of the new creation produced outbursts of song.

The early Christians belonged to a tradition, Judaism, which was keenly aware of the close connection between rejoicing and making music. That awareness is evident in the Psalms. The Jews first, and then the Christians, rejoiced by singing and making music.

> Praise the Lord!
> Sing to the Lord a new song,
> > his praise in the assembly of the godly!
> Let Israel be glad in his Maker;
> > let the children of Zion rejoice in their King!
>
> Let them praise his name with dancing
> > and make melody to him with tambourine and lyre.
> For the Lord takes pleasure in his people;
> > he adorns the humble with salvation.
>
> Let the godly exult in glory;
> > let them sing for joy on their beds.
>
> (Ps. 149:1-5)

15

Given that rejoicing and music go hand in hand, we can understand why Ralph Martin claims that "[t]he Church was born in song."[1] Nor is it surprising that music has always been prominent in the church. The news the church hears and proclaims is the good news of a rescue, and those rescued respond to their rescuer with rejoicing and thanksgiving. Moses and the children of Israel sang after they were rescued from the Egyptians.

> I will sing to the Lord, for he has triumphed gloriously;
>> the horse and his rider he has thrown into the sea.
> The Lord is my strength and my song,
>> and he has become my salvation;
> this is my God, and I will praise him,
>> my father's God and I will exalt him.
>
> (Ex. 15:1-2)

But the rescue of the Israelites only presaged the cosmic rescue set in motion by the incarnation of God's son. So Mary sang, "My spirit rejoices in God my Savior" (Luke 1:47), and Zechariah sang:

> Blessed be the Lord God of Israel,
>> for he has visited and redeemed his people . . .
> that we should be saved from our enemies
>> and from the hand of all who hate us;
> to show the mercy promised to our fathers
>> and to remember his holy covenant,
> the oath that he swore to our father Abraham, to grant us
>> that we, delivered from the hand of our enemies,
> might serve him without fear,
>> in holiness and righteousness before him all our days.
>
> (Luke 1:68-75)

And following Mary and Zechariah, Christians have never ceased to rejoice in song because their rescuer has triumphed over their captors.

Of course, there is a countersubject to this main theme of Christian song: it is an expression of sorrow and a cry for mercy. Like the main theme, the Christian church inherited it from her Jewish forebears. The Psalms are as full of cries for mercy as they are of songs of joy; paradoxi-

---

1. Martin, *Worship in the Early Church*, p. 39.

cally, music is as inextricably bound to sorrow as it is to joy. A wonderful expression of that paradox is in Psalm 137:2-4, where the Israelites sing about being unable to sing!

> On the willows there
>> we hung up our lyres.
> For there our captors
>> required of us songs,
> and our tormentors, mirth, saying,
>> "Sing us one of the songs of Zion!"
> How shall we sing the Lord's song
>> in a foreign land?

The countersubject needs to be sung lest the expression of joy in the main theme sound glib and its celebration of victory sound hollow. Christians need to remember what they have been rescued from, and they need to acknowledge what they still need rescuing from. There must be, if I may put it this way, a *Kyrie* theme in Christian song that brings out the true meaning of the main theme, *Gloria*. It is not by accident that the first two items of the Ordinary of the Mass — the *Kyrie eleison* ("Lord, have mercy") and the *Gloria in excelsis* ("Glory to God in the highest") — have stood for centuries at the beginning of Christian worship. It is because they are clearly emblematic of the two-sided response of God's people. A plaintive cry — "Lord, have mercy" — and a joyous hymn of thanksgiving — "We praise you, we bless you, we worship you, we glorify you, we give thanks to you for your great glory" — form the two sides of Christians' response to their God. Justin Martyr (ca. 100–ca. 165 CE), in his *First Apology*, recognized these two themes of the Christian song when he said that "hymns and speech" are said "with thanksgiving to Him . . . for our creation, and for all the means of health, and for the qualities of the different kinds of things, and for the changes of the seasons, and presenting Him petitions. . . ."[2] Before the face of God, Christians sing a song with two themes: one theme acknowledges their need, the other God's greatness and his marvelous deeds. But one theme is dominant in the song, and one frame of mind pervades the singer. "Joy," as James McKinnon puts it, "or more specifically, thanksgiving, is the frame of mind of the Christian singer," a frame of mind that "is a direct inheritance from Judaism."

---

2. Justin Martyr, *First Apology*, 13; pp. 30-31.

It is the continuation of the attitude of Psalms 149 and 150, in which all creation praises God for his creation. This is a central notion in late Judaism and early Christianity, for which thanksgiving is only a partially successful translation. It connoted a remembrance of the long personal relationship between Jahweh and Israel, recalling especially events such as the deliverance from Egypt, while another aspect of the idea is a special delight in the marvels of physical creation. It finds expression in the various *barakhah* of late Judaism and then in the *Eucharistia,* the central act of Christianity. It results naturally in song such as the Psalms and the ancient Christian hymn which became the *Gloria* of the Mass.[3]

Regarding this "frame of mind" or reason for music in the Judaeo-Christian tradition, McKinnon makes an important observation: the Judaeo-Christian reason for song differs from some Hellenistic ideas about music that were prominent in the world into which the church was born.

This response to Jahweh, the living God, seems to take place in a different world than that caught in the dilemma posed by Hellenistic logic, which has the superstitious seeking to beguile the deity with music and the philosopher looking only to the effect music has upon the worshiper.[4]

"To beguile the deity" nicely describes an important function of pagan ritualistic music; it falls into the category called *epiclesis.* The term itself (derived from the Greek *epikaleo*) is neutral: it simply means "to summon," "to call upon," "to appeal to." But in pagan ritual, *epiclesis* was not so benign. Johannes Quasten goes so far as to say that "all antiquity was convinced that music had the power of *epiclesis.*" And "power" is the key word. As Quasten explains, music "was understood to exercise a magical influence over the gods, so that it became a means by which men controlled the deities."[5]

Christian ritual also includes *epiclesis.* For example:

And we pray you
to send your Holy Spirit

---

3. McKinnon, "The Church Fathers and Musical Instruments," p. 118.
4. McKinnon, "The Church Fathers and Musical Instruments," p. 120.
5. Quasten, *Music and Worship in Pagan and Christian Antiquity,* pp. 18, 2.

on the offering of your holy Church,
to bring together in unity
all those who receive it.
May they be filled with the Holy Spirit
who strengthens their faith in the truth.
May we be able thus to praise and glorify you
through your Child Jesus Christ.[6]

But, unlike pagan *epiclesis,* there is no magical power in it — musical or otherwise. The Holy Spirit is not beguiled into filling those who pray. Christian *epiclesis* is petitionary, not manipulative, and in a peculiar way it asks for what is already granted. Boris Bobrinskoy explains:

> [T]he Holy Spirit remains permanently on the Eucharistic community [and] his quickening gifts are poured on it freely without ceasing, [but] this supply has nothing of the automatic about it: it is always the fruit of the Church's prayers, her ardent invocation in the sacraments. . . . So there is no opposition between the action of grace (eucharist) and invocation (epiclesis). Separation of the two is merely formal: the affirmation and the desire complete one another, the narration and the invocation join one another in the Church's liturgy, which, starting from the fullness bestowed once for all in the historical Easter and Pentecost, makes her way towards the longed-for and awaited fullness of the last Advent. It is in this way that every Eucharist is an action of grace, a proclamation of the benefits achieved by God. No less is it in its completeness an epiclesis, an ardent prayer of the Eucharistic community.[7]

Two key passages in the New Testament are clear about the relationship between music and "Spirit filling." "Spirit filling" does not come as the result of singing. Rather, "Spirit filling" comes first; singing is the response. Writing to the Ephesians, Paul says: "And do not get drunk with wine, for that is debauchery, but be filled with the Spirit, addressing one another with psalms and hymns and spiritual songs, singing and making melody to the Lord with all your heart, giving thanks always and for everything to God the

---

6. *The Apostolic Tradition of Hippolytus of Rome;* quoted from *The Springtime of the Liturgy,* p. 131.

7. Bobrinskoy, "The Holy Spirit in the Liturgy," p. 127.

Father in the name of our Lord Jesus Christ" (Eph. 5:18-20). And to the Colossians he writes: "Let the word of Christ dwell in you richly, teaching and admonishing one another in all wisdom, singing psalms and hymns and spiritual songs, with thankfulness in your hearts to God" (Col. 3:16).

Clear as these passages are in declaring that Christian singing is a response to the Word of Christ and to being filled with the Spirit, it is hard to keep from turning the cause and effect around. Music, with its stimulating power, can too easily be seen as the cause and the "Spirit filling" as the effect. It is so tempting to see the reverse of what Paul says that D. M. Stanley translated Ephesians 5:18b-19: "Seek instead to be filled with the Spirit, by reciting songs, hymns, inspired canticles, by singing to the Lord and chanting his praises with all your heart. . . ." Then he commented: "On Paul's view, it is through the liturgical recitation of such hymns that the community becomes 'filled with the Spirit.'"[8] Such a reading of the passage gives song an undue *epicletic* function and turns it into a means of beguiling the Holy Spirit. But Paul is clear about the difference between Christian and pagan music, as is Arnobius (died ca. 330), whose scathing bit of satire is reminiscent of Elijah's satirical comments to the prophets of Baal on Mt. Carmel:

> Are the gods moved by . . . the clanging of brass . . . and the shaking of cymbals? And by tambourines . . . ? And the clatter of castanets, does this bring it about that when the divinities hear it, they think that they are honored and stop being boiling mad? And like little brats who forget their silly whining out of fright induced by the sound of rattles, are the omnipotent deities in the same way hushed up by the sound of pipes, and, their indignation mollified, do they relax at the rhythm of the cymbals?
>
> What is the meaning of those morning ditties which you sing, joining your voices to the music of the pipe? The gods above fall asleep, I suppose, and they are supposed to return to their posts. What about those slumber songs with which you bid them an auspicious good night? They just will not rest and go to sleep, and so that they may be beguiled into doing so, they need to hear soothing lullabies.[9]

In addition to setting Christian song apart from the magical *epicletic* function of pagan music, the prefatory phrases in the Ephesians and

---

8. Quoted from William S. Smith, *Musical Aspects of the New Testament*, p. 166.

9. Arnobius, *Against the Pagans* VII, 32; pp. 514-515.

Colossians passages, "be filled with the Spirit" and "let the word of Christ dwell in you," are important for another reason. I noted above that the reason for Christian song is joy and that the reason for Christian joy is deliverance. But how do we know this deliverance? The pains of earthly life remain. Life still has its petty frustrations and its profound sorrows. There is no end of sickness, hunger, war, and death. Infants still die, children are still abused, and the poor are still oppressed. We all remain, as Tertullian put it, subject to "doctors and debt." So he asks, "How can you possibly think that you are freed from the Ruler of this Age, when even his flies still crawl all over you?"[10] How, in the face of all this and more, can one know that there is deliverance, indeed, that it has already been accomplished? That knowledge comes only from the Word by the witness of the Spirit. The Word and the Spirit reveal the reality of the rescue, and so, despite what appearances might say to the contrary, Christians know redemption and can join the great hymn of joy and thanksgiving, the "new song" to the Lamb. Christian song is not an opiate that numbs one to the ills of this life and thus provides a false comfort. It is a response of joy to what is known through the Word and the Spirit.

Another aspect of Christian song comes out clearly in those same verses from Ephesians and Colossians: the song's direction or, if you will, its audience. Actually, there are two directions, two audiences. The primary direction is Godward: God is the audience of Christian song, which is a response to what God has done. And so Paul explicitly says in both passages that Christians should sing "to the Lord" and "to God." But equally explicit is another direction, another audience: sing to "one another." Paul emphasizes the latter because edification is an essential ingredient in Christian life and worship. He writes to the Corinthians: "When you come together, each one has a hymn, a lesson, a revelation, a tongue, or an interpretation. Let all things [including singing] be done for building up" (1 Cor. 14:26).

Sarah Spence makes an interesting observation about the Latin words *orans* and *oratio*, which shows the interrelatedness that early Christians saw between the two directions of their song.

> [O]ratio has two different meanings. In classical Latin the word means "speech" [i.e., to one another] — hence our word *oration* —

---

10. Quoted from Brown, *The Body and Society*, p. 84.

and an *orans* was anyone who spoke officially, for legal or even religious purposes. In Christian and medieval Latin the word means "prayer" [i.e., to the Lord]. Most dictionaries suggest that there is a clear distinction between the two uses of the word, but the usage of the early Church Fathers suggests something less absolute. . . . The two meanings are not as distinct as the dictionaries seem to imply. The two uses — and the two concepts involved — were, it would seem, linked in some degree.

Prayer may thus have been seen at first as a form of oration . . . and the *orans* can be understood not just as someone praying [to God] but also as someone orating [to the people].[11]

The dual direction of religious song was not new with the church; it was another inheritance from Israel. The Psalms contain references to it —

For this I will praise you, O Lord, among the nations,
and sing to your name.

(Ps. 18:49)

— as does the *Gloria* sung by the angels to the shepherds:

Glory to God in the highest,
and on earth peace among those
with whom he is pleased.

(Luke 2:14)

Although the New Testament says virtually nothing about the direction of the church's song toward humans in connection with evangelization, the psalm just quoted clearly has the singer being heard beyond the circle of believers. Psalm 96:3 even makes singing "among the nations" imperative:

Declare his glory among the nations,
his marvelous works among all peoples!

We can take it for granted that the church, which knows of more marvelous deeds than the Psalmist knew, is called upon to sing "his glory among the nations."

There is one seemingly minor incident of singing "among the nations"

---

11. Spence, *Rhetorics of Reason and Desire*, p. 64.

reported in the New Testament. When Paul and Silas were in jail in Philippi, the author of Acts tells us that they "were praying and singing hymns to God, and the prisoners were listening to them" (Acts 16:25). Is this just casual reporting, or does the narrator want to tell us something about Christian song? I think he is telling us that Christian song, even when being sung "among the nations," is primarily sung "to God." Whatever the circumstances, God is always the primary audience; but another audience — the prisoners, the nations — is also listening.

In the same passages from Ephesians and Colossians referred to above, Paul points to one other aspect of Christian song. In both passages he says that Christians should sing "with all your heart" or "in your hearts." This could be taken to mean silent singing, a phenomenon advocated by mystic Jews and neo-Platonists of the early Christian era. For example, Philo of Alexandria, a Hellenist-educated Jew at about the time of Jesus, wrote that "one cannot truly offer thanks to God as the vast majority of men do, with external effects, consecrated gifts and sacrifices . . . but rather with songs of praise and hymns — not such as the audible voice sings, but such as are raised and re-echoed by the invisible mind."[12] He went on to say that, before the high priest went into the holy of holies, he took off his long and colorful robe, which was adorned with bells. Philo interpreted that to mean that God is not to be worshiped with colorful adornment or music because, "if the soul has opened itself totally in word and deed and is filled with God, then the voices of the senses and all other burdensome and hateful noises cease."

In the same vein, the neo-Platonist Porphyry advocated silent singing to the Supreme Being.

> To the god who is above all, as a certain wise man has said, we must offer nothing sensible, nor incense, nor anything articulate; for there is nothing material which is not straightway impure to the immaterial being. Hence no speech is appropriate to him, whether spoken or uttered within, if the soul happens to be defiled by some disturbance; rather we must worship him with pure silence and unsullied thoughts.[13]

12. Quoted from Quasten, *Music and Worship*, p. 54.
13. Eusebius, quoting Porphyry, quoting Apollonius of Tyana: *Music in Early Christian Literature*, p. 100.

But mystical silent singing is not what Paul had in mind when he said "sing . . . in your hearts." Silent singing does not make sense in the context of these passages because the congregation sings "to one another." Neither does it fit with the principle of 1 Corinthians 14:26 that "all things be done for building up." Furthermore, Porphyry's low view of everything material is incompatible with the Christian doctrines of creation and incarnation. According to McKinnon, what Paul intended was simply to emphasize "the interior disposition of the singer."[14] No doubt he is right; but there is more to the phrase than that. Its fuller meaning is brought out by William S. Smith, whose discussion we will follow here.[15]

Smith relates singing "in your hearts" to the "sacrifice of praise" mentioned in Hebrews 13:15: "Through him [Jesus], then, let us continually offer up a sacrifice of praise to God, that is, the fruit of lips that acknowledge his name." This "sacrifice of praise" has some relationship to the idea of "spiritual sacrifice" that had developed in pagan philosophy. But the New Testament does not devalue the physical as much of the pagan thought of its time did, and therefore it does not disparage "the employment of the *tongue* in audible praise. . . ." So the significance of spiritual sacrifice

> for the musical praise of the church is not that praise should be silent, internal. It is rather that the musical part of the worship service, instead of being a mere rendition or performance, is to be conceived in terms of sacrifice, an offering, and that not of some mere thing, but of *self* in the praise of, and thanksgiving to, God.

And this offering of self in musical praise involves the whole person, including the body. Far from excluding audible song, New Testament singing "in your hearts" includes it as an integral part.

The mind is also involved in the offering of self in musical praise. Paul declares this most explicitly in 1 Corinthians 14:15b: "I will sing praise with my spirit, but I will sing with my mind also." At least by implication, Colossians 3:16, with its references to "the word of Christ" and "teaching and admonishing," also points to the use of the mind in musical praise. But what is more explicit in Colossians is "what it is with which the mind is engaged — the 'theater' of the mind's operations." By relating the church's song to the word of Christ, the verse makes it clear that it "has its

14. McKinnon, "The Church Fathers and Musical Instruments," p. 118.
15. Smith, *Musical Aspects of the New Testament*, pp. 163ff.

roots in the objective facts of divine redemption and revelation." Christian song keeps "the mind of the worshipper . . . directed outwards, upon Christ and upon concrete acts and deeds of God."[16]

With the mind and the body, emotion is also involved. Whether, as Smith seems to imply, Paul means "emotion" or "feeling" when he says "in your heart," or whether "heart" suggests the whole person, there is no disagreement that the emotions are also an aspect of the singing that Paul is advocating. Since that is the case, Smith succinctly sums up the essence of Christian song, as defined in the key verses from Ephesians and Colossians: "Thus the 'heart' of man responds in thankfulness to the facts of revelation and redemption which engage his mind and which his tongue is reciting."

In his Epistle to the Romans, Paul hints at yet another characteristic of the church's song: "May the God of endurance and encouragement grant you to live in such harmony with one another in accord with Jesus Christ, that together you may with one voice glorify the God and Father of our Lord Jesus Christ" (15:5-6). Does "with one voice" refer directly to singing? Probably not — at least not exclusively. But no one can doubt that it articulates a principle that the church took very seriously for her singing. The importance of singing "with one voice" was a constant refrain among the early Christian writers. Listen to some of its recurrences during the first few centuries of the Christian era. Clement of Rome (ca. 96):

> In the same way [as the angels] ought we ourselves, gathered together in a conscious unity, to cry to Him as it were with a single voice. . . .[17]

Clement of Alexandria (ca. 150–ca. 215):

> The union of many in one, issuing in the production of divine harmony out of a medley of sounds and division, becomes one symphony following one choir-leader and teacher, the Word, reaching and resting in the same truth, and crying Abba, Father.[18]

Eusebius of Caesarea (ca. 260–ca. 340):

16. A. B. Macdonald, *Christian Worship in the Primitive Church*, p. 203.
17. *The First Epistle to the Corinthians* 34; pp. 36-37.
18. *Exhortation to the Heathen* IX; p. 197.

And so more sweetly pleasing to God than any musical instrument would be the symphony of the people of God, by which, in every church of God, with kindred spirit and single disposition, with one mind and unanimity of faith and piety, we raise melody in unison in our psalmody.[19]

Ambrose (ca. 339-397):

[A psalm is] a pledge of peace and harmony, which produces one song from various and sundry voices in the manner of a cithara....

A psalm joins those with differences, unites those at odds and reconciles those who have been offended, for who will not concede to him with whom one sings to God in one voice? It is after all a great bond of unity for the full number of people to join in one chorus. The strings of the cithara differ, but create one harmony (symphonia).[20]

Unity was an important matter to the early Christians, and, as these quotations show, almost from the beginning music was an expression of, a metaphor for, and a means toward unity.

Unity is important for identity. Any group needs something distinctive that all its members have in common and that sets them off from those who do not belong. Peter says, "Once you were not a people, but now you are God's people" (1 Pet. 2:10). What makes Christians a "people" is that they are "in Christ," and in Christ they are "in the Father." Jesus prayed fervently that all believers might be "one as we are one":

Holy Father, keep them [the disciples] in your name, which you have given me, that they may be one, even as we are one. . . .

I do not ask for these only, but also for those who will believe in me through their word, that they may all be one, just as you, Father, are in me, and I am in you, that they also may be in us, so that the world may believe that you have sent me. The glory that you have given me I have given to them, that they may be one even as we are one, I in them and you in me, that they may become perfectly one, so

---

19. On Psalm 41 4; quoted from Music in Early Christian Literature, p. 98.

20. Commentary on Psalm 1 4; quoted from Music in Early Christian Literature, pp. 126-127.

that the world may know that you sent me and loved them even as you loved me (John 17:11b, 20-23).

Obviously, unity was important to our Lord; it is equally obvious that this is something for his followers to take seriously. Paul's image of the church as the body of which Christ is the head, as well as the image in Revelation of the church as the bride of Christ, are obvious efforts to depict the unity of believers with Christ and with each other. The sacrament of the Lord's Supper also depicts that unity. With regard to the Lord's Supper, Paul says, "Because there is one bread, we who are many are one body, for we all partake of the one bread" (1 Cor. 10:17). And the prayer of consecration of the ancient Christian liturgy asks:

> For just as this bread,
> once scattered upon the hills,
> has been brought together and become one,
> so too, deign to gather your Church
> from every people, from every land,
> from every town, village, and house,
> and make of her a single Church, living and catholic.[21]

It is not surprising, then, that "with one voice" became an ideal for Christian song, an ideal that found its natural expression in unison, communal singing.

The church sings her song "with one voice." That "one voice," however, includes more than just her members on earth. Both the Old and New Testaments present the picture of all God's creatures joining in praise.

> Sing for joy, O heavens, for the Lord has done it;
> shout, O depths of the earth;
> break forth into singing, O mountains,
> O forest, and every tree in it!
>
> (Isa. 44:23a)

> Praise the Lord!
> Praise the Lord from the heavens;
> praise him in the heights!

---

21. *The Euchology of Serapion of Thumis;* quoted from *The Springtime of the Liturgy,* p. 195.

Praise him, all his angels;
    praise him, all his hosts!
Praise him, sun and moon,
    praise him, all you shining stars!

Praise the Lord from the earth,
    you great sea creatures and all deeps,
fire and hail, snow and mist,
    stormy wind fulfilling his word!
Mountains and all hills,
    fruit trees and all cedars!
Beasts and all livestock,
    creeping things and flying birds!
Kings of the earth and all peoples,
    princes and all rulers of the earth!
Young men and maidens together,
    old men and children!

                                      (Ps. 148:1-3, 7-12)

According to Otto Piper, Old Testament passages such as this one show that "Jewish religion kept a close watch over the portals of heaven and refused access to it to all mortals" so that "heavenly and earthly worship might be parallel but they could not be blended."[22] Be that as it may, in the New Testament heaven and earth definitely blend. Hebrews 12:22-23 is particularly clear about the unity of earth and heaven in worship: "But you have come to Mount Zion and to the city of the living God, the heavenly Jerusalem, and to innumerable angels in festal gathering, and to the assembly of the firstborn who are enrolled in heaven. . . ." And, of course, Revelation depicts the cosmic nature of the church's singing. In his vision John heard the "new song" sung by "every creature in heaven and on earth and under the earth and on the sea, and all that is in them . . ." (Rev. 5:13).

In summary, the song the church sings, as described in the New Testament, is a joyful response to the works of God, stimulated by the Word and the Spirit. It is sung by humans to God and to each other, with the saints and angels and all creation.

---

22. Piper, "The Apocalypse of John and the Liturgy of the Ancient Church," p. 11.

CHAPTER 3

The Church in a Pagan Society

As obedient children, do not be conformed to the passions of your former ignorance, but as he who called you is holy, you also be holy in all your conduct, since it is written, "You shall be holy, for I am holy."

I Peter 1:14-16

The early Christians had not packed their bags for a long trip. When Christ failed to reappear in the time of their hopes they found it necessary to come to terms with the world. Christianity was a religion of commitment: it called people from the world's preoccupation to life in a daring new dimension. . . . [W]e see the Church and its individual disciples attempting to assert that the Church was in reality as in ideal, holy.

Martin Marty

The church in the Apostolic Age fit with a modicum of comfort into existing patterns of society. Of course, there was much in the society around her that the church needed to stand against. But since it was seen as just another sect of the Jews, the early Christian church found itself able to exist within the patterns of an officially tolerated, though popularly despised, religion. Furthermore, conditions in the Roman Empire lent themselves to the spread of the church.

The church was born during a remarkably peaceful period that had begun with Caesar Augustus (27 BCE–14 CE) and continued throughout most of the first century and beyond. As late as the early third century, Origen remarked about the importance of the *pax Romana* for the spread of Christianity.

> There is abundance of peace which began at the birth of Christ [in the time of Caesar Augustus], God preparing the nations for his teaching, that they might be under one prince, the king of the Romans, and that it might not be more difficult, owing to the lack of unity between the nations due to the existence of many kingdoms, for Jesus' apostles to accomplish the task laid upon them by their Master, when he said: "Go and teach all nations." Now the existence of many kingdoms would have been a hindrance to the preaching of the doctrine of Jesus throughout the entire world because of men everywhere engaging in war, and fighting for their native country, which was the case before Augustus, and in periods still more remote.[1]

Given this situation, it is not surprising to hear a positive view of the state coming from New Testament writers such as Paul and Peter. The thirteenth chapter of Paul's letter to the Romans is the classic statement of this positive view: "Let every person be subject to the governing authorities. For there is no authority except from God, and those that exist have been instituted by God" (13:1). Peter's first letter says essentially the same thing: "Be subject for the Lord's sake to every human institution; whether it be to the emperor as supreme, or to governors as sent by him to punish those who do evil and to praise those who do good" (1 Pet. 2:13-14).

But already in 64 CE, there was a phenomenon that signaled the beginning of the end of the relatively peaceful church-state relationships: the persecution of Christians under Nero when he needed a scapegoat for the great fire of Rome. The Roman historian Tacitus reported that, when Nero found himself to be the object of rumors about how the fire started, he

> substituted as culprits, and punished with the utmost refinements of cruelty, a class of men loathed for their vices, whom the crowd styled Christians. . . . First, then, the confessed members of the sect were arrested; next, on their disclosures, vast numbers were convicted, not so much on the count of arson as for hatred of the human race. And

---

1. *Against Celsus* II, 30; quoted from Davies, *The Early Christian Church*, pp. 34-35.

derision accompanied their end: they were covered with wild beasts' skins and torn to death by dogs; or they were fastened on crosses, and, when daylight failed, were burned as lamps by night.[2]

The persecution under Nero marked the beginning of a century and a half during which Christians were faced with the threat of persecution. Although actual persecution by no means took place at all times in all places, the threat of persecution was constant. As Martin Marty puts it, "Local ferment was almost constant, and the universal picture is . . . fairly represented as latent storm and erupting storm. . . ." Against this background of state hostility toward the church, we can understand why there is another side to the New Testament's view of the state. The "apocalyptic cast of Mark 13 and Revelation 13 jars [the] uneasy resolution" found in Paul and Peter; in fact, "Paul, too, may be hinting at distaste for the Empire in his early references to the anti-Christ in First Thessalonians. . . ."[3]

A second event that signaled a change in the church's place in the Roman Empire was the fall of Jerusalem to Titus in 70 CE. Events immediately preceding the fall of Jerusalem included the murder of James in the year 62 by the Jewish high priests, supported by the mob, and then the Jewish revolt of 66. These events spelled an end to the Jerusalem church and left Christianity without a focal point. Together with the Neronian persecution, these events made it clear that the church would no longer enjoy any security from attachments to either the Roman Empire or Judaism. Christians were now a "third race."

Furthermore, Christians were beginning to realize that Christ's second coming would not necessarily be immediate, but that the church might be facing a long period between his first coming and his second coming, during which it would be in the world and need to face the challenges coming from that world. Indeed, one of the urgent questions facing the church was what its relationship to this world should be. Jesus' followers "are in the world" but they "are not of the world" (John 17:11, 16). How could this tension be worked out in the various areas of life, including music?

Christian writings from the second century are fairly scarce, but we can still find in them certain main strands of the church's attempt to deal with the world. Very prominent in the church's effort was what we might call

2. *Annals* XV; Vol. 4, pp. 283, 285.
3. Marty, *A Short History of Christianity,* p. 38.

definition. If the church was a "third race," what made it a distinctive race, and how could that distinctiveness be made clear? Put another way, how was it holy, and how was it separate? For the church, like Israel, was called both to holiness and to be a separate people. Peter writes: "But as he who called you is holy, you also be holy in all your conduct, since it is written, 'You shall be holy, for I am holy'" (1 Pet. 1: 15-16). Also Paul, quoting Isaiah, says: "Therefore go out from their midst, and be separate from them" (2 Cor. 6:17). Christians are "sojourners and exiles" (1 Pet. 2:11) who have no "lasting city" here (Heb. 13:14).

By the year 200 there were several concrete ways in which the church had achieved definition. It had a fixed canon of Scripture that was the foundation of thought and action for all Christians. From this canon it derived a standard statement of belief, a relatively fixed and distinctive liturgy, and a well-defined moral code. In fact, it is in the area of behavior that the second-century church exerted a great amount of effort and emphasis. Moral duties and obligations, modes of behavior, and what we now call "lifestyle" were of paramount importance. On the basis of Scripture,

> Christians were to *abstain* from all lusts; they were to *put off*, i.e. renounce, heathen idolatry and sin, and *put on* or clothe themselves with righteousness and virtue; they were to be watchful and, in particular, pray; they were to *subject* themselves in a graded series of social relations: wives submitting to husbands, children to parents, slaves to masters, and all to the civil power; they were to *withstand* temptation and persecution.[4]

These early Christians emphasized social duties to the poor, the widows, and the orphans. So strong was its emphasis on moral obligations that the second-century church has come under criticism for being too legalistic and for transforming Christ's ethic based on love back to a set of codes reminiscent of the Old Testament. For example, as Marty points out,

> The Gospels show Christ breaking the codes of Judaic legalism in his casual disregard for ritual observance. The sons of the bridegroom were to rejoice in his presence. The asceticism of John the Baptist was overshadowed by the participation in banquets and wedding parties by Jesus and his followers. That ethic which St. Augustine outlined in

4. Davies, *The Early Christian Church*, p. 65.

one line: Love, and then do as you will, had been obscured in the early Church. . . .[5]

But Marty tempers his criticism by going on to say that "formal patterns of isolation from worldly pressures seemed necessary," and that some of this moral stringency is already found "as early as the canonical Epistle of James."

One reason why the church of the late first and early second century thought it necessary to emphasize moral behavior was that libertinism was a threat to the church almost from its beginnings. Paul had to combat it, and so did Peter (in his second letter), Jude, and John (in Revelation). But even if we are willing to grant that strict moral codes were necessary to combat libertinism in the second century, and even if we recognize that there is a morally stringent side to the New Testament that must be taken as seriously as the doctrine that we are no longer "under the law," we still might think that early Christian rules for living were unnecessarily austere. Charles Williams was no doubt correct when he said, "To us the most relaxed morals of the church of the second century are austere enough."[6] The moral stringency of early Christians is probably the biggest hurdle we face in trying to appreciate them. The degree of stringency that they seem to be outlining for future Christians is not something to which we take kindly; it is certainly not something we think is necessary for the Christian life today.

Since the early Christians' moral stringency also affects their views on music, we need to investigate it for this study. Of course, we could simply ignore it by saying that the early Christians got off on the wrong track and that, thank God, somewhere along the way later Christians found the right track. But if we were to do that, we would never find out whether early Christians have anything to teach us. As a start toward dealing with this hurdle, let me present a line of thought that comes from both Charles Williams and Martin Marty.

Marty points out that, of the varied responses "to the call for holiness, retreat drew the smallest minority." We need to remember that those who separated themselves most drastically from this world — martyrs, hermits, and monks — were a small minority. Even then, the most austere road to holiness was not the road most traveled; yet the bulk of early Christian

---

5. Marty, *A Short History of Christianity,* p. 46.
6. Williams, *The Descent of the Dove,* p. 32.

writing that has survived to our day comes from those who took that less-traveled road. We should not dismiss them for that reason, for they did provide the church with something valuable: they provided the church, in Marty's words, "with a note of judgment and of conscience that cannot be dismissed. They had picked up a strand in the authentic fabric. . . ." But they erred in pulling on that strand

> with such strength that it twisted the whole garment. This distorted the question of Christian vocation, complicating it for those who chose not to go to the desert or the cell. The martyr and the monk, then, each had a place, but each in his color detracts from the pastel and gray response of holiness in congregational life and daily calling. Perhaps it was most difficult to be holy there where no beasts roared or fire flamed, where no demons fluttered around the ears of saints — but where the structures of evil pervading life called for higher witness to the way of the cross. The varying hopes for holiness were like ropes. They bound some in misery to stakes. They corralled others in cells. But for most they were stretched across poles of church and world: it is never easy to walk a tightrope.[7]

Marty's idea fits well with what Charles Williams calls the "rigorous view" and the "relaxed view." Insofar as Marty and Williams differ, the difference lies in that Williams makes it clearer that distortion can occur if either view gains the upper hand.

> In morals, as in everything, there are two opposite tendencies. The first is to say: "Everything matters infinitely." The second is to say: "No doubt that is true. But mere sanity demands that we should not treat everything as mattering all that much. Distinction is necessary; more-and-less is necessary; indifference is necessary." The contention is always sharp. The Rigorous view is vital to sanctity; the Relaxed view is vital to sanity. Their union is not impossible, but it is difficult; for whichever is in power begins, after the first five minutes, to maintain itself from bad and unworthy motives. Harshness, pride, resentment encourage the one; indulgence, falsity, detestable good-fellowship the other.[8]

7. Marty, *A Short History of Christianity*, p. 50
8. Williams, *The Descent of the Dove*, p. 31.

The church needs both kinds of responses and needs to recognize both. Williams' beautiful idea of the "exchanges of Christendom" holds the two views together. It recognizes that "the lovely refreshments of this world in some may not be without their part in the lordly rigours of the others," and that "the exchanges of Christendom are very deep; if we [who live by the 'relaxed' view] thrive by the force of the saints, they too may feed on our felicities."[9]

In defining themselves over against the world, the early Christians did not feel compelled to differ from the world in everything. Although Christians were a new people, some of the ingredients that went into their makeup were old. Not everything that had gone before needed to be rejected. For example, Christian ethics had much in common with Jewish and Stoic ethics. A classic statement of Christian continuity with the world comes from the unknown author of the second-century *Epistle to Diognetus.*

> The difference between Christians and the rest of mankind is not a matter of nationality, or language, or customs. Christians do not live apart in separate cities of their own, speak any special dialect, nor practice any eccentric way of life. The doctrine they profess is not the invention of busy human minds and brains, nor are they, like some, adherents to this or that school of human thought. They pass their lives in whatever township — Greek or foreign — each man's lot has determined; and conform to ordinary local usage in their clothing, diet, and other habits.[10]

Lest this be misconstrued to indicate too thorough an identification of the church with the world, we should be clear that the main burden of this epistle was to contrast Christian moral conduct with what prevailed in the world. Still, it is significant that the author was ready to point out the common ground.

Probably the most important area in which early Christians tried to find common ground was in pagan philosophy. The New Testament model for this search is Paul, who, on Mars Hill in Athens, quoted from two of the Greeks' own poets. Even so, Christian acceptance of elements of pagan philosophy was generally slow in coming. Two tendencies emerged within

9. Williams, *The Descent of the Dove,* p. 32.
10. *Early Christian Writings: The Apostolic Fathers,* p. 144.

the church during the second century, which would contend with each other throughout its history: on the one hand, there were those who tried to keep the thought of the church from being tainted by any pagan philosophy; on the other hand, there were those who thought that pagan philosophy held much of value that the church would ignore to its detriment. They thought that, where pagan philosophy was true, it could help them build bridges that would aid pagans in crossing over into the church, and could also aid Christians themselves in understanding and formulating their own beliefs. Ideally, the two tendencies can balance and correct each other, but they can also lead to heresy. During the second and third centuries, extreme Hellenism led to Gnostic heresies, and extreme denial led to the Montanist heresy. But Christians could go some distance in either direction and still be within the boundaries of orthodoxy. We can take Justin Martyr and his pupil Tatian as second-century representatives of the two tendencies.

Justin Martyr was the bridge-builder. His spiritual journey began as a pagan who carefully studied the various philosophies — Pythagorean, Stoic, Aristotelian, and eventually Platonic. He was most impressed by the Platonists. In his *Dialogue with Trypho*, he says:

> The perception of incorporeal things quite overwhelmed me and the Platonic theory of ideas added wings to my mind, so that in a short time I imagined myself a wise man. So great was my folly that I fully expected immediately to gaze upon God, for this is the goal of Plato's philosophy.[11]

But an old man whom he met walking on the beach shook his faith in Plato and the other philosophers. So he asked the old man, "If these philosophers do not know the truth, what teacher or method shall one follow?"

> "A long time ago," he replied, "long before the time of those so-called philosophers, there lived blessed men who were just and loved by God, men who spoke through the inspiration of the Holy Spirit and predicted events that would take place in the future, which events are now taking place. We call these men the prophets. They alone knew the truth and communicated it to men, whom they neither deferred

---

11. *Dialogue with Trypho* II, 6; pp. 6-7.

to nor feared. With no desire for personal glory, they reiterated only what they heard and saw when inspired by a Holy Spirit."[12]

The arguments of the old man joined with Justin's admiration of the Christian martyrs to bring him to Christianity.

> For I myself too, when I was delighting in the teachings of Plato, and heard the Christians slandered, and saw them fearless of death, and of all other things which are counted fearful, saw that it was impossible that they could be living in wickedness and pleasure. . . .
>
> For I myself, perceiving the wicked disguise which the evil demons had cast over the divine doctrines of the Christians, in order to avert others from joining them, laughed both at those who framed these falsehoods, and at the disguise itself, and at popular opinion. And I confess that I both pray and with all my strength strive to be found a Christian. . . .[13]

When Justin became a Christian, he did not abandon his philosophic interests; symbolically, he continued to wear the cloak that identified him as a philosopher. He accepted the teachings of Christianity as true, but he also saw that much of that truth could be found in pagan philosophy as well. Christianity completed the partial truths discovered by the philosophers, and on that basis Justin became the first Christian philosopher, an important trailblazer for many who followed. It is ironic that this conciliatory man died as a martyr; and because of the kind of person he was, his martyrdom shows all the more clearly that there are limits to conciliation. He was willing to look for common ground and to acknowledge it when he discovered it, but he would not deny his God. Therefore, for refusing to sacrifice to the gods, he was put to death in the year 165.

Tatian (fl. ca. 160), a student of Justin, took a very different stance toward pagan philosophy. Quite simply, he would have nothing to do with it, and he did not approve of other Christians dealing with it either.

> Where Justin was normally conciliatory, Tatian was uncompromising. Where Justin saw a relative value in the pagan philosophies, Tatian saw none. . . . Tatian was an angry man, and he found in the

---

12. *Dialogue with Trypho* VII, 1; p. 14.
13. *The Second Apology* 12, 13; pp. 82-83.

universality, apparent simplicity, and directness of the Christian message the means to belabor the civilization that had disappointed him. His attack was leveled not only at pagan religion, but at the Roman system of law and government. . . . Tatian was at heart a rebel, and had no place for the Roman Empire or its rulers in his scheme of values.

His acceptance after 165 of an extreme ascetic (Encratite) interpretation of Christianity involved also his rejection of the orthodox Christian values represented by his master Justin. . . . He had scant use for a Christianity that was prepared even on its own terms to live with the world.[14]

There is little about music in the surviving writings of Justin and Tatian, or, for that matter, in the whole of Christian writing before Tertullian and Clement of Alexandria. The little that has survived, however, shows continuity with the themes of the New Testament and a foreshadowing of themes that will become particularly strong in the fourth century.

"With thanksgiving to Him" — in that succinct phrase Justin Martyr clearly indicates the New Testament's view of the Christian song: it is sung to God from a grateful heart. That its Godward direction was also clear to a pagan, Pliny the Younger, is revealed in a famous passage from a letter he wrote to the Emperor Trajan: Christians, he said, "were accustomed to assemble on a set day before dawn and to sing a hymn among themselves to the Christ, as to a god. . . ."[15] There is abundant evidence that Christians recognized that in singing to God they were part of a cosmic host of singers. Origen wrote: "So we sing to God and his only begotten as do the sun, the moon, the stars and the entire heavenly host. For all these form a sacred chorus and sing hymns to the God of all and his only begotten along with those among men who are just."[16] Clement of Rome and Tertullian associate this idea especially with the *Sanctus*. Clement wrote to the Corinthian church:

> Think of the vast company of His angels, who all wait on Him to serve His wishes: "Ten thousand times ten thousand stood before him," says Scripture, "and thousand thousands did Him service, cry-

14. Frend, *The Rise of Christianity*, pp. 174-175.

15. Pliny the Younger, Letter IX, xcvi; quoted from *Music in Early Christian Literature*, p. 27.

16. *Against Celsus* VIII, 67; quoted from *Music in Early Christian Literature*, p. 38.

ing, 'Holy, holy, holy is the Lord of hosts; all creation is full of his glory.'" In the same way ought we ourselves, gathered together in a conscious unity, to cry to Him as it were with a single voice, if we are to obtain a share of His glorious promises. . . .[17]

And Tertullian wrote:

Certainly it is right that God should be blessed in all places and at all times because it is every man's duty to be ever mindful of His benefits, but this wish takes the form of a benediction. Moreover, when is the name of God not holy and blessed in itself, when of itself it makes others holy? To Him the attending hosts of angels cease not to say: "Holy, holy, holy!" Therefore, we, too — the future comrades of the angels, if we earn this reward — become familiar even while here on earth with that heavenly cry of praise to God and the duty of our future glory.[18]

From very early we can find explicit liturgical awareness of the union of human and angelic voices, particularly in the *Sanctus* and the words that surround it. The liturgy of Saints Addai and Mari is one of the earliest witnesses to the *Sanctus* in the Eucharistic prayer, perhaps as early as the third century.

Priest: Your majesty, O Lord, a thousand thousand heavenly beings adore; myriad myriads of angels, and ranks of spiritual beings, ministers of fire and spirit, together with the holy cherubim and seraphim, glorify your name, crying out and glorifying [unceasingly calling to one another and saying]:

People: Holy, holy, [holy, Lord God almighty; heaven and earth are full of his praises].

Priest: And with these heavenly armies we, also even we, your lowly, weak, and miserable servants, Lord, give you thanks because you have brought about us a great grace which cannot be repaid. For you put on our human nature to give us life through your divine nature; you raised us from our lowly state; you restore our Fall; you restored our immortality; you

17. *The First Epistle to the Corinthians* XXXIV; pp. 36-37.
18. *On Prayer* III; p. 161.

forgave our debts; you justified our sinfulness; you enlightened our intelligence. You, our Lord and our God, conquered
our enemies, and made the lowliness of our weak nature to
triumph through the abundant mercy of your grace.[19]

Other musical references from second- and third-century writings
show the ancient penchant for musical imagery, a penchant that early
Christian writers exercised fully. Here are two examples. In the first, from
Ignatius of Antioch, the harp is used as an image of harmony in the
church's hierarchy. Also to be noted again is the New Testament theme of
singing with "one voice . . . to the Father." Although the musical language
in it is largely allegorical, the phrase "sing aloud" suggests that literal singing is also meant.

> [I]t is proper for your conduct and your practices to correspond
> closely with the mind of the bishop. And this, indeed, they are doing;
> your justly respected clergy, who are a credit to God, are attuned to
> their bishop like the strings of a harp, and the result is a hymn of
> praise to Jesus Christ from minds that are in unison, and affections
> that are in harmony. Pray, then, come and join this choir, every one of
> you; let there be a whole symphony of minds in concert; take the tone
> all together from God, and sing aloud to the Father with one voice
> through Jesus Christ. . . .[20]

In the second example, Athenagoras likens the cosmos to a harmonious instrument: "Now if the cosmos is an harmonious instrument set in
rhythmic motion, I worship him who tuned it, who strikes its notes and
sings its concordant melody, not the instrument."[21] I will deal with the
idea that the cosmos is musical (i.e., "the music of the spheres") in the
chapters on Clement of Alexandria and St. Ambrose, so I need not develop
that here. But I should note that the theme of worshiping the Creator
rather than the creation is a common one. The church fathers often criticized pagan religion for falling into the trap of worshiping creatures, and
this kind of musical image typically accompanies that criticism.

---

19. *Prayers of the Eucharist*, pp. 42-43.
20. *Epistle to the Ephesians* IV, p. 62.
21. *Supplication for the Christians* 16; quoted from *Music in Early Christian Literature*,
p. 22.

I want to cite two final references — from Tatian, who, as we might expect, speaks unfavorably about pagan music.[22]

> I do not wish to gape at many singers nor do I care to look benignly upon a man who is nodding and motioning in an unnatural way. . . .

> And this Sappho is a lewd, lovesick female who sings to her own licentiousness, whereas all our women are chaste, and the maidens at their distaffs sing of godly things more earnestly than that girl of yours.

These are early hints of the patristic polemic against pagan music, a polemic that will reach a peak in the fourth century. Given the moral stringency of the second-century church, one might well have expected that the polemic would have been strong at this time. Perhaps it was, but due to the paucity of sources and the accidents of survival, the evidence for it has vanished. Or perhaps there was less need during this time before the mass conversions of the third and fourth centuries. Whatever the explanation, it is doubtful that the second- and third-century church, which was so concerned with God's call to holiness, would have been lax in its attitude toward pagan musical practices.

Like the polemic, the other matters that appear so fleetingly in the second-century references to music will soon appear in fuller bloom. The musical concerns and interests that we glimpse in the second- and third-century church will come into clearer view around the turn of the century with Clement of Alexandria and Tertullian.

---

22. *Discourse to the Greeks* xxii, 33; quoted from *Music in Early Christian Literature,* p. 22.

CHAPTER 4

Clement of Alexandria:
Musical Cosmology and Composed Manners

Glorious their life who sing, with glad thanksgiving,
true hymns to Christ the King in all their living:
all who confess his Name, come then with hearts aflame;
the God of peace acclaim as Lord and Savior.

Clement of Alexandria
(trans. F. Bland Tucker)

C lement of Alexandria is the earliest Christian from whom we have a
sizable amount of writing about music. In fact, upon opening Clement's writings in Volume 2 of the Ante-Nicene Fathers, one immediately
encounters several columns of small print comparing mythological singers, such as Amphion, Arion, and Orpheus, with the "new song." This
might seem colorful and intriguing to some readers today, but would
many be inclined to acknowledge that it could possibly have any relevance
anymore? Before giving up on Clement's opening passage, however, we
should at least find out a little about him and his writings — and the purpose of his writings.

We do not know where or exactly when Clement was born. Athens was
perhaps his birthplace, sometime around the middle of the second century. We can gather that he was probably born to non-Christian parents,
because his writings suggest that he knew as an insider the religions from
which he was trying to convert his pagan readers. We know nothing about
his conversion, but given his scholarly and reflective cast of mind, it seems

most likely that he came to Christianity gradually, after carefully thinking through the pagan alternatives. He had a searching mind and was ready to wander far and wide in his quest for Christian teachers. He said that one of his major books, *Miscellanies,* was an image and outline of "those vigorous and animated discourses which I was privileged to hear, and of blessed and truly remarkable men."

> Of these the one, in Greece, an Ionic; the other in Magna Gracia: the first of these from Coele-Syria, the second from Egypt, and others in the East. The one was born in the land of Assyria, and the other a Hebrew in Palestine.[1]

In about 180, Clement came to Alexandria, a large, cosmopolitan Greek city in Egypt, probably the wealthiest city of its time. Hadrian (if the letter is authentic) wrote: "The people are mutinous, empty-headed and troublesome; their city is rich, wealthy, prosperous; everyone is busy; their only god is money."[2] No doubt Alexandria had its share of materialists, but religion — pagan, Jewish, and Christian — flourished, and so did learning. A university had been founded there by about 290 BCE, and by Clement's time its library contained three-quarters of a million volumes and must have been a great attraction to him. Within a flourishing Hellenistic culture, Alexandria also had a sizable contingent of Jews. One of them, Philo, an influential thinker noted for his synthesis of Hebrew and Greek thought, had a strong influence on Clement.

Although we know that people from Egypt were in Jerusalem at Pentecost and that an important early convert to Christianity, Apollos, was a Jew from Alexandria, we know very little about how Christianity reached Alexandria or how it multiplied there. But we do know that by the time Clement arrived there, Christianity had taken firm hold; however, it was a Christianity with a strongly Gnostic cast. Between 130 and 180, Alexandria had a succession of Gnostic bishops: Basilides, Valentinus, and Heracleon. But during the 180s orthodoxy seems to have gained the upper hand. Around 180 an orthodox teacher named Pantaenus set up what is now referred to as the Catechetical School, and in 189, Demetrius, a man of orthodox beliefs, became bishop and remained in that office for forty-three years.

1. *Miscellanies* I; p. 301.
2. Quoted from Ferguson, *Clement of Alexandria,* p. 20.

Pantaenus was Clement's final teacher on his spiritual and intellectual pilgrimage to Christianity, and Clement spoke of his teacher in glowing terms:

> When I came upon the last [of my teachers] (he was the first in power), having tracked him out concealed in Egypt, I found rest. He, the true, the Sicilian bee, gathering the spoil of the flowers of the prophetic and apostolic meadow, engendered in the souls of his hearers a deathless element of knowledge.[3]

Eusebius (ca. 260–ca. 340), author of the first history of the church, also spoke highly of Pantaenus and of his "academy of sacred learning" in Alexandria.

> At the time the school for believers in Alexandria was headed by a man with a very high reputation as a scholar, by name Pantaenus, for it was an established custom that an academy of sacred learning should exist among them. This academy has lasted till our own time, and I understand that it is directed by men of high standing and able exponents of theology, but we know that Pantaenus was one of the most eminent teachers of his day, being an ornament of the philosophic system known as stoicism. He is said to have shown such warm-hearted enthusiasm for the divine word that he was appointed to preach the gospel of Christ to the peoples of the East, and travelled as far as India.[4]

When Pantaneus went to India, Clement succeeded him as teacher at the academy (or Catechetical School). Since no writings by Pantaenus have survived, Clement's reputation has overshadowed his teacher's. Clement, in turn, would be overshadowed by his own student, Origen, who had a mind that most patristic scholars rank with Augustine's as the most powerful in the early church. In imagining this "catechetical school," we should not think of a building or a formal institution. Most likely, the teaching was done in a private house, to which the students came from far and wide to "sit at the feet" of the master, sometimes for several years. Eusebius gives us some idea of this setting as it pertains to Origen, Clement's successor:

3. *Miscellanies* I; p. 301.
4. *The History of the Church* V; p. 213.

It was in the tenth year of Alexander's reign that Origen made the move from Alexandria to Caesarea, leaving to Heraclas the school of elementary instruction for those in the city. . . .

At this time Firmilian, Bishop of Caesarea in Cappadocia, paid a remarkable tribute to Origen, showing such admiration for him that at one time he would invite him to his own region to assist his churches, at another he would go all the way to Judaea to see him and spend some time with him, in order to deepen his own spiritual life. In the same way the head of the Jerusalem church, Alexander, and Theoctistus of Caesarea listened attentively to him at all times as their only teacher, leaving to him the interpretation of Holy Writ and all other branches of religious instruction.[5]

Clement was not the powerful thinker that his pupil Origen was, but he had an inquiring mind and was exceptionally well read. His writings reveal the breadth of his reading of both the Bible and Greek literature; Robert Louis Wilken points out that there are "more than fifteen hundred references to the Old Testament alone and close to three thousand to the New Testament." He calculates that there are roughly "seven or eight biblical citations on every page of his writings." Even so, Clement kept his audience in mind by citing Greek literature even more often than biblical passages. "Yet," says Wilken, "there is a difference."

Clement cites the Greek literature to illustrate a point, to give flourish to an argument, to delight and arouse his readers. When he cites the Scriptures there is a sense of discovery, that something extraordinary is to be learned in its pages, that it is not one book among many. For Clement the Bible was a source of revelation and instruction, "our wisdom." . . .

Indeed, in Clement's writings "the Bible emerges for the first time as the foundation of a Christian culture."[6]

One of the main burdens of his writing was to bring pagans to Christianity by showing them the superiority of Christianity. In this mission he did not hesitate to appropriate what he could from pagan philosophy, especially Plato, and though he was not Gnostic, he had an affinity with some of

---

5. *History of the Church* VI; pp. 266-267.
6. Wilken, *The Spirit of Early Christian Thought*, pp. 56-57.

their tendencies and referred to Christians who had achieved intellectual depth in their faith as "true Gnostics." In short, Clement was ready to accept truth wherever he found it; he believed that all truth is God's truth.

Because Clement so frequently used the term "true Gnostic," it is necessary to describe Gnosticism and Clement's relationship to it. Gnosticism is not easy to describe, because it was more a philosophical tendency or cast of mind than an organized set of religious beliefs or ritual activities. John Ferguson lists four trends of Gnostic thought: (1) knowledge is central (*gnosis* means knowledge); (2) knowledge is redemptive; (3) "redemption is for the spirit, not for the body or even the soul"; and (4) Gnostics "build inordinately complex systems of spiritual beings."[7] Insofar as Gnostics considered the Bible, they tended to cut the Old Testament off from the New Testament: their view of the Old Testament was that it was the word of a fallen god. Furthermore, their interpretations of the New Testament were almost entirely allegorical.

Clement was not Gnostic for the simple reason that Gnosticism cannot be squared with the teachings of the Bible. So whatever similarities there might be between Clement's thought and Gnostic thought, the differences are fundamental. First, although knowledge was important in Clement's thought, faith was redemptive. In the first book of *The Instructor*, he emphasizes faith (*pistis*). In his later work, *Miscellanies*,

he sets out at length the steps by which the Christian should advance to knowledge or understanding (*Gnosis*). *Gnosis* is not in opposition to *Pistis*; rather it consists in a fuller comprehension of what is already implicit in faith. . . . Clement's purpose as a teacher and author was, broadly speaking, twofold: to convert the Gnostics of his day whose preoccupation with philosophy and sometimes with religious ideas of paganism had led them into heterodoxy or heresy; and, at the same time, to convince those of his Christian contemporaries who rejected everything in pagan thought as dangerous to belief, that it was possible for an orthodox Christian to acquire a knowledge of dialectic and the best philosophical thought — Stoicism and Platonism as understood in his day — and also a proper understanding of the physical universe. So far from harming the faith of a Christian, this knowledge would help to deepen his understanding of the truth of Christianity.[8]

7. Ferguson, *Clement of Alexandria*, p. 39.
8. Laistner, *Christianity and Pagan Culture*, pp. 58-59.

A second important difference between Clement and the Gnostics was that Clement did not think matter was evil. On the basis of the doctrine of creation, he could not disparage the physical, as the Gnostics did. No Gnostic would have said, as Clement did, that "Christian conduct is the operation of the rational soul in accordance with a correct judgement and aspiration after truth, which attains its destined end through the body, the soul's consort and ally."[9]

Finally, Clement never allowed "his speculations about aeons or spirits to threaten the oneness of God: the Supreme God was the Creator and the Father of Jesus Christ. Even amid all the allegorization of Old Testament accounts . . . the historicity of these accounts was not denied. . . ." For Clement, both the Old and the New Testaments were God's Word; and though he frequently allegorized the Old Testament, it is interesting to note that he never allegorized the New Testament. In his thought "the historical reality of the birth, death, and resurrection of Christ stood firm against any Gnostic docetism. This reality was the guarantee of redemption and the foundation of the church, which was catholic and included all sorts and conditions of men, not merely the spiritual elite."[10]

The principal surviving writings of Clement are *Exhortation to the Heathen (Protrepticus), The Instructor (Paedogogus),* and *Miscellanies (Stromata). Exhortation to the Heathen* (i.e., the Greeks) is an apologetic work that he wrote in a literary form used for centuries by Greek philosophers to convince people to adopt a way of life based on certain beliefs. Thus, in a form familiar to them, Clement appealed to educated pagans whose philosophy, though partially true, was incomplete and often in error. Christ, he tried to convince them, corrected the error and fulfilled and augmented the truth found in pagan philosophy.

With *The Instructor,* Clement had a different audience in mind: he addressed it not to pagans but to Christian believers, particularly young believers, to instruct them in Christian living. It goes into great detail about how Christians should conduct themselves in all kinds of matters — eating and drinking, attendance at baths and public entertainments, clothing and outward adornment, to name but a few — and his teaching on these matters has been criticized for being overly negative. For example, R. B. Tollington claims that Clement's "fundamental belief" is "that to make the right denials

---

9. *The Instructor* I; p. 235.
10. Jaroslav Pelikan, *The Christian Tradition,* p. 96.

is the important thing, and that the convert's first duty is to realise where he must refuse the standards and fashions of the world. . . ." This, Tollington concludes, is a "defect in Clement's ideal," a defect that occurs

> whenever restraint, prohibition, abstinence, the ascetic virtues, predominate over the more positive ideals of duty, service, activity, and love. Clement's readers or pupils are to draw the line, and abundant warnings, with typical illustrations of unpardonable excess, leave them in little doubt as to how the Christian ought to live. . . .[11]

Tollington's criticism of Clement is in line with the criticism that has often been leveled against second-century Christianity in general — that it is too legalistic. But saying that "right denials" reveal Clement's "fundamental belief" hardly seems fair when one considers Clement's intention in writing *The Instructor*. Peter Brown's assessment is more positive because he understands that *The Instructor* is based on "a deep belief that the body could convey messages as precisely as any words could do," a belief that "had lain at the heart of the pagan notion of moral refinement."

> The [moral] codes taught by philosophers . . . were appropriated and transformed by Clement. They were . . . applied to the . . . needs of the believing household. . . . Clement's writings communicated a sense of the God-given importance of every moment of daily life, and especially of the life of the household. By free acts of conscious moral craftsmanship, the believer could create, within the home, a pool of circumstantial order in the midst of an untidy world.[12]

The minute detail in *The Instructor* shows the importance of the body in Clement's thinking, a point that distinguishes his thought from Gnosticism, as we have seen. Brown concludes that "Clement's ideal of the Christian life was permeated by a deep sense of the service of God, as Creator of the universe, combined with an awareness of the presence, in the soul of the believer, of His Word, Christ an intimate companion, to Whom every detail of the believer's life must be referred. . . ."[13]

Clement's third surviving book, *Miscellanies,* is a huge, rambling work

---

11. Tollington, *Clement of Alexandria,* p. 265.
12. Brown, *The Body and Society,* p. 125.
13. Brown, *The Body and Society,* p. 128.

in which he aimed to provide material for the construction of a Christian philosophy, a "true *gnosis*" in opposition to Gnostic thought. For Clement, Scripture was the foundation for "true *gnosis*," but he believed that there was truth to be found in the pagans as well. Therefore, Christians did not need to be frightened by philosophy — "as children are by masks."[14]

Clement taught and wrote in Alexandria until 202 or 203, when he left due to the persecutions taking place under Septimus Severus, the same persecutions that cost Origen's father his life. He probably went to Cappadocia and Antioch, but nothing is known about his life in either place. He died in about 215, having left a legacy of Christian humanism that readily embraced truth wherever it was found. Tollington aptly summarizes Clement's contribution as follows:

> Never before had the early Church been told so boldly that there was good in Paganism, and that her sacred Scriptures were the highest but not the only documents which revealed the will of God. Never before in the library of a Christian man of learning had Plato and Euripides been so frankly claimed as friends. Never before had those who hesitated to come over been so encouraged to recognise the abiding value of treasures that already were their own. Inclusive, not exclusive, was the character of Clement's Christianity, and wherever he may wander in the wide field of literature, he finds unsuspected traces of the influence of the Word. . . . [Clement sought] for correspondence rather than diversity of view, [remembered] that poets often teach true theology, [believed] that a true thing deserves equal recognition whether it is uttered by an enemy or a friend, and . . . in the quiet of [his library sought] the profane as well as the sacred Scriptures with the full conviction that the field is one, and that in every quarter there is much that may be claimed for Christ.[15]

With this much of Clement's background in mind, we are now in a better position to turn to his musical thought. His *Exhortation to the Heathen* begins as follows:

> Amphion of Thebes and Arion of Methymna were both minstrels, and both were renowned in story. They are celebrated in song to this

14. *Miscellanies* VI; p. 498.
15. Tollington, *Clement of Alexandria*, pp. 176-177.

day in the chorus of the Greeks; the one for having allured the fishes, and the other for having surrounded Thebes with walls by the power of music. Another, a Thracian, a cunning master of his art (he also is the subject of Hellenic legend), tamed the wild beasts by the mere might of song; and transplanted trees — oaks — by music.[16]

Amphion, Arion, and "the Thracian" were the great singers of Greek mythology, the mythic musical superstars of the day, and the stories about them reveal the Greek belief in the power of music. Amphion's lyre-playing was so bewitching that the stones of Mount Cithaeron were said to gather around him and become the walls of Thebes. Arion, faced with death at the hands of pirates, asked them to let him sing before they killed him. Wishing to hear such a famous musician, the pirates granted his request. When he finished singing, he jumped into the sea and sank beneath the waves. But his music had attracted dolphins, and one of them picked him up and carried him on his back to safety. "The Thracian" is Orpheus, the greatest of the mythological Greek musicians. The music of Orpheus was said to tame wild animals, cause trees to uproot themselves so they could gather around to listen, and even affect inanimate objects such as stones, upon whose hardness his music had a softening affect. So moving were his singing and lyre-playing that he persuaded the lords of the dead to allow his wife, Eurydice, to return with him to the realm of the living.

In his opening of the *Exhortation* — remember that it is addressed to the Greeks — Clement is relating something that is calculated to draw his readers in. He "is strutting before his readers, brandishing his command of Greek literature to play to the gallery. But it does not take him long to come to the point. The time has come for the Greeks to hear a new song."[17] Clement gets to that point by way of a fourth mythical musician named Eunomos.[18]

I might tell you also the story of another, a brother to these — the subject of a myth, and a minstrel — Eunomos the Locrian and the Pythic grasshopper. A solemn Hellenic assembly had met at Pytho, to celebrate the death of the Pythic serpent, when Eunomos sang the reptile's

16. *Exhortation to the Heathen* I; p. 171.
17. Wilken, *The Spirit of Early Christian Thought*, p. 55.
18. *Exhortation to the Heathen* I; p. 172.

epitaph. . . . The Locrian breaks a string. The grasshopper sprang to the neck of the instrument, and sang on it as on a branch. . . .

This is a curious addition to the list of famous musicians, for Eunomos cannot be compared in musical powers to the other three. Indeed, he supposedly charmed only a grasshopper. The clue to Clement's reason for including the story of Eunomos is in his interpretation of that story. The Greeks thought that "the grasshopper . . . was attracted by the song of Eunomos"; but Clement had a different interpretation: the grasshopper "of its own accord . . . flew to the lyre, and of its own accord sang," and the minstrel adapted his song "to the grasshopper's song. . . ." Moreover, it should be noted that the grasshopper was one of those, "warmed by the sun, [that] were chirping beneath the leaves along the hills; but they were singing not to that dead dragon, *but to God All-wise.* . . ."

What did Clement mean by introducing the story of Eunomos? It is obvious that the song Clement approved of was the song the grasshoppers sang in response to God's good gifts. Eunomos's song became worthy only when he brought it into conformity with, and completed it by, the grasshopper's song, just as Greek philosophy is true only when it is in conformity with — and completed by — God's Word. With this charming story, Clement suggested the point of the work to follow.

Clement then went on to contrast the deceit of the "old song" of Orpheus and the others with the truth of the "new song," which is Christ, and called on his readers to confine "the dramas and the raving poets . . . to Cithaeron and Helicon, now antiquated." He implored them to "bring from above out of heaven, Truth, with Wisdom in all its brightness, and the sacred prophetic choir, down to the holy mount of God; and let Truth . . . deliver men from delusion. . . . And raising their eyes, and looking above, let them abandon Helicon and Cithaeron, and take up their abode in Sion."

The power of the Old Song supposedly tamed beasts, moved stones, and brought the dead back to life. Such power, however, truly belongs to the "new song," which

also tamed men, the most intractable of animals, [and] all such blocks of stone, the celestial song has transformed into tractable men. . . . Behold the might of the new song! It has made men out of stones, men out of beasts. Those, moreover, that were as dead, not being partakers of the true life, have come to life again, simply by listening to this song.

This is the main thrust of Clement's opening allegory: the "new song" is Christ, the Word of God. He is the Truth, the true Orpheus, who alone can tame the human beast, soften human hearts that are harder than stone, and bring them to life.

But there is another dimension to Clement's allegory, a dimension that he has inherited from the Greeks, especially Plato; and though he may fine-tune it, he does not reject it. This other dimension follows immediately; in fact, it is a continuation of the exclamation quoted above: "Behold the might of the new song!" For in addition to doing all the things just mentioned, "it [the "new song," i.e., Christ] also composed the universe into melodious order, and tuned the discord of the elements to harmonious arrangement, so that the whole world might become harmony."[19]

The lineage of this idea goes back to Plato and, before him, to Pythagoras, whose discoveries regarding the relationship of music to mathematics made the connection between music and cosmic order, and pointed to music as an audible case in point of the harmony of the universe. The *Timaeus*, Plato's account of creation, is a highly developed expression of the Pythagorean connection between music and cosmic order: it is based on the presupposition that the universe is intelligible — that is, it is orderly and harmonious, not chaotic or random. Therefore, it must have been created by an intelligent being — a god. When the god created the soul of the world, Plato taught, he gave it a musical-mathematical structure. When he made the human soul, he gave it the same structure — he "mixed it in the same bowl," as Plato put it. Audible music should also have the same structure. In fact, Plato said that hearing was given to us to help retune our souls that have lost their harmony.

> [A]ll audible music was given us for the sake of harmony, which has motions akin to the orbits in our soul, and which, as anyone who makes intelligent use of the arts knows, is not to be used, as is commonly thought, to give irrational pleasure, but as a heaven-sent ally in reducing to order and harmony any disharmony in the revolutions within us.[20]

19. *Exhortation to the Heathen* I; p. 172.
20. *Timaeus* XIV, 47; pp. 64-65.

Inherent in Plato's discussion, but not explicitly named, are three classes of music. Names were provided much later by Boethius (ca. 480-524), a Roman philosopher whose writings, more than any others, transmitted Greek ideas about music to the Middle Ages and beyond. Boethius named the three classes of music *musica mundana, musica humana,* and *musica instrumentalis. Musica mundana* refers to the order and harmony of the universe: a vestige of this idea remains in the line "and 'round me rings the music of the spheres," which appears in the hymn "This Is My Father's World." *Musica humana* refers to the order and harmony in and, by extension, among human beings. In this sense, a "musical" person is not what we mean by that phrase today — that is, a person with great performing skills, a fine voice, or a keen ear. Rather, it means a well-balanced or virtuous person as described by Cassiodorus (born ca. 485): "If we live virtuously, we are constantly under [music's] discipline, but when we commit injustice we are without music."[21] We retain a vestige of that idea today when we say that someone has "lost his temper." To lose one's temper literally means to go out of tune, to lose *harmonia. Musica instrumentalis,* the third class of music, simply refers to what we today call music: the ordered sounds produced by human voice and instruments. Ideally, *musica instrumentalis* should be a reflection of *musica mundana:* that is, it should be an audible manifestation of the order and harmony of the universe if it is to fulfill the function Plato gave it of tuning our out-of-tune souls.

Clement accepted the idea of *musica mundana* — that the universe is orderly and harmonious — and added that the source of the order is the Creator. For Clement, of course, the Creator was the "new song," the Word of God. In the first chapter of the *Exhortation,* Clement also clearly refers to *musica humana:* the Word also "tuned . . . man — who, composed of body and soul, is a universe in miniature." Further, Clement hinted at the power of *musica instrumentalis* to tune the soul by referring to the story of David playing for King Saul. The "zeal of David" was "fired" by "this deathless strain, — the support of the whole and the harmony of all, — reaching from the centre to the circumference, and from the extremities to the central part, [which] has harmonized this universal frame of things . . . according to the paternal counsel of God. . . ." So David, who "was so far

---

21. *Fundamentals of Sacred and Secular Learning* V, 2; quoted from *Source Readings in Music History,* Vol. 2, p. 34.

from celebrating demons in song, that in reality they were driven away by his music," cured Saul "by merely playing."[22]

This may all be very interesting and colorful, but does audible music reflect cosmic order and in turn shape human character? Not in a fallen world — at least not completely. But would anyone have thought to use music as a metaphor for cosmic order if there were not really something of that order that could be heard in music? Would intelligent and perceptive people — the poets, philosophers, and scientists — have continued to use the metaphor through the centuries if they did not perceive in it something of a higher reality? Yes, there is something in music that makes it an appropriate metaphor for cosmic order. Not all music, of course. Using the parallel metaphor of the dance, Thomas Howard has said, "One doesn't think of the frug or the panic when one thinks of the stars."[23] Likewise, there are certain kinds of music that one does not associate with the "melodious order" and "harmonious arrangement" of the universe.

When we look at Clement's references to sounding music, it is clear that his affirmations and rejections are in harmony with a belief that *musica instrumentalis* should be a reflection of *musica mundana*. On the one hand, the words he uses to describe the music he affirms are words one can easily associate with the "melodious order" and "harmonious arrangement" of the universe. On the other hand, the words he uses to describe the music he rejects are words no one would think of when he "thinks of the stars." Clement affirms music that he describes as sober, pure, decorous, modest, temperate, grave, and soothing, over against music he describes as licentious, voluptuous, frenzied, frantic, inebriating, titillating, scurrilous, turbulent, immodest, and meretricious. Here are three typical examples.

> Burlesque singing is the close friend of drunkenness. . . . For if people occupy their time with pipes, and psalteries, and choirs, and dances, and Egyptian clapping of hands, and such disorderly frivolities, they become quite immodest and intractable, beat on cymbals and drums, and make a noise on instruments of delusion. . . . And every improper sight and sound . . . must by all means be excluded; and we must be on guard against whatever pleasure titillates eye and ear, and enervates the soul. For the various spells of the broken strains and

22. *Exhortation to the Heathen* I; p. 172.
23. Howard, *An Antique Drum*, p. 113.

plaintive numbers of the Carion muse corrupt men's morals, drawing to perturbation of mind, by the licentious and mischievous art of music.[24]

[L]et amatory songs be banished far away, and let our songs be hymns to God. . . . For temperate harmonies are to be admitted; but we are to banish as far as possible from our robust mind those liquid harmonies, which, through pernicious arts in the modulations of tones, train to languor and scurrility. But grave and modest strains say farewell to the turbulence of drunkenness. Chromatic harmonies are therefore to be abandoned to immodest revels, and to florid and meretricious music.[25]

Music is then to be handled for the sake of the embellishment and composure of manners. For instance, at a banquet we pledge each other while the music is playing; soothing by song the eagerness of our desires, and glorifying God for the copious gift of human enjoyments, for His perpetual supply of the food necessary for the growth of the body and of the soul. But we must reject superfluous music, which enervates men's souls, and leads to variety, — now mournful, and then licentious and voluptuous, and then frenzied and frantic.[26]

The first sentence of the last quotation relates *musica instrumentalis* to *musica humana:* music is for the "composure of manners." One's music, Clement believed, is not merely a reflection of the kind of person one is; it is, to a certain extent, involved in shaping a person. Clement and the church fathers were in general agreement on this point, and they were united with Plato and most of the thinkers of antiquity. For that matter, they are united with most people at all times and in all places — ancient and modern, East and West, primitive and literate, sophisticated and unsophisticated, civilized and uncivilized. Of course, there have always been skeptics, too; but the biggest concentration of skeptics appears to belong to modern Western civilization. Modern Western skeptics have a strong inclination to dismiss the subject out of hand with absurdly reductionist rhetorical questions, such as, "How can a C-sharp make me evil?" The answer,

---

24. *The Instructor* II; p. 248.
25. *The Instructor* II; p. 249.
26. *Miscellanies* VI; pp. 500-501.

of course, is that a C-sharp is not music. Nor is a scale or a chord or a rhythm or a melodic motif. Music involves all of those things, but none of them is music, and no one ever claimed that those ingredients by themselves have an impact on a person's character.

Some might remember, however, that Plato allowed only certain modes in his ideal republic; all other modes were to be banished. Is that tantamount to saying that music based on certain scales is evil? No, it isn't, because Plato — and other ancients — did not equate mode with scale, as is often done nowadays in music theory classes. A mode in ancient music was much more than a scale. The best way to convey some idea of what mode meant in ancient music is to repeat an analogy made by John Hollander. He asks us to think of

a fictional situation for nineteenth-century America in which all music was extremely formalized and regimented. Let us assume that only a few keys are in use, namely, C major, F major, and B-flat minor. Let us also imagine that all musical compositions were of one of three types: either military marches and patriotic songs accompanied by brass bands; homely, sentimental songs to be accompanied by guitar, banjo, or some other plucked string; or thick, impassioned string quartets without texts at all, originally composed and usually performed by foreign musicians with unpronounceable names. If these three sorts of composition were to be invariably written in C major, F major, and B-flat minor respectively, some sense of character might easily arise for these keys. The first, or "American" key would have the advantages of "simplicity and straightforwardness" . . . in having no sharps or flats in its signature, and in being somehow appropriate for patriotic activities and sentiments. The second key would be "milder, higher and thinner" than the first, and its ethos (might it be called the "home" or "mountain" mode?) would be "warm," "relaxed," and "fond." The third key, on the other hand, would be "wild and irrational," having a key signature cluttered with flats, no text upon which to depend for ethical clarification, a generally suspicious foreign air, etc. (it might be called the "barbarous" mode). If this situation sounds strained and caricatured, it is really only a dramatically illuminated representation of the Dorian, Lydian, and Phrygian scales of the Greeks.[27]

27. Hollander, *The Untuning of the Sky,* pp. 33-34.

Mode, then, was not only scale. It included a host of other ingredients that tended to cluster together and reinforce each other in producing music's character-shaping power — ingredients such as text, occasion, performers, kinds of instruments used, and manner of performance. This whole package is what we need to have in mind when we hear Plato or Aristotle speak about modes. It is also what we must keep in mind when we hear Clement characterize music as, for example, licentious or grave. It should be noted that Clement always referred to music in the context of an occasion, and that the music he was talking about had an inseparable connection with the occasion and all that went with it.

If Clement's speculative musical thought were limited to ideas about music's relationship to cosmic order and its power to shape human character, we would not need to pay him much attention, because he would not be offering us anything we could not find in Plato and others. But Clement does offer more. First, he points to a deeper reason than character-building for making music. Christians should want to make noble music not only to shape noble character, though they should not ignore that aspect of music; but more fundamentally, Christians make music because they are thankful. Clement says, for example, that music should accompany our eating and drinking out of thanksgiving. Instead of intemperate and disorderly revelry, the Christian's meal should be a "thankful revelry." Drinking should be done "in thanksgiving and psalmody." And before eating, "we should bless the Creator of all; so also in drinking it is suitable to praise Him on partaking of His creatures. For the psalm is a melodious and sober blessing."[28]

Not only in eating and drinking, but in all of life there should be the music of thanksgiving:

> Holding festival, then, in our whole life, persuaded that God is altogether on every side present, we cultivate our fields, praising; we sail the sea, hymning. . . . The [true] Gnostic, then, is very closely allied to God, being at once grave and cheerful in all things, — grave on account of the bent of his soul towards the Divinity, and cheerful on account of his consideration of the blessings of humanity which God has given us.[29]

28. *The Instructor* II; p. 249.
29. *Miscellanies* VII; p. 533.

And his whole life is a holy festival. His sacrifices are prayers, and praises, and readings in the Scriptures before meals, and psalms and hymns during meals and before bed, and prayers also again during the night. By these he unites himself to the divine choir.[30]

If some of Clement's words describing fitting Christian music — words such as grave and sober — mislead us into thinking that he was describing something joyless, the first quotation should set us straight. Christians, according to Clement, are both grave and cheerful at once — and so is their music. As the second quotation says, their whole life is a "festival." When Clement invited the pagans to Christianity, he did not invite them to leave something joyous and exchange it for something gloomy. He invited them to leave the frenzy and impurity of the Maenads for the sobriety of the "fair lambs"[31] who celebrate the holy rites of the Word, raising "a sober choral dance." But sober is not somber. "The righteous are the chorus; the music is a hymn to the King of the Universe. The maidens strike the lyre, the angels praise, the prophets speak; the sound of music issues forth, they run and pursue the jubilant band. . . ."[32] Clement, like Plato, was concerned about the character-shaping power of music; but if music fulfilled its primary function of being part of a thankful, sober revelry, it would also contribute toward shaping sober and joyous character.

Clement also went beyond Plato by placing *musica humana* above *musica mundana*. His writings reveal that he believed human beings are image-bearers of God. In the *Exhortation* he said it plainly: "We are they who bear about with us, in this living and moving image of our human nature, the likeness of God."[33] And he said it via musical imagery: "A noble hymn of God is an immortal man."[34] Plato's god made the cosmos and then, using the same proportions but on a lower level, he made the human soul. Clement's God made the cosmos, but created man in his own image, thereby making him the crown of all creation. Humans can make music, not first of all because they have some perception of cosmic order, but be-

---

30. *Miscellanies* VII; p. 537.

31. "The Greek *amnades*, lambs, is meant as a play upon *Mainades* (Maenads, or women worshippers of Dionysus)." G. A. Butterworth notes this in his edition and translation of the *Exhortation* for the Loeb Classical Library (New York: G. P. Putnam's Sons, 1919), p. 255.

32. *Exhortation to the Heathen* XII; p. 205.

33. *Exhortation to the Heathen* IV; p. 189.

34. *Exhortation to the Heathen* X; p. 201.

cause they bear God's image. Of course, that image has been distorted by the Fall. But Christ has come and dwells in us through his Spirit, and Clement was aware of the close union between the Christian and Christ. He had a strong "awareness of the presence, in the soul of every believer, of His Word, Christ — an intimate companion, to Whom every detail of the believer's life must be referred. . . ."[35] Joined to Christ, "the one choir-leader," the "union of many in one [issues] in the production of divine harmony out of a medley of sounds and division [and] becomes one symphony. . . ."[36] This symphony is a Christian *musica humana,* of which even the music of the spheres is but an echo, and of which the best of our *musica instrumentalis* is also an echo.

35. Brown, *The Body and Society,* p. 128.
36. *Exhortation to the Heathen* IX; p. 197.

CHAPTER 5

Tertullian: Pagan Spectacles
and Christian Households

What fellowship has light with darkness? What accord has Christ with Belial? Or what portion does a believer share with an unbeliever? What agreement has the temple of God with idols? For we are the temple of the living God; as God said, "I will make my dwelling in them and walk among them, and I will be their God, and they shall be my people. Therefore go out from their midst, and be separate from them, says the Lord. . . ."

II Corinthians 6:14-17

It would be difficult to find a person who stands in starker contrast to Clement than Tertullian (ca. 160–ca. 220-30). They were close contemporaries, and the work of both was centered in major African cities — Clement in Alexandria, Tertullian in Carthage. Both were well educated, and both were converts to Christianity. But those facts pretty much exhaust the similarities — except, of course, that both served the same God with deep devotion.

We know very little about Tertullian's life. He was born in Carthage and was a lifelong resident of that city. St. Jerome said that Tertullian's father was a centurion in the Roman army, and he called Tertullian a priest; but neither of these claims has been substantiated.[1] From Tertullian's own writings we learn that he was married — he wrote a treatise *To His Wife*

1. Barnes, *Tertullian*, pp. 3ff.

(Ad uxorem) — and that he was a convert. In *On Repentance (De paenitentia)* he referred to himself as "a sinner . . . of every brand and born for nothing save repentance,"[2] and in *To Scapula (Ad Scapulam)* he hints that the steadfastness and courage displayed by persecuted Christians was an important factor in his conversion. "For all who witness the noble patience of its martyrs . . . are inflamed with desire to examine the matter in question; and as soon as they come to know the truth, they straightway enroll themselves its disciples."[3]

Despite having little knowledge of his life, we can get to know the man well through his more than thirty surviving writings, which give a vivid picture of a complex man. Among the things that come through loud and clear is his antipathy for pagan learning. As we have seen in the previous chapter, his contemporary Clement had great admiration for some pagan thought. The best of it was to the pagans what the law was to the Jews: it needed to be corrected and completed by Christ, but it was in part true and did not need to be entirely discarded. It could provide useful material for building bridges to the true faith. Tertullian, on the other hand, would not admit to any common ground. If he is known for nothing else today, many still recognize his famous outburst:

> What indeed has Athens to do with Jerusalem? What concord is there between the Academy and the Church? what between heretics and Christians? Our instruction comes from "the porch of Solomon," who had himself taught that "the Lord should be sought in simplicity of heart." Away with all attempts to produce a mottled Christianity of Stoic, Platonic and dialectic composition. We want no curious disputation after possessing Christ Jesus, no inquisition after enjoying the gospel! With our faith we desire no further belief.[4]

This famous tirade serves as a good introduction to Tertullian, for it reveals both his uncompromising stance against pagan learning and the powerful rhetoric with which he urged others to take the same stance. The irony of this statement is that it was his pagan education that disciplined his mind and gave him the rhetorical tools with which to attack pagan learning.

Tertullian was not oblivious of this, for "even in the austerist period of

2. *On Repentance* XII; p. 666.
3. *To Scapula* V; p. 108.
4. *The Prescription Against Heretics* VII; p. 246.

his life . . . he grudgingly allowed the need for some schooling." He admitted that it is "needful for the business of daily life and even for learning the truths of Christianity; and once he even admitted that there might be some good in pagan philosophy and that ignorance can be a greater danger than knowledge."[5] But he had an explanation about how some truth got into pagan philosophy: it came from the Old Testament!

> [W]here similarities exist between the doctrines of the Church and of pagan philosophers, [Tertullian was] careful to state that the latter stole such ideas from the Old Testament, which, as a source of revelation, belongs to the Christians. The ancient thinkers only distorted the God-given truths, and thus became responsible for the heresies; they are "the patriarchs of heretics."[6]

If Tertullian's intolerant attitude toward all that came from Athens does not put us off, his extreme asceticism probably will. I have observed above how extremely ascetic the early Christian outlook in general appears to us. But its general outlook was not ascetic enough for Tertullian. Martin Marty points to Clement as a typical example of the rather "legalistic mainstream"; then he adds that "the main stream did not satisfy the more ardent swimmers."[7] Tertullian most certainly was one of those more ardent swimmers. His moral stringency led him first to a strictly ascetic sect, Montanism, and, when even that proved too lax for him, he formed his own sect, the Tertullianists. He criticized the church with the same vehemence that he had formerly reserved for pagans and heretics. For doing so, he was declared a heretic.

It will come as no surprise that Tertullian is not among the more popular church fathers today. Yet he never fails to fascinate. Modern writers take great delight in applying adjectives to him and his writings: he is "passionate" and "fiery," a writer whose "splendid, torrential prose" is "unrelenting," "uncompromising," "fanatical," and "intolerant." His arguments are "brilliant" and "incisive," though they sometimes degenerate into "clever sophistry." He can "charm" his readers, but more frequently he makes them "chafe." E. K. Rand nicely captures the contradictory character of Tertullian, describing him as

5. Laistner, *Christianity and Pagan Culture*, p. 51.
6. Quasten, *Patrology* II, p. 321.
7. Marty, *A Short History of Christianity*, pp. 47-48.

vehement, irate, witty, tender, hater of shams and of culture, cultured himself, learned in letters and the law, scorner of rhetoric and master of its devices, original in thought and style, champion of the Catholic faith and self-constituted prosecuting attorney against all heretics, devotee of a sect so strict and so peculiar it landed him in heresy.[8]

Rand goes on to portray Tertullian as "a popular preacher . . . of a *fin de siecle* society" and as an example quotes this probably well-deserved diatribe against women's fashions.

> I see some of you, who change the color of your hair to saffron. They are ashamed of their own nationality; they're sorry they were not born in Germany. That's why they dye their hair. Aye, they've clapped a bad omen on their fiery locks. They think that's pretty which pollutes. I tell you, those medical concoctions ruin the hair; the constant application of any undiluted lotion ensures softening of the brain in your old age. Even the welcome heat of the sun is injurious to hair thus dried and enlivened. — Will a Christian woman dose saffron on her head as if she were a victim led to the altar? — God said, "How can you make white hair black or black hair white?" Just see how they refute the Lord. "Very good," they retort, "we make it saffron, not white or black, as an easier means of grace." Although they do try to turn white to black as well, when they feel old age approaching. Stupid! The more you try to conceal your years, the more you display them. And that's the real meaning of "eternity," is it? — the perpetual youth of your hair? That's the "incorruptibility" you shall put on in the new mansions of the Lord — guaranteed by the oil of acacia. A fine "preparation" to make for hastening to meet the Lord and leave this wicked world![9]

No amount of description will adequately portray this complex, colorful character, and so my portrait is barely a sketch. But perhaps a few more of Tertullian's own words will serve to show that he repays reading, whatever his faults. On religious freedom he said:

> It is a fundamental human right, a privilege of nature, that every man should worship according to his own convictions: one man's religion

8. Rand, *The Founders of the Middle Ages,* p. 38.
9. *The Apparel of Women* (trans. E. K. Rand), pp. 39-40.

neither harms nor helps another man. It . . . is assuredly no part of religion to compel religion. . . .[10]

On the reality of Christ's human nature:

It was hungry under the devil's temptation, thirsty with the Samaritan woman, wept over Lazarus, was troubled even unto death, and at last actually died.[11]

On the crucifixion:

The Son of God was crucified; I am not ashamed because men must needs be ashamed of it. And the Son of God died; it is by all means to be believed, because it is absurd.[12]

On Christian care for the poor:

Every man once a month brings some modest coin, — or whenever he wishes, and only if he does wish, and if he can; for nobody is compelled; it is a voluntary offering. You might call them the trust funds of piety. For they are not spent upon banquets nor drinking-parties nor thankless eating-houses; but to feed the poor and to bury them, for boys and girls who lack property and parents, and then for slaves grown old, and shipwrecked mariners; and any who may be in mines, islands or prisons, provided that it is for the sake of God's Church, become the pensioners of their confession.

Such works of love (for so it is) put a mark upon us in the eyes of some. "Look," they say, "how they love one another."[13]

On Christian marriage:

How beautiful, then, the marriage of two Christians, two who are one in hope, one in desire, one in the way of life they follow, one in the religion they practice. They are as brother and sister, both servants of the same Master. Nothing divides them, either in flesh or in spirit. They are, in very truth, two in one flesh; and where there is but

10. *To Scapula* II; p. 105.
11. *Against Praxeas* XXVII; p. 624.
12. *On the Flesh of Christ* V; p. 525.
13. *Apology* XXXIX, 5-7; pp. 175, 177.

one flesh there is also but one spirit. They pray together, they worship together, they fast together; instructing one another, encouraging one another. Side by side they visit God's church and partake of God's banquet; side by side they face difficulties and persecution, they share their consolations. They have no secrets from one another; they never shun each other's company; they never bring sorrow to each other's hearts. . . . Psalms and hymns they sing to one another, striving to see which one of them will chant more beautifully the praises of their Lord. Hearing and seeing this, Christ rejoices. To such as these He gives His peace.[14]

On abortion:

To forbid birth is only quicker murder. It makes no difference whether one take away the life once born or destroy it as it comes to birth. He is a man, who is to be a man.[15]

On martyrdom:

But go to it! my good magistrates; the populace will count you a deal better, if you sacrifice the Christians to them. Torture us, rack us, condemn us, crush us; your cruelty only proves our innocence. That is why God suffers us to suffer all this. . . . But nothing whatever is accomplished by your cruelties, each more exquisite than the last. It is the bait that wins men for our school. We multiply whenever we are mown down by you; the blood of Christians is seed.[16]

Tertullian died, probably of natural causes, at an old age, an embattled and embittered man. It is fitting that his death, like his life, was fraught with ironic contradictions. This vigorous opponent of heresy died a heretic, and the martyrdom he admired and perhaps longed for eluded him despite his outspoken attacks on paganism. This irony deepens when we remember that the conciliatory Justin met his death as a martyr.

Tertullian's references to music are not as numerous or as full as those of Clement, and it will come as no surprise that Tertullian spent no time with

14. *To His Wife* II, 8; p. 35.
15. *Apology* IX, 8; p. 49.
16. *Apology* L, 12-13; p. 227.

the kind of philosophical speculation about music that occupied Clement's attention. Neither will it be a surprise to learn that among Tertullian's references to music are some condemnations of pagan music. What may surprise is the relative scarcity of the negative comments, especially when we discover how vehement the patristic polemic against pagan music will soon become.

Tertullian's denunciations of pagan music occur in his treatise *On Spectacles (De spectaculis)*, a sweeping attack on the public spectacles that took place in the theaters and arenas that were so prominent in the life of the late Roman Empire. Tertullian divides his condemnation into two parts: in the first he shows the connections of the spectacles to pagan worship and therefore to idolatry; in the second he denounces the shows for their pernicious effect on morals. There are three main references to music in the treatise. The first reference is to the musical instruments of pagan sacrifices, the tibia and the trumpet, a statement that links the theater to pagan worship: "The path to the theater is from the temples and the altars, from that miserable mess of incense and blood, to the tune of tibias and trumpets; and the masters of the ceremonies are those two all-polluted adjuncts of funeral and sacrifice, the undertaker and the soothsayer."[17] Apart from the association with something detestable, there is nothing particularly negative in this reference to the instruments.

In the second reference, however, Tertullian relates the music of the theater to sexual immorality and makes it clear that Christians should shun it.

> Quite obviously Liber [the Latin name for Bacchus] and Venus are the patrons of the arts of the stage. Those features of the stage peculiarly and especially its own, that effeminacy of gesture and posture, they dedicate to Venus and Liber, wanton gods, the one in her sex, the other in his dress; while all that is done with voice and song, instrument and book is the affair of the Apollos and the Muses, the Minervas and Mercuries. You, O Christian, will hate the things, when you cannot but hate the authors of them![18]

The third reference follows Tertullian's rhetorical question, "Do you think that seated where there is nothing of God, he will at that moment

17. *On Spectacles* X; p. 257.
18. *On Spectacles* X; pp. 259, 261.

turn his thoughts to God?" His sarcastic answer: "But while the tragic actor declaims, he will think of the crying aloud of one of the prophets! Amid the strains of some effeminate tibia player, he will muse in himself upon a psalm!"[19] There is certainly no approval voiced in these statements; but compared, say, to the tirade against dyed hair quoted above, Tertullian's denunciation of pagan music, even in its sarcasm, is relatively mild.

What I find more instructive in *On Spectacles* are his more general arguments at the beginning of the treatise. Tertullian first points to the seductive power of pleasure: "For such is the force of pleasure that it can prolong ignorance to give it its chance, and pervert knowledge to cloak itself." Then follows the first argument: it is against those who claim that

> there can be no clash between religion, in your mind and conscience, and these great refreshments of eye and ear that lie outside us; that God is not offended by a man's enjoying himself, but that, so long as his fear of God and God's honour are unhurt, it is no guilt in its proper time and place to avail oneself of such enjoyment.[20]

In answering this argument, Tertullian first says that the answer to it is the burden of the whole treatise: "But it is exactly this which here and now we purpose to prove — that this does not square with true religion or with duty to God."[21] In other words, if he is successful in demonstrating his two main points — that the shows are idolatrous and that they have a pernicious effect on morals — then the argument above will not hold up.

But, in addition to the argument of the whole treatise, he makes a telling point: referring to martyrdom, he says that Christians were able to meet their deaths courageously because they were not attracted to the pleasures of this life. So, given a situation in which death could strike at any moment, he asks if it would not be prudent — even if it were not a divine command — to avoid becoming attached to such fleeting pleasures.

> There are those who think that Christians, a race of men ever ready for death, are trained in that stubbornness of theirs by the renunciation of pleasures, that they may find it easier to despise life, when once its ties (if the word be allowed) are severed, and they no longer

19. *On Spectacles* XXV; pp. 289, 291.
20. *On Spectacles* I; p. 231.
21. *On Spectacles* I; p. 231.

crave what they have emptied of meaning for themselves. This would make it a rule of human prudence and forethought rather than of divine command. It would truly go against the grain to die for the Lord, if such pleasures could still have continued! Though, to be sure, if it were so, stubbornness in a rule of life such as ours might well pay attention to a plan so apt.[22]

The second argument that Tertullian refutes begins with the proposition "that all things were created by God and given to man. . . ." Those making that argument drew the conclusion that all things are good,

all being the work of a good Creator; and that among [the works of the Creator] we must reckon all the various things that go to make the public shows, the horse, for example, and the lion, and strength of body and charm of voice. It follows, they urge, that a thing cannot be counted foreign to God or hostile to Him that exists by His creation, nor must we suppose a thing hostile to God's worshippers, which is not hostile to God because it is not foreign to God.[23]

Tertullian's response is right on target.

No one denies — because nobody is unaware of it and even nature tells us — that God is the creator of the universe, and that the universe is good and is given to man. But because they do not really know God — knowing Him only by natural law and not by right of sonship — knowing Him from afar and not at close quarters, — they are necessarily ignorant as to how He bids or forbids the things of His creation to be used. They are also unaware of the rival powers that confront God for the abuse of what divine creation has given for use. For where your knowledge of God is defective, you can neither know His mind nor His adversary. We have not then merely to consider by whom all things were created, but also by whom they are perverted. For in that way it will appear for what use they were created, if it once appear for what use they were not. There is great difference between the corrupted and the uncorrupted because there is a great difference between the Creator and the perverter.[24]

22. *On Spectacles* I; pp. 231, 233.
23. *On Spectacles* I; p. 233.
24. *On Spectacles* II; p. 235.

Tertullian does not stop at exposing the error of this argument; he also points out the reason people make such a manifestly foolish argument. They resort to it when they are "afraid of losing . . . some delight or enjoyment of the world!" So powerful is the claim of pleasure that

> you will find more men turned from our school [i.e., Christianity] by the danger of pleasure than by the danger of life! For even a fool does not dread death beyond a certain point — he feels it inevitable; but pleasure, a thing of such high value, even a sage does not despise; since neither fool nor sage has any delight in life apart from pleasure.[25]

Having disposed of two arguments, Tertullian turns to a final argument. This one is unlike the previous two in that they were made by "heathen opinion," whereas this argument "our own friends put forward":

> There are certain people, of a faith somewhat simple or somewhat precise, who, when faced with this renunciation of the public shows, ask for the authority of Scripture and take their ground in uncertainty, because abstinence in this matter is not specifically and in so many words enjoined upon the servants of God.[26]

Tertullian has to admit that "we nowhere find it expressly laid down: 'You shall not go to the circus, you shall not go to the theater, you shall not look at contest or show.'" But he finds the first Psalm relevant here: "Happy is the man who has not gone to the gathering of the impious, who has not stood in the way of sinners, nor sat in the chair of pestilences." But his application of this text is forced, because he tries to make its meaning too specific.

> For at the public shows there is sitting in the seat and standing in the way. For they use the word *viae* [ways] for the alleys by the barriers and around the arena, and for the gangways up and down that separate the common people's sections on the sloping sides of the amphitheatre; and *cathedra* [seat] is the term for the space in the recess assigned for chairs.[27]

25. *On Spectacles* II; pp. 233, 235.
26. *On Spectacles* II; p. 239.
27. *On Spectacles* II; pp. 239, 241.

More to the point than this attempt to satisfy those who insist on a proof text is the point Tertullian makes next: that Christians' baptismal vows should keep them from the idolatrous shows.

> When we enter the water and profess the Christian faith in the terms prescribed by its law, we profess with our mouths that we have renounced the devil, his pomp and his angels. What shall we call the chief and outstanding matter, in which the devil and his pomps and his angels are recognized, rather than idolatry? . . . So, if it shall be established that the whole equipment of the public shows is idolatry pure and simple, we have an indubitable decision laid down in advance, that this profession of renunciation made in baptism touches the public shows too, since they, being idolatry, belong to the devil, his pomp and his angels.[28]

I suspect that Tertullian's renunciation of the spectacles sounds excessively ascetic to most of us today; we are bound to ask whether he went too far with renunciation. I will deal with that question more fully after we have encountered some more early Christian reactions to the amusements of late antiquity (in which, we must remember, music was integrally involved). At this point I will simply observe that, even if Tertullian was too stringent, he was right about a couple of basic things. First, the lure of pleasure is so powerful that it beclouds our judgment. Second, human products, even though they make use of God's good gifts, need to be critically evaluated because they are products made by fallen humans. Even if Tertullian was mistaken in his evaluation of the public spectacles (and we should not be too quick to assume that he was), we have to give him credit for realizing that the Christians of his day needed to examine them carefully. And we have to give him credit, once he came to the conclusion that they were idolatrous and morally pernicious, for denouncing them courageously in the face of their great popularity.

To summarize what we know about Tertullian's position on Christian life and pagan music, we can say that, even though his direct references to pagan music are rare, his denunciation of it is without compromise because of his complete denunciation of the public spectacles of which it was a part. There is no question of separating the various components of the spectacles; they all belong inextricably together. The music that accompanied them be-

28. *On Spectacles* IV; p. 243.

longed to them and could not be torn from them and placed in a different context. So, even though his statements specifically against the music of the spectacles are few and not especially vehement, his statements about the whole apply to the parts, and there is no question he saw the whole as idolatrous and morally pernicious and thus to be shunned by Christians.

Tertullian, however, was by no means opposed to all music. Christians were not without literature and song; on the contrary, Tertullian pointed out, Christians had a "sufficiency" of their own — "sufficiency of songs and voices, not fable, those of ours, but truth; not artifice but simplicity."[29] As with his references to pagan music in public spectacles, his references to Christian music-making are scarce; but what there is reveals his commendation of the use of music in Christian households.

At this point a word of caution is in order. We should not fall into the error of assuming that, when early Christian writings mention the singing of psalms and hymns, they are referring to "church music." Some of the references are certainly in the context of liturgical singing; but very often they are not. More often, when mentioning psalms and hymns, the early Christian writers were advocating or describing the singing of that music in everyday life. For them, church music was not one thing and the music of everyday life something else. A couple of examples from Tertullian will illustrate this point.

In the place in the *Apology* where he describes public Christian worship, a context in which we might expect to find reference to psalmody, there is none.

> We meet in gathering and congregation to approach God in prayer, massing our forces to surround Him. This violence that we do Him pleases God. We pray also for Emperors, for their ministers and those in authority, for the security of the world, for peace on earth, for postponement of the end. We meet to read the books of God — if anything in the nature of the times bids us look to the future or open our eyes to facts. In any case, with those holy words we feed our faith, we lift up our hope, we confirm our confidence; and no less we reinforce our teaching by inculcation of God's precepts. There is, besides, exhortation in our gatherings, rebuke, divine censure.[30]

29. *On Spectacles* XXIX; p. 297.
30. *Apology* XXXIX; p. 175.

71

Tertullian's silence, of course, does not mean that singing did not occur in Christian worship. There is plenty of evidence elsewhere to show us otherwise. But Tertullian, for whatever reason, does not mention singing here. However, he does mention it very specifically in his treatise *On Prayer (De oratione)*, chapters 27 and 28. I quote them in full:

> Those who are more exact about prayer are in the habit of adding to their prayers an "Alleuia" and psalms of such a character that those who are present may respond with the final phrases. Assuredly, the practice is excellent in every respect which by its high praise and reverence of God is competent to offer Him, as a rich victim, a prayer that has been filled out in every detail.
>
> Now, this is the spiritual victim which has set aside the earlier sacrifice. "To what purpose do you offer me the multitude of your victims," says the Lord? "I am full, I desire not holocausts of rams, and fat of fatlings, and blood of calves and goats. For who required these things at your hands?" The Gospel teaches what God demands. "The hour is coming," He says, "when the true worshipers will worship the Father in spirit and in truth. For God is spirit," and therefore He requires that His worshipers be of the same nature. We are the true worshipers and true priests who, offering our prayer in the spirit, offer sacrifice in the spirit — that is, prayer — as a victim that is appropriate and acceptable to God; for this is what He has demanded and what He has foreordained for Himself. This prayer, consecrated to Him with our whole heart, nurtured by faith, prepared with truth — a prayer that is without blemish because of our innocence, clean because of our chastity — a prayer that has received the victor's crown because of our love for one another — this prayer we should bring to the altar of God with a display of good works amid the singing of psalms and hymns and it will obtain for us from God all that we ask.[31]

Reading this out of context, one could be excused for thinking that Tertullian is talking about liturgical prayer. The references to responses, sacrifices, worshipers, priests, and altar all have a liturgical ring. But public worship is not the context at all. In the paragraph just prior to the two quoted above, Tertullian specifically says: "When a brother has entered

31. *On Prayer* XXVII-XXVIII; pp. 185-186.

your home, do not let him go away without prayer," and "you should not attend to earthly refreshment before the heavenly." In that same paragraph he also mentions the kiss of peace, another liturgical item, but again, specifically in the context of one's house. "Or how can you say, according to the precept, 'Peace to this house,' unless you exchange the kiss of peace with those who are in the house?"[32] It is clear, then, that in these two chapters Tertullian is talking about alleluias, responses, psalms, and hymns being sung in a Christian household.

Another reference in Tertullian's writings to music in the Christian household comes in the context of the banquet. It appears in his *Apology* in answer to pagan criticism of the crimes Christians were supposedly committing at their banquets, including the charge that they were so extravagant that Christians "market as if they were to die to-morrow, and build as if they were never to die at all." Tertullian had no problem outdoing that taunt!

> But any man sees a mote in another's eye more easily than a beam in his own. With all those tribes and senates and decurions belching the air grows sour. When the Salii dine, the money lender is needed. Actuaries will have to reckon the cost of Hercules' tithes and banquets. At the Attic Apaturia, Dionysia and mysteries, conscription is proclaimed — for cooks. The smoke of a dinner of Serapis will fetch out the firemen.[33]

The taunts out of the way, Tertullian goes on to describe Christian banquets. Embedded in his description are a brief reference to singing and a humorous remark about it being a sobriety test.

> Our dinner shows its idea in its name; it is called by the Greek name for love *(agape)*. . . . If the motive of the banquet is honest, take the motive as the standard of the other proceedings required by our rule of life. Since it turns on the duty of religion, it allows nothing vile, nothing immodest. We do not take our places at table until we have first tasted prayer to God. Only so much is eaten as satisfies hunger; only so much drunk as meets the need of the modest. They satisfy themselves only so far as men will who recall that even during the

32. *On Prayer* XXVI; p. 184.
33. *Apology* XXXIX; p. 179.

night they must worship God; they talk as those would who know the Lord listens. After water for the hands come the lights; and then each, from what he knows of the Holy Scriptures, or from his own heart, is called before the rest to sing to God; so that is a test of how much he has drunk. Prayer in like manner ends the banquet. Then we break up; but not to form groups for violence nor gangs for disorder, nor outbursts of lust; but to pursue the same care for self-control and chastity, as men who have dined not so much on dinner as on discipline.[34]

In this day of radio, MTV, and ever more readily available recorded music, singing at home, or anywhere else, has been lost. With a constant barrage of recorded music in houses, cars, shopping malls, beaches, picnic areas — there are few places one can escape it — there is little sonic space for singing. But before the electronic revolution, singing at home was normal. Certainly Tertullian expected singing to occur at home; and though he warmly recommended it, he was concerned about the kind of singing that went on. For example, one of the problems of a mixed marriage, he said, was the songs a pagan husband would sing to his Christian wife.

Whose hand will she seek to clasp to hers? Whose cup will touch her lips? What kind of song will her husband sing to her and she to him? Some piece, no doubt, which is popular in theatres and taverns this will she hear, this she will surely hear, some song which sounds in the throat of the devil himself. Is there ever any mention of God? Is there any prayer to Christ?[35]

In contrast, recall Tertullian's description of the singing of Christian spouses: "Between the two echo psalms and hymns; and they mutually challenge each other which shall better chant to their Lord. Such things when Christ sees and hears, He rejoices. To these He sends His own peace."[36]

Whether among guests or between spouses, the few glimpses into Christian domestic music-making found in Tertullian's writings reveal his ideal of replacing pagan music with psalms and hymns in all of life. We have encountered the same ideal in Clement, who wrote of psalms and

34. *Apology* XXXIX; p. 181.
35. *To His Wife* II, 6; p. 31.
36. *To His Wife* II, 8; p. 35.

hymns being sung "during meals and before bed" and of praising and hymning taking place while working in the fields and sailing the seas. Different as Clement and Tertullian were, there is little that separates them when it comes to the music they renounced and the music they warmly embraced.

CHAPTER 6

Expansion and Persecution, Triumph and Trouble

Christendom had set out to re-generate the world. The unregenerate Roman world was now handed over to it. No extreme difficulties were any longer to be put in its way. . . . The old pagan rituals were not finally prohibited until the year 392, by Theodosius, and there was still a good deal of rhetorical and sincere opposition. But the no-man's land of religion, all casual and fashionable sections of the Empire, became more or less formally Christian. All insincerity became Christian. . . .

Charles Williams

The events from the middle of the third century into the early fifth century of the current era are among the most momentous in the history of the church. Indeed, they are among the most momentous in the history of Western civilization. In particular, Constantine's conversion to Christianity stands out: with his conversion in the early fourth century, the church — with unexpected suddenness — changed from being an organization suffering from concerted imperial attempts to eradicate it to being an organization enjoying imperial favor. The early Christian historian Eusebius conveys something of the heady feeling this astonishing change brought to Christians.

Men had now lost all fear of their former oppressors; day after day they kept dazzling festival; light was everywhere, and men who once dared not look up greeted each other with smiling faces and shining eyes. They danced and sang in city and country alike, giving honour first of all to God our Sovereign Lord, as they had been instructed, and then to the pious emperor with his sons, so dear to God. Old troubles were forgotten, and all irreligion passed into oblivion; good things present were enjoyed, those yet to come eagerly awaited. In every city the victorious emperor published decrees full of humanity and laws that gave proof of munificence and true piety. Thus all tyranny had been purged away, and the kingdom that was theirs was preserved securely and without question for Constantine and his sons alone. They, having made it their first task to wipe the world clean from hatred of God, rejoiced in the blessings that he had conferred upon them, and, by the things they did for all men to see, displayed love of virtue and love of God, devotion and thankfulness to the Almighty.[1]

Under the circumstances, we can forgive Eusebius his excessive elation. But without diminishing the impact Constantine's conversion had on church and empire, we must realize that "all irreligion" did not pass "into oblivion." Although the changes his conversion brought about went far and deep, we should not conclude that paganism immediately stopped being a threat or that the triumph of Christianity did not produce new problems. A battle had been won, but not the war. Paganism, the old enemy, continued to attack the church in new guises, and another enemy — heresy — emerged. Then, in the early fifth century, when the Roman Empire finally succumbed to the pressure of the invading barbarians, the church had to face the challenges coming from the customs and beliefs of peoples quite different from the Romans.

The mid-200s was a particularly chaotic time for the Roman Empire. The *Pax Romana* was disturbed by Rome's increasing struggles with barbarian foes on the borders; by the rapid succession of emperors, many of whom were assassinated; by civil wars and revolts; by the ravages of plagues and famines; and by financial woes, the decline of cities, and the state of disrepair of aqueducts, baths, roads, and markets. The succession of crises the empire faced often diverted its attention away from the church; through all of these crises the church continued to grow, even though the empire con-

---

1. *The History of the Church* X; pp. 413-414.

tinued to view it with unfavorable eyes. If, "in the first two centuries the relative peace of the empire had fostered the extension of Christianity, the unrest of the third century favoured its intensive development, since as crisis followed crisis attention was diverted from it."[2]

Furthermore, many pagans who had grown weary of their impoverished religion and were not attracted to the exotic alternatives from the East found in Christianity answers to their profoundest questions and a high moral standard by which to live. E. R. Dodds found many reasons why third-century Christianity may have attracted many pagans, and they are worth quoting at length.

> One reason for the success of Christianity was simply the weakness and weariness of the opposition: paganism had lost faith . . . in itself.
>
> Christianity, on the other hand, was judged to be worth living for because it was seen to be worth dying for. It is evident that Lucian, Marcus Aurelius, Galen and Celsus were all, despite themselves, impressed by the courage of the Christians in face of death and torture. And that courage must have been the starting point of many conversions. . . . There were, of course, other reasons for the success of Christianity. . . .
>
> In the first place, its very exclusiveness, its refusal to concede any value to alternative forms of worship, which nowadays is often felt to be a weakness, was in the circumstances of the time a source of strength. . . . Christianity made a clean sweep. It lifted the burden of freedom from the shoulders of the individual: one choice, one irrevocable choice, and the road to salvation was clear. Pagan critics might mock at Christian intolerance, but in an age of anxiety any "totalist" creed exerts a powerful attraction. . . .
>
> Secondly, Christianity was open to all. In principle, it made no social distinctions. . . . Above all, it did not, like Neoplatonism, demand education. . . .
>
> Thirdly, in a period when earthly life was increasingly devalued and guilt-feelings were widely prevalent, Christianity held out to the disinherited the conditional promise of a better inheritance in another world. . . . Porphyry remarked, as others have done since, that only sick souls stand in need of Christianity. But sick souls were numerous in our period. . . .

2. Davies, *The Early Christian Church*, p. 115.

But lastly, the benefits of becoming a Christian were not confined to the next world. A Christian congregation was from the first a community in a much fuller sense than any corresponding group. . . . Love of one's neighbor is not an exclusively Christian virtue, but in our period the Christians appeared to have practised it much more effectively than any other group. The Church provided the essentials of social security: it cared for widows and orphans, the old, the unemployed, and the disabled; it provided a burial fund for the poor and a nursing service in time of plague. But even more important, I suspect, than these material benefits was the sense of belonging which the Christian community could give.[3]

So the church grew during the third century, but not without persecution. During two periods, one in the middle of the third century and the other at the beginning of the fourth, the empire made concerted attempts to eradicate the church. Whatever other reasons might have been behind these persecutions — to find a scapegoat, to divert the attention of the populace, or because of genuine religious belief that Christianity had brought the anger of the gods upon the empire — the main reason was probably the hope that the rapidly decaying unity of the empire could be regained by requiring all people, whatever their beliefs, to sacrifice to the traditional gods, now represented mainly in the person of the emperor.

The first of the two great persecutions began in 250 under Decius. He established a policy that required all citizens to sacrifice to the pagan gods, proof of which was to be shown by a certified statement. W. H. C. Frend refers to the Decian persecution as a watershed, a time in which the church's fortunes could have gone either way.

Had the church collapsed, it could scarcely have recovered. As it was, the combination of military and economic disasters took a heavier toll on traditional pagan society than they did on the church. The latter proved triumphantly resilient. Its worldwide organization, its economic power, and its martyr-tradition were proof against persecution and mass temporary apostasies. By 256 it had become stronger than it had been before persecution broke out. The "unlawful association" *(religio illicita)* was now a rival to the empire itself.[4]

3. Dodds, *Pagan and Christian in an Age of Anxiety,* pp. 132-137.
4. Frend, *The Rise of Christianity,* p. 328.

The church's triumph over the Decian persecution brought with it a problem that we can see as a foreshadowing of later problems. Many Christians had not stood up under the pressure of persecution; so the church faced the question of what kind of disciplinary action to take toward members who had broken their baptismal vows, who had not shown the spiritual strength to be martyrs. Schisms occurred when different courses of action were taken. Some leaders, such as Novatian and Maximus, insisted on a strict policy that would allow no apostate member back into the church; others, such as Novatus and Fortunatus, favored a lax policy of re-admittance without punishment; still others, such as Cyprian, advocated a moderate policy of re-admittance along with punishment that varied in severity according to the extent of the apostasy.

We need not be concerned here with which policy won out at various times and in various places, but we can at least see in this problem the beginnings of the kinds of problems the church was about to face when its membership would grow even more rapidly. Not all members would show equal conviction, not all would possess the same understanding, and not all would have the same ideas about correct and just courses of action. How open, then, should the church be in accepting members? How insistent should it be on uniformity of belief, and how rigorous in discipline? Where should the church draw its boundaries of orthodoxy? What would constitute heresy? What behaviors could and could not be tolerated? Such questions came forward in the third century, when the membership of the expanding church came to include many whose spiritual strength was not up to the ideal of martyrdom. Further expansion would prove to make such questions even more urgent.

The last and greatest persecution of the church began under Diocletian in 303. At first his tactics were different from those of previous persecutors: he began by ordering church buildings, sacred books, and sacred vessels to be destroyed. His next move was to imprison the clergy, obviously thinking that the removal of the leaders and the sacred artifacts would bring about the end of the church. When these measures failed, Diocletian added the policy of his predecessors — requiring all citizens to sacrifice to the gods or face death. But, like his predecessors, Diocletian failed. The church once again proved too strong. In fact, Frend claims that Diocletian's attempt to snuff out the church was doomed from the start. "By the time Diocletian threw down the final challenge in 303, the battle had been lost."[5] Just ten years later, Constantine issued the "Edict of Milan," which granted freedom of worship to Christians and restored all the church's lost property. Before the end of the fourth century, Theodosius made Christianity the official religion of the empire.

During the third century, paganism still dominated the religious scene, but it was showing signs of weakening. J. G. Davies describes the situation as follows:

> The marriage of [Emperor] Septimus to Julia Domna, daughter of the hereditary priest-prince of Emesa, encouraged the further spread of the eastern cults. . . . [And] official paganism was kept alive [by] Decius seeking to bring peace to a harried empire by demanding universal sacrifice and Aurelian attempting to revivify and unify paganism by erecting a temple to the Sun-God in Rome.
>
> These, however, were isolated and, as it proved, ineffective acts. Whatever might take place at government level, paganism amongst the populace was to suffer decline; after the year 235 very few dedications were made to the gods of the empire. Moreover in the financial stringency of the time, the Mysteries were proving too expensive, and although Mithraism was still strong, particularly in the army under the Servi and the Gordonians, its exclusion of women reduced its appeal. Once popular cults were also losing their adherents. . . .
>
> There is indeed every reason to accept the accuracy of the statement of Arnobius, written at the opening of the fourth century: "the gods are neglected, and in the temples there is now a very thin attendance. Former ceremonies are exposed to derision, and the time-honoured rites of institutions once sacred have sunken before the superstitions of new religions." Here was both the opportunity for and the partial result of the advance of Christianity.[6]

If pagan religions were showing signs of weakness in the third century, the same cannot be said for pagan philosophy. Neo-Platonism flourished under Plotinus, its founder: his work "was a powerful weapon against the faith," and his students Porphyry and Iamblichus popularized his ideas and played an important role "in propping up the failing paganism. . . . Though the verdict of history was to be that they were supporting a lost cause, their

---

5. Frend, *The Rise of Christianity*, p. 328.
6. Davies, *The Early Christian Church*, pp. 112-113.

philosophical synthesis was to prove of value as a medium of Christian theological expression, especially in the hands of Augustine of Hippo."[7]

There are widely differing appraisals of the impact of Constantine's conversion on the church. Some Christians tout it as the best thing that could have happened; others lament it as a downfall from which the church has yet to recover. Neither extreme is justified. Constantine's conversion was a mixed blessing — but a blessing nonetheless. However much we admire the martyrs, we should not desire a situation in which martyrdom is common. And though it is obvious that strength comes from adversity, we must not seek adversity or be ungrateful when God sends prosperity. What Constantine did was good, and the early Christians' celebrations reported by Eusebius were warranted and fitting.

Of course, the church grew rapidly in number and in wealth after Constantine's conversion. Under his government, revenues went to support the church's works of mercy; clergy were exempt from taxes and became paid civil servants; and magnificent church buildings were erected. In addition, liturgies were expanded and became more elaborate; the structure of the clergy became more highly organized; and major achievements were made in articulating Christian beliefs, particularly those centering on the person and work of Christ and on the nature of the Trinity. The fourth century, the century of Saints Basil, John Chrysostom, Ambrose, Jerome, and Augustine, to name but a few, has been called the "Golden Age" of early Christianity because of the great flourishing of Christian writing and preaching.

But problems came in the wake of the church's newly acquired eminence. The post-Constantinian church faced growing problems with heresy. This was partly due to its increased size: greater numbers of people brought about a greater diversity of beliefs, and not all of them could fit within the boundaries of orthodoxy. The rise of heresy was also due to the greater security that the church enjoyed during this period. No longer feeling its existence threatened, the church had the leisure to come to grips intellectually with inevitable questions, especially those concerning Christ's identity and the nature of his work. The church labored long and hard to formulate its beliefs on the person and work of Christ, and also on the Trinity. Needless to say, many divergent views flourished, so heresy flourished as well. Dualistic Manichaeism, Docetism (which denied the human

7. Davies, *The Early Christian Church*, pp. 113-114.

nature of Christ), and Arianism (which denied the Trinity) all flourished during this period and competed with orthodoxy for souls. Since orthodoxy did not have a monopoly on brains, commitment, and persuasive power, heretic leaders attracted many followers. Among their tools of persuasion was music, particularly hymns that expressed their beliefs.[8]

In addition to the growing problem of heresy within, the church after Constantine continued to face the threat of paganism from without. In fact, the pagan threat was coming from both outside and inside the church, and it may have been even more acute after Constantine's conversion than it was before. At the risk of oversimplifying a complex situation, we can say that the pagan threat from outside the church came from two different sources: Eastern mystery cults and traditional Roman religious rites. Among the general populace, the exotic mystery cults were still popular, even though they were past their heyday by the third century. The worship of Dionysus, Isis and Osiris, and Attis and Cybele, for example, held

> a powerful attraction because they promised freedom from sorrow and death to their faithful, making them in some way sharers in the very nature of God. Moreover, the splendors of the feasts, the languor produced by the music of the East, the nervous tension induced by lacerations of the flesh, the excitement of the dances, and the complicated, exotic liturgies all helped to arouse religious enthusiasm and to create a feeling of brotherhood among the adepts.[9]

The more traditional Roman religious rites were kept alive mainly by the ruling classes, who, particularly in the West, showed a great reluctance to abandon their religious traditions. Wealth and a sense of loyalty to a venerable institution kept the calendar of traditional Roman sacred feasts alive. This kind of paganism developed a tenacity that came from the feeling that something treasured was slipping away.

These two kinds of pagan challenge from outside the church were joined by a pagan challenge from within. As the Christian church's membership grew, the number of members who were reluctant to abandon their former ways of life also grew. Since being a member no longer brought with it danger but — on the contrary — often brought with it fa-

8. See chapter 10, pp. 168-69.
9. Paredi, *Saint Ambrose*, p. 220.

vor, many became members out of self-interest. "All insincerity," as Charles Williams put it, "became Christian."[10] Therefore, the church came to have significant numbers of new members whose beliefs and lifestyles retained sizable vestiges of paganism.

So paganism's threat to the church did not abate after Constantine; it simply took on different guises. It threatened the church from within because of the lingering paganism of many of its newer members, and it continued to threaten the church from without because of the remaining defensive and sometimes powerful and influential pagan minority in the empire who offered "a good deal of rhetorical and sincere opposition."[11]

The quantity of musical references in Christian literature increases dramatically after the middle of the third century. This is to be expected, especially in the fourth century, because of the improved political climate for Christians. But the themes do not change a great deal; they are more full-blown due to the increased quantity, but there are no basic changes in the church's musical thought. We continue to encounter New Testament motifs with regularity. God is the primary audience. Origen says, "We sing hymns to the one God who is over all and his only begotten Word, who is God also."[12] The reason for singing to him is gratitude for deliverance. Eusebius gave as "the background to our thought" the words from Psalm 136: "For in our low estate He remembered us,/ And redeemed us from our adversaries."[13] The Spirit is the source of Christian song: "For our mind cannot pray unless the Spirit . . . first prays before it. Nor can it sing . . . unless the Spirit . . . has first searched the depths of the mind with praise and song. . . ."[14] That song is sung in the heart, but that does not mean it is sung silently. Rather, according to Niceta of Remensiana, when Paul says "'in your hearts,' he admonishes one not to sing with the voice alone and without the attention of the heart. . . ."[15] The whole person is involved. Athanasius said: "It is proper . . . to hymn God . . . with expanse of voice" because "thus it is assured that men love God with their entire strength

10. Williams, *The Descent of the Dove*, p. 50.

11. Williams, *The Descent of the Dove*, p. 50.

12. *Against Celsus* VIII; quoted from *Music in Early Christian Literature*, p. 38.

13. *Against Celsus* X, p. 385.

14. Origen, *On Prayer* II; quoted from *Music in Early Christian Literature*, p. 37.

15. Niceta, *On the Usefulness of Hymns* II; quoted from *Music in Early Christian Literature*, p. 135.

and capability."[16] These early writers frequently emphasized singing with understanding. Basil instructed: "While your tongue sings, let your mind search out the meaning of the words, so that you might sing in spirit and sing also in understanding."[17] Singing is a "bond of unity"[18] for those singing here below; it also joins them to the heavenly hosts. Cyril of Jerusalem says:

> [W]e commemorate the heavens, the earth and the sea; the sun and moon, the stars, the whole rational and irrational creation, both visible and invisible: Angels and Archangels; Virtues, Dominions, Principalities, Powers, Thrones and the many-faced Cherubim: equivalently saying with David, "O magnify the Lord with me." We commemorate also the Seraphim whom Isaiah in the Holy Spirit saw encircling the throne of God, "with two wings veiling their faces and with two their feet, while with two they did fly," as they chanted: "Holy, Holy, Holy, Lord of Hosts." It is to mingle our voices in the hymns of the heavenly armies that we recite this doxology which descends to us from the Seraphim.[19]

Musical imagery, especially allegorical interpretation of instruments, continued unabated. A passage in Eusebius recalls — but varies — Clement of Alexandria's comparison of the old song of Orpheus and the new song of Christ:

> A Greek myth tells us that Orpheus charmed every sort of animal and mollified the savagery of wild beasts by plucking on the strings of an instrument with a plectrum. Moreover, this is celebrated in a Greek chorus and it is believed that a lifeless lyre tamed these beasts and even the trees (they were oak) moved in response to music. But the all-wise and pan-harmonious Word of God, applying every sort of remedy to the souls of men afflicted with manifold vices, takes the work of his wisdom, his human nature, into his hands as if it were a musical instrument and with it plays odes and epodes for rational beings, not mindless beasts, and thus, with the medication of his in-

---

16. Athanasius, Letter to Marcellus XXVII; quoted from *Music in Early Christian Literature*, p. 53.

17. Basil, *Homily on Psalm 28* VII; quoted from *Music in Early Christian Literature.* p. 66.

18. Basil, *Homily on Psalm 1* II; quoted from *Music in Early Christian Literature*, p. 66.

19. Cyril, *Mystagogical Lectures* V, 6; pp. 195-196.

spired doctrine, he cures all kinds of savages, Greek no less than barbarian, of their wild passion and bestiality of soul.[20]

Several themes that we have heard somewhat faintly in the second and third centuries become very strong in the fourth. Two of these will be prominent in later chapters, so I will only mention them here. One theme is positive: the praise of psalmody; a second theme is negative: the polemic against pagan music that James McKinnon characterizes as uniform and vehement. A third theme is one that likely will strike a modern reader as odd because it is so at variance with prevalent notions about music. It is a theme that can be detected at the end of the passage from Eusebius quoted above: Christ cures "wild passion."

Many musical references deal with passion. For example, Isidor of Pelusium warned against misusing music "to arouse passion,"[21] and Basil warned against being "brought down to the passions of the flesh by the pleasure of song."[22] Such statements sound very strange in a culture such as ours, which places such a high premium on passion, which values intense emotion and the music that stimulates it, and which prizes excitement and the music that provides a "high" or a "rush." Against this backdrop, the church fathers seem unduly stoical in their low view of the emotions, their fear of sensual pleasure, and their suspicion of music and the other arts. There can be no denying that there is an austerity about the church fathers' thought, and it is true that it often resembles Stoicism. But before we dismiss them out of hand and view their thinking as nothing but recycled Stoicism, we need to understand what they meant by "the passions."

We would be wrong to simply equate passions with emotions. In the thought of the church fathers, not all emotions are passions, and the passions are not limited to emotions. Insofar as passions are emotions, they are obsessive or "unruly emotions like fear, anger, jealousy, and passionate love."[23] But they are more than emotions. Peter Brown puts it this way:

The "passions" are best seen as tendencies built up within the ego, which could force the sage to overreact to any situation, to cathect it

---

20. Eusebius, *Tricennial Oration* XIV; quoted from *Music in Early Christian Literature*, p. 101.

21. Isidor, *Epistle I*; quoted from *Music in Early Christian Literature*, p. 61.

22. Basil, *Homily on Psalm 1* II; quoted from *Music in Early Christian Literature*, p. 66.

23. Wilken, *The Spirit of Early Christian Thought*, p. 295.

with a change of personal, egotistic significance that distorted its true meaning. The "passions" colored perceptions of the outside world with nonexistent sources of fear, anxiety, and hope; or else they bathed it in a false glow of pleasure and potential satisfaction.

The passions, he adds, "were not what we tend to call feelings, they were, rather, complexes that hindered the true expression of feelings."[24] Similarly, Roberta Bondi defines passions as "emotions, attitudes, desires, and ways of acting . . . that blind us in our dealings with ourselves, each other, and the world, and so pervert perfectly good and useful impulses which take away our freedom to love."[25] Augustine, in his *Confessions,* explains how the passions took away his freedom before his conversion.

> The consequence of a distorted will is passion. By servitude to passion, habit is formed, and habit to which there is no resistance becomes necessity. By these links, as it were, connected to one another (hence my term a chain), a harsh bondage held me under restraint. The new will, which was beginning to be within me a will to serve you freely and to enjoy you, God, the only sure source of pleasure, was not yet strong enough to conquer my older will, which had the strength of old habit.[26]

Clement of Alexandria defined passion as "an excessive appetite exceeding the measures of reason, or appetite unbridled and disobedient to the word. Passions, then, are a perturbation of the soul contrary to nature, in disobedience to reason."[27] Evagrius Ponticus's list of passions in the fourth century fits well with Clement's definition: gluttony, avarice, lust, depression, anger, sloth, vainglory, pride. Anger is the only item on the list that is not necessarily "excessive" or "unbridled"; all the others invariably carry negative connotations.

Clement's use of the terms "unbridled" and "disobedience to reason" indicates his indebtedness to ancient Greek psychology, which distinguished two basic drives that were imaginatively depicted as horses drawing a chariot. The two horses (or drives) are desire (the appetitive drive)

---

24. Brown, *The Body and Society,* pp. 129-130.
25. Bondi, *To Love as God Loves,* p. 57.
26. *Confessions* VIII, v, 10; p. 140.
27. *Miscellanies* XIII; p. 361.

and anger (the spirited drive); both are "blind." The driver of the horses, the "charioteer," is reason, and if the "horses" become "unbridled,"

> chaos results; the energy of the horses becomes the power for various destructive passions, and the human personality is turned over to these passions which victimize it and destroy it as they repeatedly try unsuccessfully to satisfy themselves. But they can never permanently fill themselves up. . . . A life that takes its meaning from eating, or sex, or owning things [or music — cf. Augustine in chapter 11 below] can never be fulfilled because the desires can never be permanently satisfied. These desires are alternately filled and recurring over and over. This phenomenon is called "the cycle of desire."[28]

Among the Greeks it was the Stoics who aimed to eliminate the passions from their lives; they strove to achieve a state of *apatheia*. And early Christian views often seem in harmony with the Stoic ideal. Clement, for example, says: "This is the really good man, who is without passions, having, through the habit or disposition of the soul endued with virtue, transcended the whole life of passion."[29] That statement is not surprising in light of Scripture passages such as Galatians 5:24: "And those who belong to Christ Jesus have crucified the flesh with its passions and desires." But Christians could not simply adopt Stoicism. There were problems, and the key problem was that Stoicism did "not give an adequate account of what moves the soul to act."[30] The early Christians saw that desire is not only an appetitive drive that is acquisitive and self-centered, but that it is also what draws us to God. They needed love to enter the picture to solve this dilemma. Gregory of Nyssa drew a distinction between desire and love, and Robert Wilken explains Gregory's distinction this way:

> [A]s one comes into the presence of God desire gives way to love, and what was formerly sought by desire is now possessed in love. "If love is taken from us how will we remain united to God?" he asks. Desire is a restless activity, a yearning for something one craves but does not possess. Love, even though it is passionate, has within it an element

---

28. Bondi, *To Love as God Loves*, p. 60.
29. *Miscellanies* VII; p. 541.
30. Wilken, *The Spirit of Early Christian Thought*, p. 298.

of repose, of satisfaction, of joy that comes from delight in the presence of the beloved.[31]

For Augustine, too, the key is love: it is not the state of *apatheia* that is good, but the state in which the passions are right because love is right.

[T]he citizens of the holy city of God, who live according to God in the pilgrimage of this life, both fear and desire, and grieve and rejoice. And because their love is rightly placed, all these affections [passions] are right. . . . They fear eternal punishment, they desire eternal life; they grieve because they themselves groan within themselves, waiting for the adoption, the redemption of their body; they rejoice in hope, because then "shall be brought to pass the saying that is written, Death is swallowed up in victory." In like manner they fear to sin, they desire to persevere; they grieve in sin, they rejoice in good works.

Augustine goes on to say that, for the citizens of the City of God, it is "not only on their own account [that] they experience these emotions [passions], but also on account of those whose deliverance they desire and whose perdition they fear, and whose loss or salvation affects them with grief or with joy." So he concludes:

[I]f there be some of its citizens who seem to restrain and, as it were, temper those passions, they are so elated with ungodly pride, that their disease is as much greater as their pain is less. And if some, with a vanity monstrous in proportion to its rarity, have become enamoured of themselves because they can be stimulated and excited by no emotion, moved or bent by no affection, such persons rather lose all humanity than obtain true tranquility. For a thing is not necessarily right because it is inflexible, nor healthy because it is insensible.[32]

This condition in which the passions are made right by love is far removed from Stoic *apatheia*. But if, in the Greek analogy, we designate love to be the charioteer instead of reason, we are not far from Augustine's Christianized view of the passions.

It is thus apparent that, when the church fathers spoke ill of the passions and said they needed to be suppressed, or when they condemned

---

31. Wilken, *The Spirit of Early Christian Thought*, pp. 301-302.
32. *City of God* XIV, ix; pp. 452, 453, 456.

music that aroused the passions, they were speaking of the passions in the negative sense — that is, "emotions, attitudes, desires" that are not governed by reason, let alone by love. Each passion on Evagrius's list is a perversion. For example, gluttony is an obsessive or inordinate desire for food; avarice is an unreasonable desire for resources and an unloving unwillingness to share them; anger refers not to anger in general but to misdirected anger, anger that is beyond reason and unguided by love.

The church fathers recognized music's power to calm the passions (negative sense). But Evagrius meant something more profound than what "easy-listening" or dentist-office music calls to mind when he said, "Psalmody lays the passions to rest and causes the stirrings of the body to be stilled. . . ."[33] "Easy listening" could not be further from what the church fathers had in mind. Psalmody, the music that "lays the passions to rest," achieves its results by conveying truth — for example, "My help comes from the Lord, who made heaven and earth," "God is our refuge and strength," "Blessed is the man who walks not in the counsel of the wicked," "For God alone my soul waits in silence; from him comes my salvation." The calming effect of dentist-office music and easy-listening radio is an opiate that dulls one's perception, bringing one to a subpassionate level. Psalmody raises one above the passions (negative sense).

The church fathers knew of music's power to excite and inflame the passions, as well as its power to calm them; and this power made them wary of music and the other arts. In their wariness they joined a long tradition that went back to Plato. One of Plato's objections to the arts (see *Republic* X) "is their tendency to water the passions and make the less stable part of human nature prevail over the rational virtues." Though the church fathers were similarly offended, there was a different reason behind it: they "prized not so much the rational virtues as the habit of gentleness. The fruits of the Spirit are love, joy, peace, meekness, temperance, long-suffering, kindness. Christians found the opposite emotional habit in the Pagan secular arts."[34] The wild, intoxicating excitement generated by the music of pagan cults and the public spectacles was a constant target of their vehement denunciation. The church fathers would have no part of that kind of excitement. But that does not mean they denounced all moving music or failed to appreciate its beneficial uses. Chrysostom spoke ap-

---

33. *On Prayer* 82-83; quoted from *Music in Early Christian Literature*, p. 59.
34. Gilbert and Kuhn, *A History of Esthetics*, p. 122.

preciatively about music's power to arouse the soul: "[N]othing so arouses the soul, gives it wing, sets it free from the earth . . . as concordant melody and sacred song composed in rhythm."[35] Ambrose boasted about the power of his hymns to move people from heresy: "They [the Arians] say that the people are led astray by the charms of my hymns. Certainly; I do not deny it. This is a mighty charm, more powerful than any other."[36] Augustine attested to the beneficial power of those same hymns:

> How I wept during your hymns and songs! I was deeply moved by the music of the sweet chants of your Church. The sounds flowed into my ears and the truth was distilled into my heart. This caused the feelings of devotion to overflow. Tears ran, and it was good for me to have that experience.[37]

He also spoke movingly of ecstatic melismatic singing as an expression of joy in the Lord that words cannot utter.

> Sing to him in jubilation. This is what acceptable singing to God means: to sing jubilantly. But what is that? It is to grasp the fact that what is sung in the heart cannot be articulated in words. Think of people who sing at harvest time, or in the vineyard, or at any work that goes with a swing. They begin by caroling their joy in words, but after a while they seem to be so full of gladness that they find words no longer adequate to express it, so they abandon distinct syllables and words, and resort to a single cry of jubilant happiness. Jubilation is a shout of joy; it indicates that the heart is bringing forth what defies speech. To whom, then, is this jubilation more fittingly offered than to God who surpasses all utterance? You cannot speak of him because he transcends our speech; and if you cannot speak of him, yet may not remain silent, what else can you do but cry out in jubilation, so that your heart may tell its joy without words, and the unbounded rush of gladness not be cramped by syllables? Sing skillfully to him in jubilation.[38]

---

35. *On Psalm 41* I; quoted from *Music in Early Christian Literature*, p. 80.

36. *Sermon Against Auxentium* XXXIV; quoted from *Music in Early Christian Literature*, p. 132.

37. *Confessions* IX, vi, 14; p. 164.

38. *Exposition 2 of Psalm 32* 8; p. 401.

CHAPTER 7

St. Ambrose: Administrator and Mystic

The Ambrosian syllabic settings were similar to the street dances of the day.

Donald Paul Elsworth

As a certain secular teacher has said: "No one dances when sober, unless he is insane." Now if according to the wisdom of the world it is drunkenness or madness that begets the dance, what sort of warning do we expect to be given in the exempla of Sacred Scripture, where John, prophet of Christ, was beheaded at the whim of a dancer?

St. Ambrose

O f all the early Christians, St. Ambrose is the one most likely still to be associated with music in the minds of some people today. A few may have a distant memory of something called the Ambrosian Chant. More will make the association with Ambrose because they have sung some of his hymns that appear in some modern hymnbooks. Or they may have heard him referred to as the "father of hymnody." Or there may be something in a modern Christian's memory that suggests that St. Ambrose was one of the few church fathers — perhaps the only one — who did not have a jaundiced view of music and who was not squeamish about bringing popular dance music off the street and using it to enliven the stodgy chant that dominated church services.

There is a large repertory of liturgical chant that bears Ambrose's name and is still used today in Milan, where he was the bishop. But calling it "Ambrosian" more likely reflects the veneration in which tradition holds Ambrose than any actual involvement he might have had in the making of that repertory. He did write hymns, but only four can be attributed to him with certainty, and about ten more are somewhat likely to be by him.[1] We do not know who made the tunes for his hymns (if those tunes were new) or whence they were borrowed (if they were adaptations of pre-existing tunes). The hymns he introduced did become very popular and spread throughout Christendom, as did an apparently new method of singing the psalms that may have been antiphonal (two or more groups singing alternately). That is about the extent of our knowledge of Ambrose's influence on musical practice; but lack of knowledge has not prevented the development of a rather far-fetched mythology. Let me give one example.[2]

This version of the myth begins with a pictorial introduction that shows a ruined cathedral and a close-up of a flower growing next to a crumbling wall. The caption reads: "The verve and excitement has been gutted from the structures of Christianity only too often. Rules and systems, made by sincere people to preserve what they considered the finest worship music, have turned out to be suffocating. Slowly the structures crumble . . . and life springs up beside them once again." Then the main text goes on: "The days of free expression lasted a couple of centuries past New Testament times before the Church began getting sticky about music." I find it curious that the authors include Clement of Alexandria and Tertullian as representatives of the "days of free expression." Be that as it may, the authors say that after them "the problems began — problems of tightening up, regimentation, which have plagued Christians right up to the present. . . . Free, spontaneous God-music almost went down the drain. . . ." But Ambrose "reversed the tide."

But who was St. Ambrose? And how does his musical thought compare to that of other early Christian writers?

Ambrose's life is fairly well known to us thanks in large part to a biography of him by his stenographer, Paulinus. He was born in Trier, probably in

---

1. See Chapter 10, pp. 171-175, for more on the Ambrosian hymns.

2. Cf. Harold Myra and Dean Merrill, *Bach, Rock and Superschlock* (Philadelphia: A. J. Holman Co., 1972), ch. 5.

339, into an aristocratic senatorial family that had been Christian for several generations. His father was a praetorian prefect of the Gauls, but he died when Ambrose was about fourteen years old. After his father's death, he moved to Rome with his mother and siblings. The Ambrose household "was a strongly religious household, accepting asceticism as the highest Christian calling. . . . The household . . . was among the earliest of those patrician palaces devoted to Christian piety and learning where Jerome and Pelagius taught a generation later."[3]

Ambrose was educated to be a lawyer. In 368 he was employed in the prefecture of Sirmium, and in about 370 he became governor of Aemilia-Lurgia, an area that included the city of Milan. In 373, Auxentius, the Arian-leaning Bishop of Milan, died. In the election to fill his position, the struggle between the Arian and Trinitarian factions turned into a riot, and Ambrose, the governor, was called in to make peace. As he was speaking to the crowd, a child shouted, "Let Ambrose be bishop!" The whole crowd joined in the shout. Ambrose acquiesced to the wishes of the populace, but it was with great reluctance: he was not only uninterested in taking on such a responsibility, he was also unprepared. Though he was a catechumen at the time, he had never been baptized and had no particular interest in theology. Nevertheless, he was baptized and ordained bishop.

On becoming bishop, Ambrose gave up his considerable family wealth. According to Paulinus, "he bestowed all the gold and silver he possessed on the church for the poor. He even gave the church the landholdings he owned . . . and left nothing here below which he could call his own."[4] He also embarked on an intensive study of Scripture to make himself qualified for his new position. "When I was rushed from the bench of justice into the priesthood," he said, "I began to teach what I had not learned myself — the result is that I now must learn and teach at the same time."[5]

As Bishop of Milan, Ambrose was a busy man. His regular duties consisted of celebrating mass and the daily offices, preaching, administering baptism and penance, supervising the charities of the church, defending the oppressed, adjudicating civil disputes, and disciplining the clergy. He was also frequently involved in imperial politics during the reigns of

3. Frend, *The Rise of Christianity,* p. 618.

4. *The Life of Ambrose* 38; quoted from Quasten, *Patrology* IV, p. 145.

5. *On the Duties of Ministers* I, i, 4; quoted from Rand, *The Founders of the Middle Ages,* p. 78.

Gratian, Valentinian II, and Theodosius, working for the rights of the church over the empire. One particularly important confrontation occurred between Ambrose and Theodosius.

> A charioteer, idolized by the populace, attempted to rape a Gothic officer by the name of Butheric and was cast into prison. Riots took place and Butheric was killed. Theodosius sent orders for a secret massacre; soldiers were to surround the amphitheatre when the people gathered to see the games and were then to slaughter the spectators. Although the emperor relented and sent a revocation of his order, it arrived too late and seven thousand were butchered. Ambrose accordingly excommunicated him and it was only after a penance lasting several months that Theodosius was restored to communion. . . .[6]

Two goals Ambrose worked hard to achieve as bishop were eliminating the last vestiges of power remaining in the pagan aristocracy and ridding the church of heresy. His battle against paganism is epitomized by a dispute that arose when the Altar of Victory was removed from the Senate House. The altar had long resided there as a venerable symbol of Rome's religion and military power. Senators swore loyalty to the emperor at the Altar of Victory and burned incense there at the beginning of Senate meetings. Emperor Constantius had it removed, but Julian the Apostate had it brought back; Valentinian I left it, but Gratian — possibly at the instigation of Ambrose — had it removed once again. This brought a protest from the Senate, still a stronghold of ancient Roman paganism. After the assassination of Gratian, Symmachus, prefect of the city of Rome, took up the cause with Valentinian II, Gratian's successor. He made a moving plea for tradition ("Grant, I implore you, that we who are old men may leave to posterity that which we received as boys") and tolerance:

> It is right that what all adore should be deemed one. We all look up at the same stars. We have a common sky. A common firmament encompasses us. What matters it by what kind of learned theory each man looks for the truth? There is no one way that will take us to so mighty a secret. All this is matter of discussion for men of leisure.[7]

---

6. Davies, *The Early Christian Church*, p. 216.
7. Quoted from Rand, *The Founders of the Middle Ages*, p. 16.

Ambrose's response to Symmachus's arguments is preserved in letters he wrote to Emperor Valentinian II. He commends the new emperor as "a veteran in the faith" and declares that he is not doubtful regarding his faith. But he fears the power of Symmachus's eloquence. So he asks that Valentinian, in listening to his response,

> will not expect eloquence of speech but the force of facts. For, as holy Scripture teaches, the tongue of the wise and studious man is golden, decked with glittering words and shining with the gleam of eloquence, as though some rich hue, capturing the eyes of the mind by the comeliness of its appearance, dazzling in its beauty. But this gold, if you examine it carefully, though outwardly precious, within is a base metal.[8]

Responding to the argument for tradition, Ambrose puts the following words into the mouth of Rome personified:

> "I lament my downfall. My old age is accompanied by shame over that disgraceful bloodshed. But I am not ashamed to be converted in my old age along with the whole world. Surely it is true that no age is too late to learn. Let that old age feel shame which cannot rectify itself. It is not the old age of years which is entitled to praise, but that of character. There is no disgrace in going on to better things. This alone I had in common with the barbarians, that I did not know God before. Your sacrifice consists in the rite of being sprinkled with the blood of beasts. Why do you look for God's words in dead animals? Come and learn of the heavenly warfare which goes on on earth. We live here, but we war there. Let God Himself, who established the mystery of heaven, teach me about it, not man who does not know himself. Whom more than God shall I believe concerning God? How can I believe you who admit that you do not know what you worship?"[9]

Then he turns to the argument for tolerance.

> So great a secret, it is said, cannot be reached by one road. We [Christians] know on God's word what you do not know. And what you know by conjecture we have discovered from the very wisdom and

8. Letter 18; p. 40.
9. Letter 18; p. 40.

truth of God. Your ways do not agree with ours. You ask peace for your gods from the emperors; we beg peace for our emperors from Christ. You adore the works of your hands; we consider it wrong to think that anything which can be made is God. God does not wish to be worshiped in stones. Even your philosophers have ridiculed these ideas.[10]

Despite his disclaimer at the beginning of the letter, Ambrose showed no less eloquence than his opponent had, and in the end Valentinian did not restore the Altar of Victory to the Senate. Ambrose had won; paganism had lost — not only the battle but the war, at least as some historians see it. And perhaps, as Frend suggests, neither the facts nor the eloquence of Ambrose's appeal was the real cause of his victory; rather, it may have been Ambrose's tendency to play the tyrant. Had the debate been limited to what we find in Letter 18, W. H. C. Frend agrees with those who view the response as "one of the classics of the ancient world." But Letter 17, he says, reveals that "Ambrose could not resist . . . bullying tactics. . . ."

He threatened. It was an "affair of religion." He spoke "as a bishop." If Valentinian were to accept the pagan petition, Christ would not accept his gifts. The menace of excommunication together with an appeal to the memory of his dead brother, Gratian, carried the day. The petition was dismissed. Ambrose had gained an ignoble but decisive victory over the old religion. The position of Christianity as the religion of the Latin West was assured. The surrender of the pagan aristocracy to Theodosius in 389 was merely the aftermath of victory.[11]

Ambrose fought heresy as doggedly as he fought paganism. One heresy that he fought was advanced by a disgruntled monk named Jovinian. In order to understand Ambrose's opposition to Jovinian, we need to recognize that Ambrose's view of the Christian life, like that of the early church in general, was strongly ascetic. Ambrose admitted, when pressed, that both virginity and marriage are good.

Someone will say, "You, therefore, discourage marriage?" No, I encourage it and condemn those who are accustomed to discourage it,

10. Letter 18; p. 40.
11. Frend, *The Early Church*, p. 186.

so much so that I frequently speak of the marriages of Sarah, Rebecca, Rachel, and other women of old as instances of singular virtue. . . . I do not then discourage marriage, but I count the advantages of holy virginity. The latter is a service of a few only, the former of all.[12]

Even though he said he was "comparing good things with good things," when he added "so that what is better may be seen more clearly," he left no doubt which one he thought was better.

Jovinian taught the complete equality between marriage and celibacy and between eating and fasting. He also taught something like the Calvinist doctrine of the perseverance of the saints: those who have been born again in baptism cannot be turned away by Satan. Not only that, he denied the perpetual virginity of Mary. It is no wonder that church historians have sometimes called him the first Protestant. Unfortunately, the only sources of information regarding Jovinian come from treatises and letters that his enemies wrote against him. Among those sources, the treatise in which Jerome paints a most unflattering picture of his opponent stands out. That Jovinian was a disgruntled monk who left the ascetic life we need not doubt. But was he the gourmand, the dandy, and the ladies' man that Jerome and others depicted? Perhaps there were features of his lifestyle that warranted the accusation that he was "the Epicurus of the Christians"; but there can be no question that Jerome's picture is overdrawn. He abused his opponent with every foul adjective in his extensive and colorful vocabulary. He was all too ready to believe the worst abominations of a foe "who disparaged fasting and virginity — who, moreover, was providentially an exceedingly bad writer" (no small fault in Jerome's eyes!). There is no reason to believe that Jovinian was the complete voluptuary Jerome describes, one who died "amid feasts of pheasants and pork," who did not breathe out, "but belched out, his spirit."[13]

Ambrose had Jovinian condemned in Milan as a Manichean, probably an inaccurate label regardless of what Jovinian's faults might have been. How much his profligate lifestyle or — in another direction — his tendency toward a Pelagian emphasis on salvation by works contributed to Ambrose's condemnation of Jovinian, we will never know. In any case, we do know enough about Ambrose as a champion of the ascetic life to realize

12. *Concerning Virgins*, 1, 34-35; quoted from Paredi, *Saint Ambrose*, p. 148.

13. This account of Jovinian is based on, and the quotations are taken from Dudden, *The Life and Times of St. Ambrose*, pp. 393-398.

that anyone who had Jovinian's lack of enthusiasm for virginity and fasting would raise Ambrose's ire. The controversy reveals little authentic information about Jovinian, but it does reinforce, if reinforcing is necessary, Ambrose's strong tendencies toward asceticism.

During the fourth century, Arianism was one of the major heresy threats to the church. But by the time Ambrose became bishop, Arianism was on the decline — though one of its last strongholds was Milan. Emperor Valentinian I had been committed to a policy of religious freedom, so Ambrose had little opportunity to eradicate Arianism from Milan during Valentinian's reign. But after the latter died, Ambrose was able to persuade his successor, Gratian, to adopt an anti-Arian policy. However, Justina, Valentinian's widow, continued to wield some power and, like her late husband, she supported religious freedom — particularly for Arians in Milan. Twice she came into direct conflict with Ambrose over Arian claims she was seeking to enforce.

> In 385 she demanded that a church at Milan should be handed over to the Arians; Ambrose refused and soldiers were sent to take over the property; the populace almost became out of hand, but Ambrose was able to control them and Justina, realizing she was playing with fire, withdrew the troops. The next year the attack was renewed when a decree was published permitting all Arians freedom to hold religious assemblies, death being the penalty for those who withstood them. Again Ambrose stood fast, again soldiers were sent, and again the court climbed down. The death of Justina shortly afterwards meant that the Arian cause had lost its leading supporter in the West and that Ambrose's policy had triumphed.[14]

Ambrose died in 397, after having served for twenty-four years as Bishop of Milan. Amid his daily liturgical and administrative duties and his many political wrangles, he found time to write quite voluminously. His extant writings number some twenty exegetical works, six moral and ascetical works, nine dogmatic works, along with sermons, letters, and hymns. These works show his wide knowledge of Scripture and of Christian and pagan authors, both ancient ones and those contemporaneous with him. Of the nonbiblical writers, he is most indebted to Plato, Cicero, and Philo, an Alexandrian Jew. E. K. Rand says: "As Cicero translated

---

14. Davies, *The Early Christian Church*, p. 223.

Greek thought into Roman, so Ambrose translated it into Christian.... He likewise was an interpreter of Greek theology to the west."[15]

One of his greatest works is *On the Duties of Ministers (De Officiis ministrorum)*, which he modeled after Cicero's *De Officiis*. Rand points to it as an example of Ambrose's Christian humanism, his acceptance of the benefit Christians can derive from pagan thought and art.

> The *De Officiis Ministrorum* is, in a way, a new sort of apology. The danger is, not that the author will submerge Christianity in [Cicero's] Stoic ethics, but that, although he is well versed in the ancient writers, both Latin and Greek, he may turn his new weapon with deadly effect against Pagan culture, if such be his desire. "Let us return to our Moses," says Ambrose, after recounting the chivalrous conduct of Pyrrhus to the Romans, "and cull examples as superior in point of nobility as they are in point of time." One might as well feel that if the Church possessed the treasure of fine lives, high thoughts, and great art that Tertullian and Ambrose claimed for it, the world would profit by lopping off the whole record of Paganism, which, whatever its excellencies, contained much that was harmful to the progress of Christian civilization. But another conclusion is possible from the evidence gathered by Ambrose, namely, that the contemplation of the two pictures side by side was no bad thing, and that the enjoyment of the best in Pagan thought and Pagan art would help, not hinder, in the forming of Christian character. This last attitude is Christian humanism, and to this . . . St. Ambrose subscribes.[16]

There can be no question about Ambrose's impact on the church and, beyond that, on the subsequent course of Western civilization. He played a significant role in the demise of Arianism and paganism in the West. His promoting of asceticism helped to secure it a prominent place in the life and thought of the church. His strong stands against various emperors paved the way for the superiority of church over the state during the Middle Ages. His hymns (to which we will turn our attention in chapter 10) became a permanent part of the church's repertory of song, and they established certain structural features that remain the norm for congregational song to this day. And no list of Ambrose's legacy would be complete if it

---

15. Rand, *The Founders of the Middle Ages*, p. 79.
16. Rand, *The Founders of the Middle Ages*, p. 83.

did not mention his role in the conversion of St. Augustine, arguably the most influential of all the early church fathers.

The popular mythology about Ambrose would lead one to expect musical ideas from him that differ significantly from those of most, if not all, early Christian writers. The foregoing biographical sketch suggests otherwise, a suggestion that is confirmed by the musical references in Ambrose's writings. He is typical, not unique. Like all the other early Christian writers, he railed against the pagan music of his day and lavished unstinting praise on the psalmody of the church. Like Clement, he accepted the musical cosmology inherited from the Greeks, and also like Clement, he gave it a clearly Christian interpretation.

There was a uniform vehemence in the early Christian polemic against pagan music, and Ambrose was no exception. Isaiah 5:11-12 provided him with a biblical precedent for his denunciation:

> Woe to those who rise early in the morning
>   that they may run after strong drink,
> who tarry late into the evening
>   as wine inflames them!
> They have lyre and harp,
>   tambourine and flute and wine at their feasts,
> but they do not regard the deeds of the Lord,
>   or see the work of his hands.

Ambrose comments on this passage: "Woe to those who require the drink of intoxication in the morning, who ought to praise God, to rise before dawn and to meet in prayer the sun of justice, who visits his own and raises us up, if we do rise for Christ and not for wine and drink. Hymns are being sung, and you hold the kithara?" To make clear the objectionable association of the music of those instruments with drunken revelry, he adds: "I will not discuss the kithara, the psalteries and tympana, which we recognize as being frequently used at this type of banquet, in order to stir the passions by both wine and song."[17] To make matters worse, he laments, these objectionable activities were taking place precisely when people should have been offering prayer and psalmody to God. It was in the early

---

17. *On Elijah and Fasting* xv, 55; quoted from McKinnon, "The Church Fathers and Musical Instruments," p. 191.

morning, before the necessary daily activities began, and in the evening, after they had ceased, that laypeople had time for devotions. So he advises:

> At least divide your time between God and the world. When the darkness of night prevents you from performing in public the deeds of this world, then, as you have leisure time for God, give yourself to prayer, and, lest you sleep, sing psalms, thus cheating your sleep by means of a beneficial fraud. In the morning hasten to church and offer the first fruits of your pious devotion, and afterwards, if worldly necessity calls, you are not excluded from saying: "My eyes have anticipated the morning that I might meditate upon your words" (Ps. 119:148). You may now with peace of mind proceed to your duties.[18]

For this reason, he pronounces another "woe": "Psalms are being sung, and you take up the psaltery or the tympanum? Woe unto you indeed, because you relinquish salvation and choose death."[19]

Though Ambrose does not mention it in his comments on the Isaiah passage, lyre playing was also associated with prostitution, an association made clear in the following commentary on the same passage by an unknown early Christian.

> You place a lyre ornamented with gold and ivory upon a high pedestal as if it were a statue or devilish idol, and some miserable woman, rather than being taught to place her hands upon the spindle, is taught by you, bound as she is in servitude, to stretch them out upon the lyre. Perhaps you pay her wages or perhaps you turn her over to some female pimp, who after exhausting the licentious potential of her own body, presides over young women as the teacher of similar deeds. Because of her you will meet with a double punishment on the day of judgement, since you are yourself immoral, and since you have estranged this poor soul from God through evil teaching. So she stands at the lyre and lays her hands upon the strings, her arms bare and her expression impudent.[20]

18. *Exposition on Psalm 118* xix, 32; quoted from *Music in Early Christian Literature*, p. 128.

19. *On Elijah and Fasting* xv, 55; quoted from McKinnon, "The Church Fathers and Musical Instruments," p. 191.

20. Pseudo-Basil, *Commentary on Isaiah* 5, 158; quoted from *Music in Early Christian Literature*, p. 70.

Sexual immorality was stimulated not only by lyre-playing prostitutes but also by shows that were very popular in the theaters. In his *Hexameron*, a series of sermons on the six days of creation, Ambrose sees the marsh as a kind of theater.

> The marsh is self-indulgence, the marsh is intemperance, the marsh is incontinence, where are found wallowing places for lusts, the grunts of beasts, and the lairs of passions. . . . And so from every marsh, where like frogs they have sung their ancient chant of complaint, has congregated here [in the church] faith; here, too, have congregated purity of heart and simplicity of mind. . . .
>
> [In the church Christians] find delight not in the baleful songs sung by theatrical performers, songs which lead to sensual love, but in the chants of the Church. Here we hear the voice of the people singing in harmony the praises of God.[21]

Notice that, in denouncing pagan music, Ambrose points to the music that should be in its place — the psalmody of the church, music that "delights your mind" and "can cure the wounds of selfish passion."[22] This is what he wanted Christians to sing and listen to instead of the intoxicated music of the carousers, the siren songs of prostitutes, the songs of sensual love in the theaters, and, generally speaking, any music that aroused unbridled passion. In offering psalmody in place of the world's music, Ambrose was offering something for which he had lavish praise. He did not see that as a poor trade; in fact, those who do not make the trade, as Ambrose said in his commentary on the Isaiah passage quoted above, "disregard salvation and choose death." The psalms, he said, contain everything that is necessary and are a veritable spiritual treasury. Here is a sampling of Ambrose's praise of psalmody:

> A psalm is the blessing of the people, the praise of God . . . the joy of liberty, the noise of good cheer, and the echo of gladness. It softens anger, it gives release from anxiety, it alleviates sorrow; it is protection at night, instruction by day, a shield in time of fear, a feast of holiness, the image of tranquility, a pledge of peace and harmony,

---

21. *Hexameron* III, i, 4-5; p. 69.

22. *Exposition on Psalm 118* xix, 30; *Commentary on Psalm 1*, 9; quoted from *Music in Early Christian Literature*, pp. 128, 126.

which produces one song from various and sundry voices in the manner of a cithara. The day's dawning resounds with a psalm, with a psalm its passing echoes.

The Apostle admonishes women to be silent in church, yet they do well to join in a psalm; this is gratifying for all ages and fitting for both sexes. Old men ignore the stiffness of age to sing [a psalm], and melancholy veterans echo it in the joy of their hearts; young men sing one without the bane of lust, as do adolescents without threat from their insecure age or the temptation of sensual pleasure; even young women sing psalms with no loss of wifely decency, and girls sing a hymn to God with sweet and supple voice while maintaining decorum and suffering no lapse of modesty. Youth is eager to understand [a psalm], and the child who refuses to learn other things takes pleasure in contemplating it; it is a kind of play, productive of more learning than that which is dispensed with stern discipline. . . . A psalm is sung at home and repeated outdoors; it is learned without effort and retained with delight. A psalm joins those with differences, unites those at odds and reconciles those who have been offended, for who will not concede to him with whom one sings to God in one voice? It is after all a great bond of unity for the full number of people to join in one chorus. The strings of the cithara differ, but create one harmony. The fingers of a musician often go astray among the strings though they are very few in number, but among the people the Spirit musician knows not how to err.[23]

In this panegyric, Ambrose manages to incorporate just about every major New Testament and early Christian theme on music. The two audiences are here: "A psalm is the blessing of the people, the praise of God." And so is joy: "A psalm is . . . the joy of liberty, the noise of good cheer, and the echo of gladness." The singing of psalms is Spirit-inspired: "Among the people the Spirit musician knows not how to err." And singing psalms is done with "one voice"; indeed, it is a "bond of unity." Though he does not mention participation with the angelic hosts here, in one of his letters Ambrose says that those "who have taken up that praise which day and night they proclaim in hymns" are doing "the service of angels."[24]

Other early Christian themes are also explicitly present. Psalms are

---

23. *Commentary on Psalm 1,* 9; quoted from *Music in Early Christian Literature,* p. 126.
24. Letter LXIII, 82; quoted from *Music in Early Christian Literature,* p. 132.

sung "without threat from . . . the temptations of sensual pleasure." Instead, they are decent, decorous, and modest in character; they make learning palatable. And like the other early church fathers, Ambrose did not look on psalmody merely as "church music." It was music for the whole of a Christian's life: "A psalm is sung at home and repeated outdoors." Daily psalmody is something Christians can learn from the birds, who frame day and night with their joyful praise.

> It is customary for the birds at nesting time "to charm the sky with song," in joy that their allotted task is done. This usually happens, following, as it were, a ritual pattern, at dawn and at sunset, when the birds sing the praises of their Creator, at the moment of transition from day to night or from night to day. [In this pattern there is] a mighty incentive for arousing our religious devotion. For what person of natural human sensibility would not blush to terminate the day without a ritual singing of the psalms, since even the tiniest bird ushers in the approach of day and night with customary devotion of sweet song![25]

This passage hints at Ambrose's cosmic view of musical praise. Along with us humans, the birds are part of a cosmic symphony. Ambrose knew Plato's ideas about cosmic music, and though he had some reservations about some aspects of Plato's thought, he affirmed its underlying truth. In the *Hexameron* he asks why, if the movements of the heavenly spheres make actual sound, we cannot hear them. Proposed answers leave him skeptical about the "music of the spheres" producing actual sound, but he does not doubt that the whole cosmos is harmonious and therefore is musical in the most fundamental sense.

> Who, therefore, does not marvel at the fact that a world formed of dissimilar elements should rise to the level of unity in one body, that this body should combine by indissoluble laws of concord and love to link together and form a union of such discordant elements? Furthermore, who does not marvel that these elements so naturally separate should be tied together in the bonds of unity and peace as if by an indivisible compact?[26]

25. *Hexameron* V, xii, 36; p. 192.
26. *Hexameron* II, i, 1; p. 45.

Later in the *Hexameron* he uses the metaphor of the dance to express the musical nature of the universe. The elements, he says, "meet together in a dance measure of concord."[27] Although this creation in all its beauty and harmony is marvelous beyond describing, Ambrose, throughout the *Hexameron,* issues warnings against worshiping the creature (either *in toto* or in any given part) instead of the Creator. Nature does not sing her own praises; nor does her most resplendent (and therefore most likely to be worshiped) part, the sun. Together they groan "in order that there may come the adoption of sons and the redemption of the human race by which we, too, [says Nature] may be freed from servitude." While waiting, they praise "the Author . . . [singing] a hymn to the Lord God."[28]

Musica mundana has its reflection in *musica humana* in Ambrose's thought as well. But unlike the Platonists, who saw *musica humana* as the harmony between body and soul, Ambrose saw it in the structure of the body. He says that the human body "excels all things in grace and beauty," and then he goes on to note that "the body of man is constructed like the world itself."[29] But there is more to his concept of *musica humana* than physical structure. The deeper level of *musica humana* in his thought is not an imitation of *musica mundana;* it is not merely an echo of the music of the spheres (although that would be no small matter). Rather, it is an echo of God's Word and Spirit: "In the people who are the instruments of the operations of God they hear music which echoes from melodious sound of God's word, within which the Spirit of God works."[30]

In Ambrose we have a clear Christianization of the Platonic idea of cosmic music. *Musica humana* and *musica mundana,* as perfectly created, echo God's Word and Spirit. The one is not an echo of the other, but both, as echoes of the same thing, praise their Maker in harmonious chorus. Because of the Fall, however, the whole creation groans, waiting for the time when perfect harmony and peace will be restored. Yet, in the interval, the cosmic symphony and dance are not completely beyond the realm of our perception or our (and nature's) participation. One of the most beautiful passages in all early Christian literature was inspired by the harmonious joining of sea and church in praise of the Creator. Genesis says

27. *Hexameron* III, iv, 18; p. 81.
28. *Hexameron* IV, i, 4; pp. 128-129.
29. *Hexameron* VI, ix, 54-55; p. 268.
30. *Hexameron* III, i, 3-5; p. 70.

that God saw that the sea was good, and Ambrose had no trouble under-standing why. His description of the sea reveals his keen eye for the beau-ties of creation.

> The aspect of this element is beautiful, either when the sea foams with its surging white caps and mounting billows, or when it bedews the rocks with its snowy spray, or even when under a balmy breeze it shimmers, often in this case presenting itself to the beholder from afar in colors of purple, suggesting serene tranquility. Such is the as-pect of the sea when it does not beat the nearby shores with the on-rush of its waves, but when the waters greet it, as it were, in a fond embrace of peace. How gentle is the sound, how pleasing the splash of the water, how pleasant and rhythmic the wave-beats! Notwith-standing all this, I am of the opinion that the beauty of such a cre-ation is not to be estimated by the standard of our own eyes, but is to be gauged in the design of the work as a whole by its conformity and agreement with the intention of its Creator.[31]

But Ambrose saw and heard more.

> [The sea] is the secret strength of moderation, the practice of re-straint, the retreat of seriousness, the port of security, the tranquility of the age, the sobriety of this world, the incentive of worship to de-vout and faithful men, so that when the singing of psalms chimes with the sound of gently breaking waves, the isles clap their hands and the tranquil choir of the sacred waves echo with the hymns of the saints. . . . Aye, the Sea is the Church, which pours forth from its doors in waves the crowds of the faithful, and echoes with refluent waves of the people's prayer, with the responses of psalms, the sing-ing of men, of women, of children, a crashing surf of concordant song. And what of the wave that washes sin away and the life-giving breezes of the Holy Spirit?[32]

This is truly a "Christian version of the idea of world harmony," a "prose hymn" that reveals an "upward striving from the visible world har-mony to the invisible will of the Creator." In it "nature and man unite in a

---

31. *Hexameron* III, v, 21; pp. 82-83.
32. *Hexameron* III, v, 23; trans. E. K. Rand, p. 98.

concert of softly singing waves and pious songs"; and in it Ambrose leads us imperceptibly "from the musical harmony of the sea to the harmonious agreement between Creator and creation, to the harmony between sacred nature and pious mankind, to the harmony of the divine service, of grace, of purification from sin. . . ."[33]

Passages such as this prompted E. K. Rand to call Ambrose a mystic deep inside the successful administrator. When "we break through the daily round, the outer triumphs of the great Bishop of Milan, we find . . . one of the Saints that know mystic rapture, one of the pure in heart that see God."[34] It is no wonder that one who had heard something of the purity of the ancient song of creation could not countenance the old songs of this world. The "new song" sung by the redeemed creation could not be part of the sensual, frenzied music of an old world. And when we read the *Hexameron* and "find in the inner soul of him a child of the Muses," it is no wonder that he became the "father of hymnody" for the Western church.

33. Spitzer, *Classical and Christian Ideas of World Harmony,* pp. 20-23.
34. Rand, *The Founders of the Middle Ages,* p. 101.

CHAPTER 8

St. John Chrysostom: Christian Households amid the Devil's Garbage Heap

And as swine flock together where there is mire, but where there is aroma and incense there bees abide, so demons congregate where there are licentious chants, but where there are spiritual ones there the grace of the Spirit descends, sanctifying mouth and mind. This I say not only that you may yourselves sing praises, but also that you may teach your wives and children to do so, not merely while weaving to lighten the work, but especially at the table.

St. John Chrysostom

Give me chastity and charity. . . .

Book of Common Prayer

John, later dubbed Chrysostom ("golden mouth") for his eloquence in the pulpit, was born in Antioch of Christian parents in about 350. His father was an army officer, a position lucrative enough to provide a comfortable living for the family and a good education for John. When his father died, John was still an infant and his mother, Anthusa, was only twenty years old. In one of his treatises John recalls what his mother told him about her early widowhood.

My child [she said], it was not the will of Heaven that I should long enjoy the benefit of your father's virtue. For his death soon followed the pangs which I endured at your birth leaving you an orphan and me a widow before my time to face all the horrors of widowhood, which only those who have experienced them can fairly understand. For no words are adequate to describe the tempest-tossed condition of a young woman who, having but lately left her parental home, and being inexperienced in business, is suddenly racked by an over-whelming sorrow, and compelled to support a load of care too great for her age and sex. For she has to correct the laziness of servants, and to be on the watch for their rogueries, to repel the designs of rela-tions, to bear bravely the threats of those who collect the public taxes, and harshness in the imposition of rates. And if the departed one should have left a child, even if it be a girl, great anxiety will be caused to the mother, although free from much expense and fear: but a boy fills her with ten thousand alarms and many anxieties every day, to say nothing of the great expense which one is compelled to in-cur if she wishes to give him a good education.[1]

The courage with which Anthusa faced these hardships and the success with which she maintained her household and saw to John's education prompted Libanios, one of John's pagan teachers, to remark, "Great heav-ens, what remarkable women are to be found among the Christians!"[2]

John studied under a philosopher named Andragathius and, more im-portantly, under the famous Stoic rhetorician Libanios; he proved to be a very bright student. The fifth-century church historian Sozomen wrote that when Libanios "was on his death-bed, he was asked by his friends who should take his place. 'It would have been John,' he replied, 'had not the Christians taken him from us.'"[3]

When John was eighteen, he abandoned his study with pagan teachers. According to his early biographer, Palladius,

he revolted against the sophists of word-mongering, for he had ar-rived at man's estate and thirsted for living knowledge. At that time the blessed Meletius the confessor, an Armenian by nationality, ruled the church at Antioch. He took notice of the bright lad and was im-pressed by the beauty of his character so he had him constantly near

1. *On the Priesthood* I, 5; p. 34.
2. Kelly, *Golden Mouth*, p. 7.
3. *A History of the Church* VIII, ii; p. 376.

him. He observed him with prophetic eye as it were, and he could envisage the young man's brilliant future. He was admitted to the mystery of the washing of regeneration, and after about three years attendance upon the bishop he was appointed reader.[4]

At this point in his life, John thought that he could not safely live a Christian life amid the temptations of the city while "his youthful nature was bursting within him." So he decided to become a hermit in the mountains, to battle "with the crags of voluptuousness."[5] But his mother, with heart-wrenching entreaties, persuaded him to stay with her until she died. John later recalled her words to him:

> I held on as I was [she said], in the midst of the storm and uproar, and did not shun the iron furnace of widowhood. My foremost help indeed was the grace from above; but it was no small consolation to me under those terrible trials to look continually on your face and to preserve in you a living image of him who had gone, an image indeed which was a fairly exact likeness.
>
> On this account, even when you were an infant, and had not yet learned to speak, a time when children are the greatest delight to their parents, you afforded me much comfort. Nor indeed can you complain that, although I bore my widowhood bravely, I diminished your patrimony, which I know has been the fate of many who have had the misfortune to be orphans. For, besides keeping the whole of it intact, I spared no expense which was needful to give you an honorable position, spending for this purpose some of my own fortune, and of my marriage dowry. Yet do not think that I say these things by way of reproaching you; only in return for all these benefits I beg one favor: do not plunge me into a second widowhood; nor revive the grief which is now laid to rest: wait for my death: it may be in a little while I shall depart. The young indeed look forward to a distant old age; but we who have grown old [she was probably in her early forties] have nothing but death to wait for. When, then, you shall have committed my body to the ground, and mingled my bones with your father's, embark for a long voyage, and set sail on any sea you will:

---

4. Palladius, *Dialogue on the Life of St. John Chrysostom;* p. 35.
5. Palladius, *Dialogue on the Life of St. John Chrysostom;* p. 35.

then there will be no one to hinder you: but as long as my life lasts, be content to live with me.[6]

According to Palladius, in 373, presumably after his mother's death, John went "to the nearby mountains [where] he met up with an old man, Syrus, who exercised great self-discipline, and John strove earnestly to imitate his severe lifestyle." He stayed with Syrus about four years, until "he suppressed temptations more easily." Then

> he retired to a cave all alone, eager to dwell in obscurity. There he stayed for twenty-four months, most of that time not partaking of sleep while he thoroughly learned the covenants of Christ to dispel ignorance. He never relaxed for that two-year period, not in the days nor at night, and his gastric organs became lifeless and the proper functions of the kidneys were impaired by the cold. Since he could no longer take care of himself alone, he went back once more to the haven of the Church [in Antioch]. And this is proof of the Savior's providence that he was taken away from the ascetic life by his sickness brought on by such strict habits, forcing him to leave his caves for the benefit of the Church.[7]

Back in Antioch John was ordained, first as deacon in 381, then as priest in 386.

Located in northern Syria about twenty miles from the Mediterranean coast, Antioch was a thriving city bounded by the Orontes River, by a fertile plain that supplied ample food, and by Mount Silpius, home of many Christian hermits. In the fourth century this magnificent city was at the peak of its splendor.

> With its many public baths, its fountains, its grand private homes, its numerous markets, Antioch required two aqueducts to serve the opulent life of its citizens, who in the words of one ancient historian "thought only of festivals, of good living, and of continuous theaters and circus plays."
>
> For centuries Antioch had charmed visitors with its magnificence and delighted inhabitants with its comforts. . . . She seemed without

---

6. *On the Priesthood* I, 5; p. 34.
7. Palladius, *Dialogue on the Life of St. John Chrysostom*; p. 35.

peer, "the fair crown of the east," and her famous citizens, brilliant culture, and handsome buildings exhibited the highest accomplishments of Greek civilization.[8]

The church in Antioch during the fourth century was beset by rival factions within and strong opponents without. Antioch still had a large contingent of Arians, and even the Nicene Christians were divided into competing factions. In one of his homilies John complained: "They all met together in earlier times and sang psalms in common. This we do also now: but then among all there was one soul and heart: but now not in one single soul can one see that unanimity, rather much disputing is everywhere."[9]

Judaism was also strong. Its threat to the church in Antioch was the impetus for some of John's most venomous words, words that reveal an unfavorable side of his character. For, though the danger of Christians sliding back into Judaism was real, that in no way justified the venom the Jews received from John. His tongue, his greatest strength, was also his greatest weakness: when he was riled up, this gentle and holy man gave his tongue free rein. Let loose, his tongue was second to none in abusing an opponent.

In addition to Judaism, John had to worry about the threat of pagan Hellenism. Antioch, the city where followers of Jesus were first called Christians, had a sizable Christian population, but the general ambience of the city was still pagan. Pagan temples and shrines were prominent architectural features of the cityscape. Along its streets, in its public buildings, and in the palaces of the wealthy, the subjects of pagan mythology and religion could be seen in the abundant mosaics and statues. The calendar of pagan festivals punctuated the life of the citizens; in addition, the theater and the circuses were extremely popular. Above all, education was thoroughly pagan.

> The backbone of the educational system was the study of the Greek classics, a body of literature that immersed the young boy in the legends and myths of ancient Greece. Though much time was devoted to grammar, vocabulary, style, and the organization of speeches, the themes and examples were taken from the myths and legends of ancient Greece. Parents and teachers alike understood that literature

8. Wilken, *John Chrysostom and the Jews*, p. 2.
9. *Homily XXXVI on 1 Corinthians*, 7; p. 220.

did not simply teach language and style or sharpen a boy's aesthetic sense; it formed his character and outlook on life.[10]

At the end of his portrait of Antioch during John's time, Robert Wilken concludes that "Antioch was still a pagan city, for those features of its life that transmitted and nurtured the values of its citizens and molded the character of its young people — education, social custom, literature, art and architecture, legends and myths — were still untouched by Christianity."[11]

For twelve years John ministered to the citizens of Antioch. His main duty was preaching in the principal church of the city, a duty that he carried out with great relish and with great concern for the Antiochene householders who made up his audience. "He identified with them with the instinctive . . . sensitivity of a great *rhetor.* . . . [He said] 'I know no other life but you and the care of souls.'" He preached with the hope that his preaching and holy example would bring about a "reform of the Christian household" that would in turn create "a new form of urban community."

> The poignant, tragically unrealized wish of his life was to be able to speak to Antioch as a totally Christian city. The themes of marriage, of the household, and of sexuality bulk so large in his sermons because it was through such themes that John wished to express a new view of the civic community.[12]

One of the great burdens of John's preaching was care for the poor. He saw the suffering and degradation of the poor close at hand, and he saw it in stark contrast to the luxurious and uncaring lifestyle of the rich. In his sermons John frequently mentioned the plight of the poor in Antioch. Hungry and cold, they were forced into begging on the streets and sleeping on a little straw. At the same time, many Christians were among the very wealthy, living on spacious lands in splendid palaces amid lavish furnishings. They wore luxurious clothing and expensive jewelry; they sponsored sumptuous banquets featuring rich delicacies and debauched entertainment. But they refused the outstretched hand of the beggars. John said to them: "It is not for stretching out your hands that [your prayers] will be heard. Stretch

---

10. Wilken, *John Chrysostom and the Jews*, p. 20.

11. Wilken, *John Chrysostom and the Jews*, p. 24.

12. Brown, *The Body and Society*, pp. 306, 309.

forth your hands, not to heaven but to the poor."[13] And he said further: "When you are weary of praying, and do not receive, consider how often you have heard a poor man calling, and have not listened to him."[14]

John wondered out loud how a Christian lady could walk past a beggar with the price of several meals dangling from her ears.[15] The poor man, he told his congregation, inhabits the same world, looks at the same sun, and has the same soul as each of them; moreover, he has the same Lord and is "a partaker with you of the same mysteries, called to the same heaven . . . ; having a strong claim, his poverty, and his want of necessary food." John upbraided his parishioners for being unwilling to give anything to the poor, while the wanton Saturnalia revelers "that wake you with flutes and pipes in the winter season, and disturb you without purpose or fruit, depart from you receiving many gifts."[16]

One of John's most scathing sermons on giving to the poor paints a most distressing picture of the life of the destitute in Antioch and of the insensitivity of the wealthy.

> Paul suffered hunger that he might not hinder the Gospel; we have not the heart to touch what is in our own stores, though we see innumerable souls overthrown. "Yea," says one, "let the moth eat, and let not the poor eat; let the worm devour, and let not the naked be clothed; let all be wasted away with time, and let not Christ be fed. . . ." What madness is this . . . to fill your chests with apparel, and overlook him that is made after God's image and similitude, naked and trembling with cold, and with difficulty keeping himself upright.
>
> "But he pretends," says one, "this tremor and weakness." And do you not fear lest a thunderbolt from heaven, kindled by this word, should fall upon you? (For I am bursting with wrath: bear with me.) You, I say, pampering and fattening yourself and extending the stations to the dead of night and comforting yourself in soft coverlets, do not deem yourself liable to judgement, so lawlessly using the gifts of God: (for wine was not made that we should get drunk; nor food, that we should pamper our appetites; nor meats, that we should distend the belly). But from the poor, the wretched, from him that is as

13. *Homily I on II Timothy;* quoted from Brown, *The Body and Society,* p. 311.
14. *Homily XI on I Thessalonians;* quoted from Brown, *The Body and Society,* p. 310.
15. Brown, *The Body and Society,* p. 312.
16. *Homily XXXV on Matthew;* p. 235.

good as dead, from him you demand strict accounts . . . ? Why, if he plays the hypocrite, he does it of necessity and want, because of your cruelty and inhumanity, requiring the use of such masks and refusing all inclination to mercy. . . .

And why speak I of nakedness and trembling? For I will tell a thing yet more to be shuddered at, that some have been compelled even to deprive their children of sight at an early age in order that they might touch our insensibility. For since when they could see and went about naked, neither by their age nor by their misfortunes could they win favor of the unpitying, they added to such great evils another yet sterner tragedy, that they might remove their hunger; thinking it to be a lighter thing to be deprived of this common light and that sunshine which is given to all, than to struggle with continual famine and endure the most miserable of deaths. . . .

There are other poor men . . . having often tried to deal with us by piteous gestures and words and finding that they availed nothing, have left off those supplications and thenceforward our very wonderworkers are surpassed by them, some chewing the skins of worn-out shoes, and some fixing sharp nails into their heads, others lying about in frozen pools with naked stomachs, and others enduring different things yet more horrid than these, that they may draw around them the ungodly spectators. And you, while these things are going on, stand laughing and wondering the while and making a fine show of other men's miseries, disgracing our common nature. . . . Still you ask then, tell me, to what end is hell-fire? Nay, ask not that any more, but how is there one hell only? For of how many punishments are not they worthy, who get up this cruel and merciless spectacle and laugh at what both they and yourselves ought to weep over. . . .[17]

Many Christians apparently thought that works of charity were the special province of the monks. John informed his congregation that works of charity and the modest and chaste lifestyle that needed to accompany them were not reserved for the "solitaries" on Mount Siplius. The same ideals that shaped monastic life should shape the Christian household.

The Beatitudes of Christ [John said] were not addressed to solitaries only. . . . For if it be not possible, in the married state, to perform the

---

17. *Homily XXI on 1 Corinthians*; pp. 123-124.

duties of solitaries, then all things have perished, and Christian virtue is boxed in. Why, it is just this that makes me sigh, that you think that monks are the only persons properly concerned with decency and chastity. This notion has been the ruin of us all.[18]

But a Christian household, ruled by married chastity and generous charity, was not an easy thing to build. Those households had to grow in the midst of the pagan life of Antioch, which, to John, "was a 'Devil's garbage tip,' piled high outside the simple walls of Christian houses." As Peter Brown has so aptly put it, the "undiminished, deeply profane vigor [of the city of late antiquity] mocked John's rhetoric." Often these households did not even get off to a Christian start.

> The forms of marriage ceremony celebrated in Antioch made brutally plain how far from fourth-century reality John's hopes had remained. When they joined their sons and daughters in marriage, the Christian families of the fourth century still breathed a heavy, civic air. A public procession led the unveiled bride through the city to her husband's house. Songs and dances referred in no uncertain terms to love and to sexual exploits. . . . Priests were rarely invited to these occasions; and those who came were advised to leave early. For a moment, the raucous, whirling world of the theater burst through the walls of the Christian household.[19]

If the theater entered the Christian household at the wedding, its enticements tempted the household every day of its life. So it is not surprising that John frequently and vehemently spoke out against the theater in his sermons. This was not simply because the theater was "exuberantly immoral"; it was because "John sensed in the theater the perfect rival to the sense of community that he himself propounded so frequently."[20]

Even though John's goal of a Christian Antioch made up of Christian households was not to be realized, the combination of his holy life and eloquent preaching did have an impact. John was loved by many, and there is no reason to doubt what Sozomen said about John's success: "Many of those

18. From homilies on Hebrews and Matthew; quoted from Brown, *The Body and Society,* p. 311.

19. Brown, *The Body and Society,* p. 313.

20. Brown, *The Body and Society,* p. 314.

who heard the discourses of John in the church were thereby excited to the love of virtue and to the reception of his own religious sentiments. But it was chiefly by the bright example of his private virtues, that John inspired his auditors with emulations."[21] Whatever the balance of success and failure in Antioch, there can be little doubt that his years there were good ones.

But John Chrysostom's life took an unexpected and, as it turned out, tragic turn in 397, when the Patriarch of Constantinople died and John was chosen to be his successor. Despite his aversion to accepting the position, he relented and was consecrated Patriarch in 398. He immediately set about instituting reforms that were consistent with his beliefs. But those reforms proved to be the source of his undoing because they were very unpopular with both the imperial court and the clerics. Peter Brown describes the situation as follows:

> Constantinople . . . was a world capital. . . . Its patriarch had to be "representative"; he had to preside with benign good nature over the one city in the Roman world that could boast an impeccably Christian origin. In such a role, John was a resounding failure. . . . Instead of entertaining on a lavish scale, as a good bishop should, he dined alone. . . . He persuaded Olympias [the head of a nunnery] to focus her use of wealth even more austerely than before on the needs of the poor, thus cutting back on those sections of the budget that had provided pensions for retired gentlewomen and entertainment and funds for visiting ecclesiastical dignitaries. He founded a leper colony on the edge of a fashionable suburb.[22]

Needless to say, John made some enemies.

Yet John's biographer, Palladius, speaks in glowing terms about his reforms and their success: "Because of all these reforms the church was flourishing more excellently from day to day. The very color of the city was changed to piety; everyone looked bright and fresh with soberness and Psalm-singing." Palladius even mentions people abandoning the circuses and theater: "[H]orse-crazed men and theater fans have abandoned the courts of the devil and hastened to the fold of the Savior out of love for the piping of the Shepherd who loves His sheep."[23]

---

21. *History of the Church* VIII, ii; p. 376.
22. Brown, *The Body and Society,* pp. 317-318.
23. Palladius, *Dialogue on the Life of St. John Chrysostom;* p. 40.

John also had some success against heresy. Sozomen provides an interesting episode in John's battle with the Arians:

> The Arians, having been deprived of their churches in Constantinople during the reign of Theodosius, held their assemblies without the walls of the city. They assembled by night in the public porticos, and sang in parts certain hymns which they had composed in vindication of their own tenets; and, at break of day, marched in procession, singing these hymns, to the places in which they held their assemblies. They proceeded in this manner on all solemn festivals, and on the first and last days of the week. . . . John was fearful lest any of his own people should be led astray by witnessing these exhibitions, and therefore commanded them to sing hymns in the same manner.

On at least one occasion, these competing processions resulted in a fight between the Arians and the orthodox. The eunuch of the empress was wounded by a stone thrown at him. According to Sozomen, this kindled the "resentment of the Emperor . . . and he put a stop to the Arian assemblies." But the orthodox retained "the custom of singing hymns . . . to the present day." Like John's other actions, this one both won admirers and made enemies. As Sozomen tells it,

> The institution of these processions, and the faithfulness of his ministrations in the church, endeared John to the people; but he was hated by the clergy and the powerful on account of his boldness and candour; for he never failed to rebuke the clergy when he detected them in acts of injustice, nor to exhort the powerful to return to the practice of virtue when they abused their wealth, committed impiety, or yielded to voluptuousness.[24]

One of the "powerful" whom John offended was Empress Eudoxia. Though she had paid for the cost of the processions and had appointed her eunuch to organize them, John did not hesitate to rebuke her for seizing a widow's piece of property. When she joined forces with John's other new enemies and his longtime opponent, Bishop Theophilus, John was up against an alliance that would bring about his death within a few years. As a result of some trumped-up charges of treason, John was exiled to

---

24. *History of the Church* VIII, 8; pp. 388-389.

Bithynia; but this must have been the shortest exile in history. He was almost immediately recalled — according to Palladius, it was the following day — because of an uproar of protest among the people and because of some kind of calamity (perhaps an earthquake) in the palace. But John was back in Constantinople for only two short months when he again incurred the wrath of Eudoxia: this time it was because he criticized her for erecting a silver statue of herself in the square outside the cathedral and for celebrating its unveiling with loud music, disorderly dancing, and indecent amusements. So the palace exiled John again, this time to Caucasus in Armenia.

After a few years, people from Antioch began making pilgrimages to see John in exile, so the palace sentenced him to banishment further away, to Pityus, an isolated place on the Black Sea. John died before he got there. According to Palladius,

> The soldiers of the praetorian prefect guarded him and rushed him along at high speed, saying that those were their instructions. Should he die on the way before arrival, the officers would receive a promotion. . . . [One of them] had but one desire, to bring about John's death as miserably as possible. For example, he started out without consideration in the midst of a tempestuous rainstorm, so that streams of water ran down his back and chest. On another occasion the extreme heat of the sun must have been the occasion of delight to this man who knew full well that John suffered from it, because he was bald like Elisha. Should they come to a city or town where there was the refreshment of a bath, the wretched man would not allow even a moment's delay. But John kept on like a shining star despite these hardships, his emaciated body being as though it were an apple turning ripe in the sun on the topmost branch of the tree.

They got as far as Comana, where there was a shrine of the martyr Basilicus. John had a vision in which Basilicus appeared to him and said, "Have courage, brother, tomorrow we shall be together."

> John accepted this as a reliable oracle for the morrow and calling them together he bade them remain until the fifth hour. They did not believe him and marched on, and when they had gone about thirty *stades* they returned to the martyr's shrine they had left as John had an acute attack.

When they got there, John donned a white robe, took communion, and offered

> his last prayer using his usual formula: "Glory to God for all things."
> Then he signed himself at the last Amen. *He raised up his feet* [like
> Moses], those beautiful feet [of the preacher] that hastened for the
> salvation of those who choose repentance and for chastising those
> who cultivate sin so freely.[25]

References to music in John's surviving writings are more copious than those in any other early Christians' writings, partly because his surviving writings themselves are among the most copious we have. But it is also because of the nature of his surviving writings: they are mainly sermons. Furthermore, they are sermons with a pastoral purpose, so they deal with problems of everyday morality more than with questions of doctrine. And since music was very much a part of the warp and woof of daily life, John frequently had occasion to refer to it in his sermons. Perhaps because they are in sermons, John's references to music contain nothing of speculative, cosmological musical thought. However, as we have seen in Ambrose's sermons in the *Hexameron,* musical cosmology is not necessarily an incompatible topic for sermons. More likely, the absence of thoughts on musical cosmology in John's sermons is due to his lack of interest in the subject. In this respect, the Greek John is more like the Latin Tertullian than like the Greek Clement; and the Latin Ambrose is more like the Greek Clement than like the Latin Tertullian.

Among John's references to music, I will concentrate on those relating to the theme at the heart of so much of his sermonizing, the building and maintenance of the Christian household as the foundation for a Christian society. The Christian household begins with marriage. But as I have observed above, the wedding festivities of Christians in Antioch were often more pagan than Christian. Christians were reluctant to abandon objectionable pagan customs at their weddings. These customs included music that was objectionable to John, and he denounced it whenever he dealt with weddings. A sermon on Acts provides a typical denunciation: in it John speaks of the "Bacchic frenzy" of the festivities, more becoming to brutes than to men. There was in these wild festivities, he said, "much

---

25. Palladius, *Dialogue on the Life of St. John Chrysostom;* pp. 72-73.

pomp of the devil," including "cymbals, auloi and songs full of fornication and adultery."[26]

John's Twelfth Homily on 1 Corinthians contains his most extensive castigation of pagan marriage festivities as they were practiced by Christians. Among the "ridiculous things" that took place were "dancing, and cymbals, and flutes, and shameful words, and songs, and drunkenness, and revellings, and all the Devil's great heap of garbage." It was hardly the way John wanted to see the Christian household started, because "from the very commencement of her marriage" the bride was "instructed in imprudence" and found "herself put forward in the midst of wanton and rude men." "What [John asks] will not be implanted in the bride from that day forth? Immodesty, petulance, the love of vainglory: since they will naturally go on and desire to have all their days such as these. Hence our women become expensive and profuse; hence are they void of modesty. . . ."[27]

John describes the spectacle made of the bride as she was paraded through the marketplace amidst the "besotted" and "profligate" men who rivaled each other in uttering foul words; those who "found the largest store of railings and the greatest indecencies" were considered victorious. The parade continued well into the night, preventing even those who were "in their houses and plunged in deep sleep from remaining ignorant of these proceedings; that being wakened by the pipe and leaning to look out of the lattices, they may be witnesses of the comedy such as it is." John concludes with a paragraph focused directly on the music that accompanied these proceedings:

> What can one say of the songs themselves, crammed as they are with all uncleanness, introducing monstrous amours, and unlawful connections, and subversions of houses, and tragic scenes without end . . . ? And, what is still more grievous, that young women are present at these things . . . and in the midst of wanton young men acting a shameless part with their disorderly songs, with their foul words, with their devilish harmony. Tell me then: do you still inquire, "Whence come adulteries? Whence fornications? Whence violations of marriage?"[28]

26. *Homily XLII on the Acts of the Apostles* 3; quoted from *Music in Early Christian Literature*, p. 85.

27. *Twelfth Homily on 1 Corinthians*; p. 69.

28. *Twelfth Homily on 1 Corinthians*; p. 70.

If pagan wedding festivities threatened to get marriages off on the wrong foot, the enticement of the theater was a constant threat to the stability of households. John lamented about Christians who ran to the theater instead of to church, who ran after a star of the stage rather than after Christ, and who left "the fountain of blood" for "the fountain of the devil, to see a harlot swim, and to suffer shipwreck of the soul."[29] He feared that the adulteries on the stage would lead to real adulteries, "for nothing is more full of whoredom and boldness than an eye that endures to look at such things."[30]

The music of the theater was just as loathsome to John as the action on the stage.

> And that which the barbarian threatened, saying, "You shall eat your own dung," and what follows; this do these men also make you undergo, not in word, but in deeds; or rather, somewhat even much worse. For truly those songs are more loathsome even than all this; and what is yet worse, so far from feeling annoyance when you hear them, you rather laugh, when you ought to abominate them and fly.[31]

John goes on to describe the whole show of which the "loathsome songs" were a part. He tells of its themes of adultery, "stolen marriages," prostitution, and "youths corrupting themselves"; of "foul sayings" and "gestures fouler still"; of unnatural and unchaste dress, hairstyle, gait, and "flexure of limbs." The whole thing was a "tumult" filled with "satanic cries." In short, he says, the whole thing is "full of the most extreme impurity"; these spectacles stir up the populace and make "tumults" in the cities. "For youth, when it has joined hands with idleness, and is brought up among such great evils, becomes fiercer than any wild beast."[32]

John knew that these spectacles were not without their pernicious effect: "For even all the mire that is poured out for you, by the speeches, by the songs, by the laughter, you collect and take every man to his home, or rather not to his home only, but every man even into his own mind." Those who attend the theater have no time "to hear Paul" and "to gain the sense

---

29. *Homily VII on Matthew* 7; p. 48.
30. *Homily VI on Matthew* 10; p. 43.
31. *Homily XXXVII on Matthew* 8; p. 248.
32. *Homily XXXVII on Matthew* 8; p. 249.

of [their] wrong actions" when "drunk . . . ever and incessantly with the spectacle." John asks the pertinent questions:

> For when will you be able to become good, bred up as you are with such sounds in your ears? When will you venture to undergo such labors as chastity requires, now that you are falling gradually away through this laughter, these songs, and filthy words?[33]

Then, as now, there were those who claimed that they were unharmed by the spectacles. John had a hard time believing that, knowing that "if even now you are chaste, you would have become more chaste by avoiding such sights." But even if he granted that someone would be "nothing hurt by their pastime in that place," he still saw two problems: "In the first place, even this is a hurt, to spend one's time without object or fruit." In other words, at best it was a waste of time; there were better things to do. In the second place, one's presence gave support to the activity and could cause a brother or sister to stumble. "For as surely as, if there were no spectators, there would be none to follow these employments; so, since there are, they too have their share of the fire due to such deeds. So that even if in chastity you were quite unhurt . . . , yet for others' ruin you will render a grievous account."[34]

Thus John saw that wanton music and the shows of the theater were a dire threat to chastity. He wanted his congregation to have nothing to do with the theater and its music, including those who thought they were immune to its effects. But the spectacles were not only a threat to chastity; John saw them as a direct link to a lack of charity as well. Just prior to the portion of Homily 37 on Matthew that I have been quoting, John says that "harlot's songs," among other worldly enticements, make the mind "unclean," "worse than any filth." But they also "close it up." In particular, they close it up to the apostles; and a mind that is closed to the apostles will close its doors to the poor. So John asks:

> [O]f what indulgence should we be worthy, showing so much inhospitality, and shutting our doors against them that are in need, and before our doors, our ears? or rather not against the poor only, but against the apostles themselves? For therefore we do it to the poor, because we do it to the very apostles. For although Paul is read, you

33. *Homily XXXVII on Matthew* 7-8; p. 248.
34. *Homily XXXVII on Matthew* 9; p. 250.

do not attend; although John preaches, you do not hear: when will you receive a poor man, who will not receive an apostle?

In order then that both our houses may be continually open to the one [the poor], and our ears to the others [the apostles], let us purge away the filth from the ears of our soul. For as filth and mud close up the ears of the flesh, so do the harlot's songs . . . close up the ear of the mind, worse than any filth; nay rather, they do not close it up only, but also make it unclean.[35]

In addition to the way one's attachment to the theater and its songs closes one's ears to God's apostles and therefore to their calls to help the needy, the theater affects one's willingness to give to the poor — because it is also an economic drain. John preached against "forsaking your workshops, and your crafts, and your incomes from these, and in short everything, for the sake of continuing" in the theater[36] and against those who "spend without limit on that wicked choir of the devil."[37]

At the end of Homily 37, John gives some trenchant advice to his listeners, who, "when there is a question of precedent, claim to take first place of the whole world, forasmuch as our city first crowned itself with the name Christian."[38] He tells those proud Christians, who were also proud citizens of the Roman Empire, to "imitate the barbarians, if no one else; for they verily are altogether clean from seeking such sights."

What excuse then can we have after all this, we the citizens of Heaven, and partners in the choirs of the cherubim, and in fellowship with the angels, making ourselves in this respect worse even than the barbarians, and this, when innumerable other pleasures, better than these are within our reach?

If you desire that your soul may find delight, go to the park, to a river flowing by, and to lakes, take notice of gardens, listen to grasshoppers as they sing, be continually by the tombs of the martyrs, where is health of body and benefit of soul, and no hurt, no remorse after pleasure, as there is here.

You have a wife, you have children; what is equal to this pleasure?

35. *Homily XXXVII on Matthew* 7; p. 248.
36. *Homily VI on Matthew* 10; p. 42.
37. *Homily XXXVII on Matthew* 8; p. 249.
38. *Homily VII on Matthew* 7; p. 49.

You have a house, you have friends, these are the true delights: besides their purity, great is the advantage they bestow. For what, I pray you, is sweeter than children? what sweeter than a wife, to him that will be chaste in mind?

To this purpose, we are told, that the barbarians uttered on some occasion a saying full of wise severity. I mean, that having heard of these wicked spectacles, and the unseasonable delight in them; "Why the Romans," they say, "have devised these pleasures, as though they didn't have wives and children;" implying that nothing is sweeter than children and wife, if you are willing to live honestly.[39]

But John had even better models than the barbarians to hold before his congregation. He held up to them the ideals of the monks — though there was a difference. "I do not," said John, "make it a law that you are to occupy the mountains and the deserts." The Christian householders had spouses and children; but Scripture's demands of chastity and charity were not meant for monks alone. It made John sigh that his congregation thought only monks needed "to be concerned with decency and chastity"; what had ruined all, he claimed, was that they thought "that the reading of the divine Scriptures appertains to monks only." Christian householders in the city, as much as the monks in the mountains, were required "to be good and considerate and chaste."[40]

Christian householders, like the monks, were to fill their lives with the psalms. John described the singing of the monks in glowing terms.

These who are the lights of the world, as soon as the sun is up, or rather even long before its rise, rise from bed, healthy, and wakeful, and sober . . . ; having risen then straightway from their beds, cheerful and glad, and having made one choir, with their conscience bright, with one voice all, as out of one mouth, they sing hymns to the God of all, honoring Him and thanking Him for all His benefits, both particular and common.

He then asked, rhetorically, whether there was any "difference between a choir of angels and this choir of men on earth singing the words, 'Glory to God in the highest, and on earth peace, good will among men.'"[41]

39. *Homily XXXVII on Matthew* 9; pp. 249-250.
40. *Homilies VII and II on Matthew;* pp. 49, 13.
41. *Homily LXVIII on Matthew* 3; p. 418.

Christian householders were not excluded from that singing. Wherever they were, whatever their activity, they could join the song. John knew the attraction of music and how it fills people's lives. In his *Exposition of Psalm 41*, he wrote with obvious approval of the folk music that people sing in all of life's activities.

> To such an extent, indeed, is our nature delighted by chants and songs that even infants at the breast, if they be weeping or afflicted, are by reason of it lulled to sleep. Nurses, carrying them in their arms, walking to and fro and singing certain childish songs to them, often cause them to close their eyes. For this reason travelers also, driving at noon the yoked animals, sing as they do so, lightening by their chants the hardships of the journey. And not only travelers, but also peasants often sing as they tread the grapes in the wine press, gather the vintage, tend the vine, and perform their other tasks. Sailors do likewise, pulling at the oars. Women, too, weaving and parting the tangled threads with the shuttle, often sing a certain melody, some-times individually and to themselves, sometimes in concert. This they do, the women, travelers, peasants, and sailors, striving to lighten with a chant the labor endured in working, for the mind suf-fers hardships and difficulties more easily when it hears songs and chants.

After this beautiful appreciation of lullabies and work songs, he adds:

> Inasmuch as this kind of pleasure is thoroughly innate to our mind, and lest demons introducing lascivious songs should overthrow ev-erything, God established the psalms, in order that singing might be both a pleasure and a help. From strange chants harm, ruin, and many grievous matters are brought in, for those things that are las-civious and vicious in all songs settle in parts of the mind, making it softer and weaker; from spiritual psalms, however, proceeds much of value, much utility, much sanctity. . . .[42]

Unfortunately, Christians in Antioch knew the songs of the world better than they knew the psalms. John challenged his congregation: "Who of you that stand here, if he were required, could repeat one Psalm, or any

---

42. Quoted from *Source Readings in Music History,* Vol. 2, p. 14.

other portion of the divine Scriptures? There is not one." And it was bad enough that they did not know Scripture; what made it worse was that they did know, all too well, "what belongs to Satan."

> And it is not this only that is the grievous thing, but that while you have become so backward with respect to things spiritual, yet in regard of what belongs to Satan you are more vehement than fire. Thus should any one be minded to ask of you songs of devils and impure effeminate melodies, he will find many that know these perfectly, and repeat them with much pleasure.[43]

Therefore, it was very important that the teaching and learning of psalms and hymns be a high priority in the Christian household. In his wonderful *Address on Vainglory and the Right Way for Parents to Bring Up Their Children,* John told parents to let their children "learn to sing hymns to God" so that they would not spend their leisure "on shameful songs and ill-timed tales."[44] And in his *Exposition on Psalm 41,* he urged men to learn the psalms "not only that you may yourselves sing praises, but also that you may teach your wives and children to do so, not merely while weaving, to lighten work, but especially at the table."[45]

John gives us a glimpse of the Christian household singing at the table, both before and after the meal, "rising from the feast together with one's wife and children, to sing sacred hymns to God." All standing, they would sing a psalm together: "'For you, Lord, have made me glad through your work; I will triumph in the works of your hands.' Then after the psalmody let there be added a prayer, in order that along with the mind we may also make holy the house itself." Everyone could participate in the singing, for no one would

> be blamed if he be weakened by old age, or young, or have a harsh voice, or no knowledge at all of numbers [i.e., the theoretical aspects of music]. What is here sought for is a sober mind, an awakened intelligence, a contrite heart, sound reason, and clear conscience. If having these you have entered into God's sacred choir, you may stand beside David himself.

43. *Homily II on Matthew* 10; p. 13.
44. *Address on Vainglory;* p. 101.
45. Quoted from *Source Readings in Music History,* Vol. 2, p. 14.

This practice should become habitual, for "once we have acquired this habit, neither through free will nor through carelessness shall we neglect our beautiful office." Custom will compel us, he says, "even against our will, to carry out this worship daily." And not only at mealtime at home, but anytime and anywhere, for in psalm singing

> [t]here is no need for place or for season; in all places and at all seasons you may sing with the mind. For whether you walk in the market place, or begin a journey, or sit down with your friends you may rouse up your mind or call out silently. . . . If you are an artisan, you may sing sitting and working in your shop. If you are a soldier, or if you sit in judgement, you may do the very same. One may also sing without voice, the mind resounds inwardly. For we sing, not to men, but to God, who can hear our hearts and enter into the silences of our minds.[46]

Unlike his Latin contemporary Ambrose, John did not write hymns. Nevertheless, as Peter Brown points out, "his rhetoric of compassion survived" in the music of the Byzantine church.

> Themes taken directly from his sermons, or from sermons composed in his spirit, entered the great urban chants of the Byzantine church. The *kontakia* of Romanos Melodes, composed in the early sixth century, embraced the urban community in a spider-fine web of common feeling. They instilled, with heartfelt artistry, a sense of shared suffering, of shared fasting, of a shared duty to free the city's poor.[47]

Particularly interesting is Romanos's hymn *On the Ten Virgins*, which says that Christ considered the devotion shown to him in love for people higher than that shown him in the practice of virginity. In the hymn Christ says:

I renounce the fasts	of those who show no mercy.
I accept the prayers	of those who eat with kindness.
I hate all virgins	who shun human feeling.
I love the married	who love their fellow-creatures.

---

46. Quoted from *Source Readings in Music History*, Vol. 2, p. 16.
47. Brown, *The Body and Society*, p. 321.

Romanos knew how often he and we all fall short. So he added this prayer:

> I do not do what I now say, and what I urge the people.
> For this reason, I fall down. Oh Savior, give me tears,
> Contrition in my heart, and in all those who hear me.[48]

48. Quoted from Brown, *The Body and Society*, pp. 321-322.

CHAPTER 9

Rejection: The Music of a Pagan World

I know where you dwell, where Satan's throne is. . . .

Revelation 2:13

B y now it should be abundantly clear that there was a great deal of hostility among the early Christian writers toward some of the music in the world around them. I have quoted above James McKinnon's characterization of their polemic against it: their response is characterized by "vehemence and uniformity." The uniformity is especially striking considering how different those writers were in other respects. Whether they were Greek-speaking or Latin-speaking, pre- or post-Constantine, conciliatory or antagonistic toward pagan learning, lifelong Christians or converts — whatever their background or personality, they agreed that Christians should distance themselves from some of the music of the surrounding culture. We have seen nothing to make us doubt McKinnon: the polemic was indeed uniformly vehement. But was the situation really so bad that the proper Christian response had to be surgery? That is, was it necessary to cut out large areas of the music of pagan society? Or were the early Christian writers misguided by an overly austere mentality when they launched their polemic?

The world into which the church was born was the Roman Empire, an enormous amount of territory surrounding the Mediterranean Sea (the "Roman Lake"), radiating as far north as Britain and as far east as the Caspian Sea, and including a welter of peoples, customs, and religions. Dom Gregory Dix called it a "great crucible" into which were poured all the streams of culture welling up out of the dimness of pre-history; from Egypt and Mesopotamia, even in lesser degree from Persia and in thin trickles from the alien lands of India and China; in Anatolia from the long-dead Hittite empire . . . and Ionia, and from semitic Tyre and Carthage. All these, with the raw cultures of the North and West, were formed by the dying flame of Hellas and the hardness of Rome into the unified Mediterranean world of the first and second centuries — the *Civitas Romana*. Into that had flowed all the forces of antiquity.[1]

In the second century the Roman historian Tacitus commented that in this crucible "all things hideous and shameful from every part of the world meet and become popular."[2]

Such was the world that the early church needed to live *in* while not being *of* it; such was the world the church needed to convert and transform; such was the world the church needed to teach to sing the "new song." All of the peoples in the bubbling Roman crucible made music, raising their voices and playing their instruments to their gods. They sang and played and danced on many occasions in their daily lives. The church needed to measure the abundance of songs in the world against the standard of New Testament ideals. What could be embraced? What could be appropriated? What needed to be rejected?

There were three main elements in the Roman Empire with which the church needed to reckon, and all three had musical components. The first was the mixture of pagan religions and cultures so vividly described by Dix. The second element was Greek thought, the "dying flame of Hellas." The third, not explicitly mentioned by Dix, was the Jewish tradition out of which Christianity grew. We have already seen examples of the Christianization of Greek musical thought in Clement and Ambrose. That went along with their acceptance, with reservations and modifications, of Greek — or, more specifically, Neo-Platonic — philosophy. In the next chapter we will take up the church's appropriation of Jewish psalmody; in this chapter we will take a closer look at the music of the pagan society at which the church fathers aimed their polemic.

---

1. *The Shape of the Liturgy*, p. 385.
2. *Annals* XV, xliv, 3; quoted from Meeks, *The Moral World of the First Christians*, p. 25.

In ancient pagan religious ritual, music typically had one or more of three magical functions: *euphemia* — to produce good omens; *apostrophe* — to ward off evil demons or the anger of the gods; and *epiclesis* — to summon the gods. At its lowest level, *euphemia* may have been merely the covering up of unpleasant noises, which seems to be the case in Plutarch's description of a particularly gruesome pagan rite involving child sacrifice.

> [T]he mother stood by without a tear or moan; but should she utter a single moan or let fall a single tear, she had to forfeit the money, and her child was sacrificed nonetheless; and the whole area before the statue was filled with a loud noise of flutes and drums so that the cries of wailing should not reach the ears of the people.[3]

But simply covering up unwanted noises cannot have been the main reason for music at sacrifices. First of all, one can question whether the music would have been loud enough to cover the noise of screaming children or bellowing bulls. But even if it were loud enough, we would not have an explanation why music was used at the offering of incense or libations. The cries of victims did not need to be drowned out at either of these, and music was invariably used at both.

The deeper purpose of *euphemia* can be learned from a statement by Pliny: at a sacrifice the "piper plays so that nothing at the prayer is heard."[4] This means that the music prevented anything extraneous from being heard by the god, anything that would anger rather than placate the god. The music was part of a prayer that needed to be exact if it was going to be effective. The phrases immediately preceding Pliny's statement about the piper make that clear:

> We see also that our chief magistrates have adopted fixed formulas for their prayers; that to prevent a word's being omitted or out of place a reader dictates beforehand the prayer from a script; that an-

---

3. *De superstitione* 171; quoted from McKinnon, "The Church Fathers," pp. 11-12. For some reason unknown to me, most translators mistranslate the Greek *aulos* and the Roman *tibia* as "flute." This gives a completely wrong picture to modern readers because they, rightly, do not associate loud, raucous music with flutes. When "flute" is used in these translations, think of an oriental double-reed instrument, or a modern oboe if you like, but one with an especially wild and penetrating tone.

4. *Nat. Hist.* XXVIII, iii, 11; quoted from McKinnon, "The Church Fathers," p. 12.

other attendant is appointed as a guard to keep watch, and yet another is put in charge to maintain strict silence.

The *apotropaic* function, the warding off of evil spirits, is clear from many statements about noisemakers, particularly bells or gongs or cymbals, that were used at various pagan rites. In the *Fasti* of Ovid we read about the clashing of "Temesan bronze" as the spirits of the dead are asked to leave the house.[5] This belief in the *apotropaic* function of clanging metal was deeply rooted in the populace. John Chrysostom had to warn his congregation against believing that bells could ward off evil spirits. "What shall we say," he asked them, "about the amulets and the bells which are hung upon the hand . . . when they ought to invest the child with nothing else save the protection of the Cross?"[6]

The third magical function, *epiclesis,* the summoning of the god, I have already discussed in chapter 2 (pp. 18-21).

According to McKinnon, the magical functions of music had lost their significance by the early Christian era. By that time the original significance of instrumental music at pagan rituals had been lost and remained only "as formalistic cult features like fillets and barley-meal. . . . [They had] become part of the 'dead matter' of paganism."[7] It is true that, by early Christian times, many pagans had abandoned some of their earlier beliefs. But the claim that belief in the magical power of music was only "dead matter" is hard to credit fully. Censorius, a pagan writing in 238 CE, says that music pleases the gods. Although his statement is not exactly a description of *epiclesis* in the narrow sense, it is not far removed; for pleasing a god is but one short step from summoning a god. This is what he said:

Music is pleasing to the gods, for if it were not pleasing to the gods . . . the flutist would not attend prayers of supplication offered in sacred shrines; the triumph in honor of Mars would not be celebrated to the accompaniment of flute music or the trumpet's blast; the cithara would not be dedicated to Apollo, nor would flutes and other instruments be dedicated to the Muses; flutists would not be permitted to perform in public, to eat on the Capitol or to roam about the city on

5. *Fasti,* ll. 441-444; quoted from McKinnon, "The Church Fathers," p. 15.
6. *Homily XII on First Corinthians;* p. 71.
7. McKinnon, "The Church Fathers," p. 23.

the Ides of June, drunken and disguised in whatever they choose to wear.[8]

Apparently, beliefs like these were still prevalent enough so that Arnobius and Chrysostom did not see them as "dead matter." They thought the issue was alive enough to warrant a satirical jibe aimed at pagans and a solemn warning for Christians. McKinnon is certainly correct, however, in seeing that belief in these magical powers of music was not the most dangerous of the threats that pagan music posed for the early Christians. A greater threat — and hence one that occasioned much more early Christian comment — was the threat from the ecstatic, orgiastic music of the mystery religions from the East.

The mysteries reached a peak of popularity during the early centuries of the Christian era because, like Christianity, they offered the comfort of life hereafter. Some, such as Mithraism, were highly moral, disciplined, and wholesome in character. But most of them featured ecstatic, even frenzied and orgiastic, rites. Ecstatic rituals were not uncommon in Greek and Roman societies, going back centuries before the Christian era. The rituals associated with the worship of Dionysus or his Roman equivalent, Bacchus, are the classic examples of this type. Drunken revelry, wild music, frenzied dancing, and flagellation and mutilation were their hallmarks. During the second century BCE, Bacchic rites flourished briefly in Rome before they were suppressed by the government. But suppression did not eradicate them; instead, they re-emerged later as a kind of chic, hedonistic fad among the Roman upper classes. In the homes of the rich, Dionysiac associations met

> like the other numerous religious associations of Late Antiquity . . . under the pretext of honoring some god, in order to enjoy themselves and feast. Wine-drinking and banqueting are especially fitting in the Dionysiac associations since Dionysus is considered at this time to be the god of wine and intoxication. Sexual symbols are maintained as the central symbols of the cult but certainly could not, as among simple people, be thought of merely as bringers of fertility; for the well-to-do townspeople they must have had a piquant attraction.[9]

---

8. *De die natali* XII, 2; quoted from Quasten, *Music and Worship*, p. 1.
9. McKinnon, "The Church Fathers," pp. 32-33.

While the wealthy were dabbling in the voluptuous and erotic vestiges of Dionysiac worship, the common people were more attracted by the promises of redemption that came from the oriental mystery religions, as well as by the exotic rituals of those religions, which were replete with wild music and dance that aroused a great deal of religious enthusiasm. The most degenerate and Dionysiac of the mysteries, and one of the most popular, was the one devoted to the Syrian goddess Cybele: in the rites of Cybele, frenzied music and dancing brought on a state of ecstasy (or "divine madness") that led to the castration of the *Gallae,* those who would be priests of Cybele. In a description of this rite by the second-century Greek satirist Lucian, we read about a curious crowd, gathered to observe this rite, getting caught up in the frenzy. At one point, Lucian relates, "a young man seized by this madness rips the clothing from his body and dashes into the middle with a loud cry and, snatching one of the swords that stands ready for just such a purpose, he castrates himself."[10]

Of course, offensive activities were not a part of all pagan ritual and did not occur every day. Nevertheless, as McKinnon notes, in early Christian times "the worst aspects of religious orgy were sufficiently widespread throughout the Empire . . . to come to the attention of all observers."[11] If they did not participate in or observe the actual rites, they at least saw them enacted in the theater, as Augustine had.

> I myself, when I was a young man, used sometimes to go to the sacrilegious entertainments and spectacles; I saw the priests raving in religious excitement, and heard the choristers; I took pleasure in the shameful games which were celebrated in honour of gods and goddesses, of the virgin Coelestis, and Berecynthia [Cybele], the mother of all the gods. And on the holy day consecrated to her purification, there were sung before her couch productions so obscene and filthy for the ear — I do not say of the mother of the gods, but of the mother of any senator or honest man — nay, so impure, that not even the mother of the foul-mouthed players themselves could have formed one of the audience. . . . If these are sacred rites, what is sacrilege? If this is purification, what is pollution?[12]

---

10. *De Dea Syria* 50; quoted in Quasten, *Music and Worship,* p. 37.
11. McKinnon, "The Church Fathers," pp. 34-35.
12. Augustine, *The City of God* II, iv; p. 43.

Of course, religious ritual was not the only place in Roman society where music was heard; it was everywhere. In fact, music historians see evidence for a proliferation of music during the late Roman Empire. The theaters and arenas rang with music; minstrels entertained at the baths and in the streets; highly trained slaves made music in the houses of the wealthy; virtuosi competed in contests; and some Romans still enjoyed the singing of lyric poetry to the accompaniment of the lyre. And as in all civilizations before the advent of electronic media, people sang as they worked.

The great quantity of music in late Roman society is not a sign of its quality. In that time, as now, great popularity seldom accompanied high quality. The overall picture of music in the Roman Empire is a picture of decadence; in fact, as early as Cicero (first century BCE) there were complaints about decline. "Imposing sternness" had given way to "modern tunes," to which audiences "leap up and twist their necks and turn their eyes."[13] Cicero was not alone in seeing decline. Quintilian and Seneca saw

> in the newfangled music signs of moral as well as of artistic degeneration, and look back nostalgically to a time when music was more serious or more sacred, a time when, after a patrician banquet, the lute would circulate among the guests, who performed songs in praise of heroes and of gods; when dances were not lascivious in character, but ceremonial and religious. Under the Empire, it appears, a more sensual quality came to pervade both vocal and instrumental music, the songs and dances of private feast and public spectacle alike.[14]

Virtuosi contests featuring the latest stars were part symptom and part cause of the decline. These contests did not foster good art; instead, mere technique was deemed the highest value. Those who could blow the loudest and the longest were prized, and because they were prized, they developed the insolence and arrogance that stars usually develop. They also became rich. The lure of the stage attracted Emperor Nero, who may or may not have actually "fiddled" while Rome burned, but who certainly tried his hand at the contests. The following account of Nero's musical aspirations, written by the Roman historian Suetonius, is worth quoting at length for the light it sheds on this aspect of Roman music-making.

13. *Laws* II, xv, 39; p. 419.
14. Dronke, *The Medieval Lyric,* p. 13.

Having gained some knowledge of music . . . as soon as he became emperor he sent for Terpnus, the greatest master of the lyre in those days, and after listening to him sing after dinner for many successive days until late at night, he little by little began to practise himself, neglecting none of the exercises which artists of that kind are in the habit of following, to preserve or strengthen their voices. For he used to lie upon his back and hold a leaden plate on his chest, purge himself by the syringe and by vomiting, and deny himself fruits and all foods injurious to the voice. Finally encouraged by his progress, although his voice was weak and husky, he began to long to appear on the stage, and every now and then in the presence of his intimate friends he would quote a Greek proverb meaning "Hidden music counts for nothing." And he made his debut at Naples, where he did not cease singing until he had finished the number which he had begun, even though the theatre was shaken by a sudden earthquake shock. In the same city he sang frequently and for successive days. Even when he took a short time to rest his voice, he could not keep out of sight but went to the theatre after bathing and dined in the orchestra with the people all about him, promising them in Greek, that when he had wetted his whistle a bit, he would ring out something good and loud. He was greatly taken too with the rhythmic applause of some Alexandrians, who had flocked to Naples from a fleet that had lately arrived, and summoned more men from Alexandria. Not content with that, he selected some young men of the order of the knights and more than five thousand sturdy commoners, to be divided into groups and learn the Alexandrian styles of applause . . . and to ply them vigorously whenever he sang. . . . [Their] leaders were paid four hundred thousand sesterces each.

Considering it of great importance to appear in Rome as well, he repeated the contest . . . and when there was a general call for his "divine voice," he replied that if any wished to hear him, he would favour them in the gardens; but when the guard of soldiers which was then on duty seconded the entreaties of the people, he gladly agreed to appear at once. So without delay he had his name added to the list of the lyre-players who entered the contest. . . . Having taken his place and finished his preliminary speech, he announced through the ex-consul Cluvius Rufus that "he would sing Niobe"; and he kept at it until late in the afternoon, putting off the award of the prize for that event and postponing the rest of the contest to the next year, to have an excuse for singing oftener. . . . He even thought of taking part in private performances among the professional actors, when one of the praetors offered him a million sesterces. He also put on the mask . . . having the masks fashioned in the likeness of his own features or those of the women of whom he chanced to be enamoured. Among other themes he sang "Canace in Labor," "Orestes the Matricide," "The Blinding of Oedipus" and the "Frenzy of Hercules."[15]

Even making allowances for the fact that this is about the emperor, it is not hard to imagine this kind of craving for the spotlight by any other Roman virtuoso. We might also imagine how little of this account would need to be changed to make it fit, say, a Baroque castrato or a contemporary rock star.

The shows at the theaters were the most popular entertainments during the late Roman Empire, unless that distinction went to the violent and bloody games in the amphitheaters. Many writers, pagan and Christian, have furnished evidence of the Roman citizens' craving for the theater. The two principal kinds of theater were pantomime and farce, and music was an indispensable part of both. Pantomime appealed largely to the aristocracy; its subjects were mythological, and its character was sensuous, erotic, and lascivious. "Many of the *pantomimi* attained to an extreme refinement in their degenerate and sensuous art. They were, as Lucian said . . . erudite of gesture."[16] Farce appealed largely to the bourgeoisie. Like the prevalent popular entertainment of our own day, television and the movies, farce was characterized by violence:

> The Roman taste for bloodshed was sometimes gratified by mimes given in the amphitheater, and designed to introduce the actual execution of a criminal. Martial, *de Spectaculis,* 7, mentions the worrying and crucifixion of a brigand in the mime Laurelus, by order of Domitian. . . .[17]

And farce was also characterized, of course, by sex:

---

15. *Lives of the Caesars* VI; pp. 115-119.
16. Chambers, *The Medieval Stage,* p. 6.
17. Chambers, *The Medieval Stage,* p. 4, n. 5.

The favourite theme . . . was that of conjugal infidelity. Unchaste scenes were represented with astonishing realism. Contrary to the earlier custom of the classical stage, women took part in the performances, and at the *Floralia,* loosest of Roman festivals, the spectators seem to have claimed it as their right that the *mimae* should play naked.[18]

Other venues for lascivious music and dance were the tavern and the wealthy household. Musical slaves were imported from all around the Roman Empire, the most popular being dancing girls from Egypt or Syria.

Dancing girl of Syria, her hair caught up with a fillet:
Very subtle in swaying those quivering flanks of hers
In time to the castanet's rattle: half-drunk in the smoky tavern,
She dances, lascivious, wanton, clashing the rhythm.[19]

The popularity of dancing girls is revealed by an incident that occurred in 383 CE, reported by Ammianus Marcellinus. First he complains about the low esteem in which serious thought is held, compared to frivolous music:

. . . the few houses that were formerly famed for devotion to serious pursuits now teem with the sports of sluggish indolence, re-echoing to the sound of singing and the tinkling of flutes and lyres. In short, in place of the philosopher the singer is called in, and in place of the orator the teacher of stagecraft, and while libraries are shut up forever like tombs, water-organs are manufactured and lyres as large as carriages, and flutes and instruments heavy for gesticulating actors.

Then, to illustrate just how low things had sunk, he tells what happened when some foreigners in a city had to be expelled because there was not enough food to go around. This selection makes it clear where the city's values lay:

[T]hose who practised the liberal arts (very few in number) were thrust out without a breathing space, yet the genuine attendants upon actresses of the mimes, and those who for the time pretended to be such, were kept with us, while three thousand dancing girls,

18. Chambers, *The Medieval Stage,* pp. 4-5.
19. *Copa Surisca,* ll. 1-4; *Medieval Latin Lyrics,* p. 13.

without even being questioned, remained here with their choruses, and an equal number of dancing masters.[20]

Even if the music-making in wealthy households was not always sensuous or lascivious in character, it was part of a life of luxury that had become obscene. The most vivid picture of the opulence and decadence of aristocratic society during the early years of the Christian era can be found in the story "Trimalchio's Dinner," one of the surviving fragments of the *Satyricon* by Gaius Petronius (died 66 CE). Although we need to make allowances because the story is a satire, it had to be close enough to a portrayal of a real situation to make its point. Morris Bishop describes the *Satyricon* as "the first picaresque novel, an episodic, satiric, realistic picture of a society. . . ."[21] As "an arbiter in all questions of sensual taste" at Nero's court,[22] Petronius was well qualified to portray a society largely governed by the Epicurean philosophy "Eat, drink, and be merry, for tomorrow we die."

In the story Trimalchio "keeps a clock in his dining-room and a bugler to sound the hours, so he'll always know how fast life is slipping away."[23] During the party Trimalchio sings an Epicurean ditty with a familiar theme:

What is man? Why, nothing at all!
And when we answer the final call
We'll be in that same circumstance;
So let us live, while we got the chance!

The story of "Trimalchio's Dinner" is told by a narrator who, with two friends, has been invited to the party. When they arrive, they mix

with groups of sportsmen and [exchange] wise-cracks. Then we noticed an old bald fellow [Trimalchio] in a red sweat-shirt playing ball with a bunch of long-haired slave-boys. . . . When he dropped a ball he did not bother to pick it up; a slave with a sackful of balls threw out a fresh one to the players. We noticed other novelties. Two eunuchs stood at opposite sides of the ring. One held a silver chamber-

20. *Books of History* XIV. vi. 18 and 19; pp. 47, 49.
21. *A Classical Story Book*, p. 201.
22. Dill, *Roman Society from Nero to Marcus Aurelius*, p. 123.
23. All the quotations are taken from *A Classical Storybook*, pp. 201-216.

pot. . . . At [a] signal [from Trimalchio] a eunuch deftly posed the chamber-pot for the player. Having relieved himself, Trimalchio called for a basin of water, daintily dipped in his fingers, and wiped them on a slave-boy's hair.

Next they go to the baths, where Trimalchio has a rubdown "with cloths of the softest wool." When his masseurs, fighting over the towel, spill his fine Falernian wine, he laughs and says they poured out "a libation to his health." After the bath they go into Trimalchio's house, the lavish and ostentatious decor of which rivals his lavish and ostentatious clothes and jewelry. Trimalchio, propped up on pillows, is carried around to the accompaniment of music. When all are at the table, Alexandrian slaves pour iced water on the guests' hands and trim their toenails. "They didn't do their rather disagreeable task in silence; they sang all the time." This made the narrator "curious to find out if the whole corps of slaves were singers"; so he asked for a drink. "A slave popped up," he tells us, "and filled my order with a shrill singsong. All the other requests were honored in the same way. You would have thought it a theatrical performance rather than a family dinner."

The dinner is a seemingly endless stream of exotic courses, all of which are served to the accompaniment of music. During the meal the diners wash their hands in wine, and silver dishes that are dropped on the floor are swept away with the table scraps. The food is lavish beyond description, and it is served on incredibly costly and bizarre vessels, such as the donkey of Corinthian bronze with two baskets and the tray with four statuettes of Marsyas "with spicy garum-sauce trickling down from their bellies onto the fish swimming in a little fishpond."

I will not belabor Trimalchio's dinner. I have described enough for the reader to get the picture without hearing further details about the elaborate courses of food, the inhumane treatment of slaves, the "floorshows," and the end of the banquet, when Trimalchio, dressed in his burial shroud and accompanied by a funeral march says, "I'm dead. Now say something nice about me."

Even if Petronius's satire stretches the truth, other sources leave little doubt that decadent luxury was not uncommon at banquets. In Minucius Felix's dialogue entitled *Octavius*, Caecilius ridicules Christians for refraining from "honest pleasures." He says to Octavius: "You do not attend the shows; you take no part in the processions; fight shy of public banquets; abhor sacred games."[24] In response, Octavius replies that "morals and modesty" give Christians "good reason to abstain from the vicious delights" and the "pernicious attractions" of such events.[25] Clement of Alexandria reprimanded Christians who, like chameleons, change according to their surroundings. Leaving church, where they "hymned immortality," he says, they are found "wickedly singing this most pernicious palinode, 'Let us eat and drink, for tomorrow we die.'" They lay aside "the inspiration of the assembly" and "become like others with whom they associate."

> After having paid reverence to the discourse about God, they leave within [the church] what they have heard. And outside they foolishly amuse themselves with impious playing, and amatory quavering, occupied with flute-playing, and dancing, and intoxication, and all kinds of trash.[26]

In his *First Homily on Colossians,* Chrysostom describes and contrasts two banquets — "one for the blind, the halt, the maimed in hand or leg, the barefoot, those clad with but one scanty garment, and that worn out," the other for "grandees, generals, governors, great officers, arrayed in costly robes. . . ."[27] Although these banquets are fictitious, John Chrysostom's description of the one for the "grandees" has the ring of truth. Those to whom he was preaching would have recognized it as something they had participated in, observed, or at least heard about. At that banquet the vessels are made of silver and gold; the "wine jars line in order, glittering . . . with gold," and the couch around the table is "smoothly laid all over with soft drapery." Expensive food is served by numerous servants, "in the flower of life," dressed "in garments no less ornamented than those of the guests." The dinner is followed by "flutes, and harps, and pipes" by which "the Demons are hymned," followed by a show of prostitutes, who "are a pleasure to look upon." The house becomes a "brothel" filled with "unchaste pleasure, loose laughing, drunkenness, buffoonery, filthy language" and, no doubt, sensuous music and dancing. Chrysostom's description fits exactly with the picture painted by J. P. V. D. Balsdon, which was derived from abundant Roman sources: "Lively and dissolute parties" were

24. *Octavius* XII, 5; p. 347.
25. *Octavius* XXXVII, 11; p. 431.
26. *The Instructor* III, p. 290.
27. *First Homily on Colossians,* pp. 260ff.

replete with performances by "buffoons . . . effeminate men, dancing girls from Syria or, best of all, from Cadiz."[28]

Noise pollution in the form of somebody else's unwelcome music seems to have been a problem even before the days of electronic media. Cicero describes the music-making in the house of a certain Chrysogonus, who had "so many artists, that the whole neighborhood [rang] with the sound of vocal music, stringed instruments, and flutes, and with the music of banquets by night."[29] There is at least a hint in his narrative that the neighbors did not always appreciate the music reverberating through the neighborhood. Martial became so sick of music at the table that he said that the best entertainment is where there is no tibia player to drown out the conversation.[30] Apparently, one could not even be guaranteed an escape from the din of popular music by taking a day at the beach. Seneca tells about drunks wandering along the beach and the "riotous reveling of sailing parties," which make the lakes "a-din with choral song."[31]

We will never know how large a part of the whole musical scene these kinds of musical nuisance and degeneracy were. But the uniform witness from a variety of sources does indicate that it was definitely considerable and probably dominant. However, there is also evidence pointing to the existence of nobler musical art, though it was apparently peripheral and on the wane.

The venerable art of the *citharode,* who sang the praises of heroes and gods to the accompaniment of a plucked stringed instrument, was not completely dead yet. The appreciative description by the Roman rhetorician Quintilian is obviously from an eyewitness. "Do not harpists simultaneously exert the memory and pay attention to the tone and inflexions of the voice, while the right hand runs over certain strings and the left plucks, stops or releases others, and even the foot is employed in beating time, all these actions being performed at the same moment?"[32] We can read of lyrical poetry by great poets such as Vergil and Catullus being sung to the lyre, and the songs of Horace sung by choirs of boys and girls. Pliny's letters inform us that his published poems "are in everybody's hands; they

---

28. Balsdon, *Life and Leisure in Ancient Rome,* p. 49.
29. *In Defense of Sextus Roscius of Ameria* XLVI, 134; pp. 243.
30. Martial, *Epigrams* IX, 77.
31. Seneca, Epistle LI; p. 339.
32. Quintilian, *On the Instruction of an Orator* I, xii, 3; p. 193.

are even sung to harp or lyre accompaniments. . . ."[33] His wife, too, he says, "sings my verses and sets them to her lyre. . . ."[34]

Finally, even if there were no evidence for it, we could assume that, wherever the musical slaves or professionals did not dominate the scene, the people of the Roman Empire, like people everywhere, had their folk music that they sang at work and play. But we need not assume it; there are references in the literature, including one quoted from John Chrysostom in the preceding chapter (p. 127). Here is another, this time from Quintilian:

> Indeed nature itself seems to have given music as a boon to men to lighten the strain of labour: even the rower in the galleys is cheered to effort by song. Nor is this function of music confined to cases where the efforts of a number are given union by the sound of some sweet voice that sets the tune, but even solitary workers find solace at their toil in artless song.[35]

The early Christian writers aimed no polemic at the nobler art music or the folk music of their day. Had they been opposed to it, they would no doubt have spoken against it. Their denunciations of music were not general; rather, they were aimed at a few well-defined targets: the music of the popular public spectacles, the music associated with voluptuous banqueting, the music associated with pagan weddings, and the music of pagan religious rites and festivities. As we have already seen, they were not alone in their denunciations. They joined their voices with those of pagan Romans who were painfully aware of the decay of their civilization. Emperors such as Tiberius, Marcus Aurelius, and Julian the Apostate were aware of the ethical threat posed by the theater. Julian said:

> No priest should, in any place, attend these licentious theatrical shows . . . nor introduce [an actor] into his own house, for that is altogether unfitting. Indeed, if it were possible to expel such shows completely from the theatres and give back a pure stage to Dionysus I should certainly have attempted zealously to carry this out; but since I thought that this was impossible, and that even if it were possible it would, for other reasons, not be expedient, I abstained entirely from

33. Letters VII, iv; p. 493.
34. Letters IV, xix; p. 299.
35. Quintilian, *On the Instruction of an Orator* I, x, 16; p. 167.

this ambition. I do expect, however, that priests should withdraw themselves from the obscenity of the theatres and leave them to the crowd. Therefore let no priest enter a theater, or have an actor or a charioteer for his friend; and let no dancer or mime approach his door.[36]

Barbarians, too, when they encountered Roman popular entertainments, were appalled. And as we saw in the preceding chapter, John Chrysostom chastised his congregation for being less upright than the barbarians when it came to the theater. "Imitate at least the barbarians," he told them, "for they truly are altogether clean from seeking such sights." There were other writers who pointed to the barbarians' abhorrence of the theater. According to Salvian, the fall of the theater "was not because Christians had learned to be faithful to their vows and to the teaching of the Church; but because the barbarians, who despised the spectacula, and therein set a good example to degenerate Romans, had sacked half the cities, while in the rest the impoverished citizens could no longer pay the bills."[37] And Cassiodorus suggested "that the greater menace to the continuance of the theatre lay in the taste of the barbarians than even in the ethics of Christianity."[38]

It appears beyond doubt, then, that the degeneracy the early Christian writers saw in the theater and in other areas of pagan life around them was not the result of overwrought, puritanical imaginations, but was an accurate assessment of the state of affairs. Their call for Christians to separate themselves from the banal, the rude, and the immoral elements in the culture around them was a call to bring Christians into conformity with the teachings of the New Testament. Christian freedom is an important strand in New Testament — especially Pauline — theology. But lest that teaching be taken as a license for any kind of human activity or behavior, there is a morally restrictive side to New Testament teaching as well. Right from the beginning, there were those in the church who took Paul's teaching and distorted it into an antinomian heresy. No matter that Paul himself denounced such heretics and explicitly denied what they inferred from his teaching (Rom. 3:8; 6:1); and no matter that he clearly set out parameters

36. Julian, Epistle 89; quoted from Wellesz, *A History of Byzantine Music and Hymnography*, p. 84.

37. Chambers, *The Medieval Stage*, p. 19.

38. Chambers, *The Medieval Stage*, p. 40.

within which Christian freedom could operate (I Cor. 6–10) — antinomians still found a foothold in the church. Throughout the history of the church there have been those who "have found it easy to shelter their sins beneath 'the imputed righteousness of Christ', have used a phrase like 'not under the law but under grace' to blur the otherwise disturbing fact that God is holy and that there is such a thing as the moral stringency of Jesus. . . ."[39]

The New Testament writers knew the moral stringency of Jesus' teaching. The Epistles of Jude and 2 Peter, and the letters to Pergamum and Thyatira in Revelation 2, make particularly strong denunciations of those who seek to ease the morally stringent side of the gospel by accommodating themselves comfortably to their pagan surroundings. Jude used the figure of Balaam as a type of those who accommodate themselves to the world: "Woe to them! For they walked in the way of Cain and abandoned themselves for the sake of gain to Balaam's error . . ." (Jude v. 11). According to E. M. Blaiklock, "Balaam in the imagery of the passage, stands for the breakdown of separation, the effacement of those differences which mark and set apart the people of God, and the mingling of sacred and profane."[40] In the letter to Pergamum in Revelation 2, John links the followers of Balaam with the Nicolaitans: "You have some there who hold the teaching of Balaam. . . . Likewise you also have those who hold to the teaching of the Nicolaitans" (Rev. 2:14-15). The Nicolaitans "were libertines who counseled less rigid practices, a less uncompromising stand, a wider measure of participation in the pagan life of the wide Greek and Roman world, a gentler religion, less austere, less unsociable."[41] John again denounces this accommodating attitude in the letter to Thyatira. "You tolerate that woman Jezebel, who calls herself a prophetess. By her teaching she misleads my servants into sexual immorality and the eating of food sacrificed to idols" (Rev. 2:20).

> Jezebel . . . was the seal of a trade alliance. No other close relations were possible with Phoenicia, and there is no doubt that Ahab's Israel derived immense wealth from business conducted with the busy heathen on the coast. . . . But prosperity is not always good for a nation. With Tyrian goods came Tyrian gods. With Jezebel came Baal. It is

---

39. Stewart, *A Man in Christ*, p. 195.
40. Blaiklock, *The Christian in Pagan Society*, p. 22.
41. Blaiklock, *The Christian in Pagan Society*, p. 23.

possible, therefore, that the choice on Carmel involved more than theology. When the people chose Jehovah it is not impossible that they precipitated an economic depression. A break with Jezebel was a break with Tyre. . . .

The woman in Thyatira, a clever woman with a gift of speech who professed to interpret God's will, offered, in the same way, prosperity at the price of compromise with heathendom. She was a Nicolaitan who believed in establishing a compromise with surrounding society.[42]

The leaders of the early church were not seduced by the error of the Nicolaitans and other libertines. They realized that there could be no easy commerce between the church and the world, between Jerusalem and Athens, between Christ and Belial. "[N]othing could have saved the infant Church from melting away into one of those vague and ineffective schools of philosophic ethics except the stern and strict rule laid down by St. John. An easy-going Christianity could never have survived; it could not have conquered and trained the world."[43] But the church did survive — and more. The strength with which the early Christians stood over against what was evil in the culture around them, including its music, resulted in as thorough a transformation of culture as this sinful world is likely to see. It transformed a decadent Roman Empire into the Christian Middle Ages.

42. Blaiklock, *The Christian in Pagan Society,* pp. 26-27.
43. Blaiklock, *The Christian in Pagan Society,* p. 29.

CHAPTER 10

Affirmation: Psalms and Hymns

Let our songs be hymns to God.

Clement of Alexandria

If you yearn for songs, you have the Psalms.

Didascalia Apostolorum

The church fathers were vehement in their rejection of some of the music in the pagan Roman society around them; but they balanced that negativity with a nearly unanimous and usually enthusiastic affirmation of another kind of music. The balance is clear in St. Basil's counsel to young people:

> The passions born of illiberality and baseness of spirit are naturally occasioned by this sort of music. But we must pursue that other kind, which is better and leads to better, and which, as they say, was used by David that author of sacred songs, to soothe the king in his madness. And it is said that Pythagoras, upon encountering some drunken revelers, commanded the aulos player who was leading the song to change the mode and to play the Dorian for them. They were so sobered by this music that tearing off their garlands they returned home ashamed. Others dance to the aulos in the manner of Corybantes and Bacchants. Such is the difference in filling one's ears with wholesome

or wicked tunes! And since the latter type now prevails, you must have less to do with it than with any utterly depraved thing.[1]

The "latter type that now prevails" refers to the bacchanalian music of pagan religious rites, the theater, weddings, and orgiastic parties; "that other kind" was chiefly represented by the Psalter. But it is worth noting that there is also an implied approval of the Dorian music that Pythagoras's aulos player played. However wide or narrow the extent of the church fathers' affirmation, at its center was a fervency about praising God in song that they inherited from the New Testament. In particular, their writings overflow with praise of psalmody.

The fathers' enthusiastic promotion of psalm-singing reached an unprecedented and unsurpassed peak in the fourth century, when church fathers such as St. Basil, St. John Chrysostom, and St. Ambrose gave it their unstinting praise. They mustered all of their considerable eloquence to urge the faithful to sing the psalms daily. Listen, for example, to what Basil said about the psalms.

All Scripture is inspired by God and is profitable. . . . But the Book of the Psalms embraces whatever in all the others is helpful. It prophesies things to come, it recalls histories to the mind, it gives laws for living, it counsels what is to be done. And altogether it is a storehouse of good instructions, diligently providing for each what is useful to him. For it heals the ancient wounds of souls and brings prompt relief to the newly wounded; it ministers to what is sick and preserves what is healthy; and it wholly removes the ills, howsoever great and of whatsoever kind, that attack souls in our human life; and this by means of a certain well-timed persuasion which inspires wholesome reflection. . . .

A psalm is the tranquility of souls, the arbitrator of peace, restraining the disorder and turbulence of thoughts, for it softens the passion of the soul and moderates its unruliness. A psalm forms friendships, unites the divided, mediates between enemies. For who can still consider him an enemy with whom he has sent forth one voice to God? So that the singing of psalms brings love, the greatest of good things, contriving harmony like some bond of union and uniting the people in the symphony of a single choir.

---

1. *Exhortation to Youths* vii; quoted from *Music in Early Christian Literature*, p. 69.

A psalm drives away demons, summons the help of angels, furnishes arms against nightly terrors, and gives respite from daily toil; to little children it is safety, to men in their prime an adornment, to the old a solace, to women their most fitting ornament. It peoples solitudes, it brings agreement to market places. To novices it is a beginning; to those who are advancing, an increase; to those who are concluding, a confirmation. A psalm is the voice of the Church. It gladdens feast days, it creates grief which is in accord with God's will, for a psalm brings a tear even from a heart of stone.[2]

While Basil obviously tends toward hyperbole to make his point, it is certainly true that throughout the history of music the psalms have held a special place in the church. Undergirding all of Basil's praise and his specific reasons for valuing psalms stands a feature that makes them unique: they are at once God's word to us and our words to him. As Joseph Gelineau put it, "Psalmody never loses its double character of word of God and prayer of the community," and it has "always been given special preference."[3] That is no exaggeration. Though Gelineau's claim cannot hold up in every instance, there can be no doubt that the psalms have been the most widely used and universally loved texts that Christians have sung. If the psalms have not been the preferred texts to sing at all times and in all places, they have rarely been neglected. Usually they have been prominent; sometimes they have been dominant; and at some times in some places they have been the only texts Christians sang in public worship.

The psalms, of course, came to the church from the Jews. There is little that is known with certainty about their origin and early history, but the psalmody that the earliest Christians inherited would have come from the Jewish psalmody that they sang and heard in their own time. The earliest Christians (before 70 CE, when the Temple was destroyed) would have been familiar with Temple psalmody. But as Edward Foley points out,

[not] all, or even most of the psalms were related to Temple worship. Very few of the psalms have specific and identifiable liturgical references that allow them to be linked with any certainty to worship or, more particularly, to worship in the Temple. While the structure and

2. *Homily on the First Psalm* 1 & 2; quoted from *Source Readings in Music History,* Vol. 2, pp. 11-12.

3. Gelineau, *Voices and Instruments in Christian Worship,* p. 68.

content of some psalms suggests that they were employed in the rituals of the Temple, and the Mishnah remembers that certain others were sung on particular days in the Temple, not all of them were employed there, and other texts besides the psalms were sung in Temple worship.[4]

The few references in the Old Testament historical and prophetic books do not give us a very good idea about what the music in Temple worship was like. And since none of that music was written down, we will never know much about it. Beyond knowing that it was in the hands of the Levites and that it included instrumental accompaniment as well as singing, there is little we can say with certainty about it. We can surmise that, at least for the Second Temple, the singing of psalms at the sacrifices was quite an elaborate affair, performed by trained singers and instrumentalists.

We have a somewhat clearer picture of Temple worship around the time of Jesus because of some fairly detailed description found in the Mishnah, an edition of the Talmud from about 200 CE. Every day of the year there was a solemn sacrifice in the morning and another in the afternoon; on sabbaths and feast days there were additional sacrifices. Services began with the priests blowing three blasts on their silver trumpets. Then

> the great gate of the sanctuary was opened, the lamb was slaughtered and its limbs made ready for the sacrifice. At this point the participants retired for prayer to the Chamber of Hewn Stone. . . . They recited three items: (1) the Ten Commandments; (2) the *Shema*, "Hear, O Israel" [Deut. 6:4-9]; and (3) a number of benedictions which constituted the nucleus of what would become the eighteen benedictions of the *Tefillah* [prayers]. . . .
>
> The service continued as two priests chosen by lot went to the Sanctuary for the solemn incense offering before the Holy of Holies. As they moved across the court towards the Sanctuary an officer threw down a large rake, the *magrefah*, with a legendary loud clatter. This was the signal for the participants to prepare for the final acts of the service, and accordingly the Levite musicians assembled on the *duchan*, a platform adjoining the people's portion of the inner court towards the east. While the incense was being offered the people both within and without the Temple court prayed. After performing the

---

4. Foley, *Foundations of Christian Music,* pp. 37-38.

offering the chosen priests withdrew from the Sanctuary and together with the other priests blessed the people from the Sanctuary steps. The limbs of the lamb were then carried up the altar ramp and cast upon the fire. Two priests gave three blasts on their trumpets, the *segan* waved a cloth, the Temple officer who was "over the cymbals" clashed them together, and as the libation of wine was poured on to the fire the Levites sang a psalm accompanied by the string instruments *nevel* and *kinnor*. The morning service — and the afternoon service as well — ended with the conclusion of the psalm.[5]

This description of the Temple liturgy confirms the impression about Temple psalmody left by Old Testament sources: (1) it was part of a highly formalized liturgy; (2) it was closely associated with the sacrifice; (3) it was performed by the Levites, that is, by specially trained musicians; and (4) it was accompanied by stringed instruments, that is, by the softer instruments that could support the singing but would not cover the words.

The last feature is an indication that Jewish psalmody was word-oriented, a characteristic that set it apart from the music of the sacrificial rites of the Israelites' pagan neighbors. Pagan sacrificial music typically featured the frenzy-inducing sound of the loud double-reed instruments and the rhythms of orgiastic dancing. Words were superfluous. Temple music was different from pagan music in all these respects: words were primary in it, and they governed the rhythms; instrumental accompaniment was by stringed instruments that supported the monophonic vocal line, perhaps with some heterophonic embellishments, but never covering or distracting attention away from the words; instruments were used independently only for signaling purposes, as when trumpets and cymbals signaled the beginning of the psalm and the places at the end of sections where the worshipers should prostrate themselves.

Synagogues are the other places we usually associate with Jewish psalmody. The singing there was very different from that in the Temple. The gatherings in the synagogues were not for sacrifice and did not require priests and Levites. Therefore, synagogue psalmody was not part of an elaborate liturgical ceremony and was not in the hands of specially trained musicians. It was undoubtedly simple — probably little more than a slightly embellished recitation — and did not make use of instruments.

5. McKinnon, "The Question of Psalmody," pp. 162-163.

Questions arise when we seek to determine when the chanting of psalms became a regular feature of synagogue gatherings. There has been widespread agreement among scholars for some time that psalmody played an important role in Jewish synagogues during pre-Christian times, and that the chanting of psalms in early Christian worship was a carryover from synagogue practice. Richard Hoppin's explanation is typical of that view:

> Christianity began as an offshoot of the Jewish religion, and the first Christians attended both the synagogue services and their own private gatherings. It is not surprising, then, to find that the new sect retained many features of the Jewish liturgy, adapting them as needed to fit the new faith. . . . From the musical point of view, the most important borrowings from the synagogue were the chanting of Bible readings and the solo singing of psalms with congregational responses.[6]

This makes sense because, before the Christian era, synagogues were thought to be primarily places of worship where the four main activities were scripture reading, a discourse on the reading, prayer, and chanting psalms. These were also the main ingredients in the pre-Eucharist part of early Christian worship. Thus a conventional conclusion has been that early Christian psalmody was an inheritance from synagogue practice.

However, that hypothesis rests more on reasonable assumptions and conjecture than on concrete evidence. Surviving evidence reveals that Scripture reading and discourse on it were regular occurrences at synagogue gatherings.[7] For example, there are the familiar accounts, in Luke 4:14-30 and Acts 13:14-43, of Jesus and Paul in the synagogue. Jesus read from and commented on a passage in Isaiah; and Paul, after hearing the readings from the Law and the Prophets, spoke to the assembly in response to the invitation from the rulers to anyone who had "a word of exhortation for the people." But there is no evidence that prayer and psalmody were regular, fixed activities in the synagogue. Praying no doubt took place, but no text refers to the synagogue as a "house of prayer," as is true of the Temple. And no passage in the New Testament says that anyone went to the synagogue to pray. When a text says that people went to pray, it is invariably to

6. Hoppin, *Medieval Music*, p. 30.

7. What follows is based on the research of James McKinnon, "The Question of Psalmody," and J. A. Smith, "The Ancient Synagogue, the Early Church and Singing."

the Temple or to a house; when it says that they went to the synagogue, they went there to speak or debate. The picture that emerges of the synagogue in Jesus' time and the early Christian era is more of a public forum for reading, studying, and discussing the Law and the Prophets, as well as a place to settle disputes in what we might think of as secular matters.

After the Temple was destroyed in 70 CE, changes took place in the synagogues. With the Temple no longer in existence, synagogues began to take over some of the elements of formal worship from the Temple — excluding, of course, the sacrifices. For example, it seems that, after the destruction of the Temple, the *Shema* ("Hear, O Israel, the Lord our God, the Lord is One") and the *Tefillah* (a series of eighteen prayers beginning "Blessed art thou, O Lord") moved into the synagogues and eventually became regular features of synagogue liturgy. Regular chanting of psalms is as noticeably absent as formal prayer from the sources of information we have about the synagogue in pre-Christian and early Christian times. It seems likely that psalms would have sometimes been among the Scripture readings, though technically they were not a part of the Law and Prophets, which are explicitly mentioned in our sources, but part of the *Hagiographa* ("Writings"), the third part of the Hebrew Scripture. As Scripture readings, they would have been intoned in a simple recitation formula like the other readings.

Owing to the psalms' poetic qualities, their recitation may have tended to be more melodious and lyrical; but as a regular, fixed, and distinctively musical part of the activities in the synagogues, psalmody seems to have been a latecomer. In fact, the earliest concrete evidence for psalmody as a distinct musical ingredient in synagogue liturgy comes from an eighth-century treatise, *Sopherim,* which lists the daily psalms used in the synagogue. They were to be chanted at the end of the synagogue service, preceded by a clear reference to Temple psalmody: "This is the first [or second, etc.] day of the week, on which the Levites used to say. . . ." Particularly interesting, as McKinnon points out, is that even at this late date, it was "found necessary . . . to contrive some justification for [the psalms'] use in the absence of sacrifice,"[8] another indication that it took a considerable amount of time after the destruction of the Temple for psalmody as a specific musical-liturgical activity to find its way into synagogue worship.

8. McKinnon, "The Question of Psalmody," p. 183.

All indications are that early Christian psalmody was similar in style, method of performance, and character to the psalmody that eventually made its way into the synagogues as a regular feature of worship. It was simple, performed by "amateurs," and completely devoid of instrumental accompaniment. Given the Temple psalmody's close association with sacrifice, which was no longer necessary after Christ's final sacrifice, and the early church's lack of opportunity for the institutional development of trained choirs and instrumental ensembles like those of the Levites, it is not surprising that the early church did not follow the lead of the Temple in its psalmody. But, if it did not come from the Temple, and synagogue psalmody was a later development, where did early Christian psalmody come from?

That question betrays a hidden assumption that has lurked in scholars' minds for a long time, the assumption that psalms were exclusively — or at least primarily — music for worship in the Temple, synagogue, or church. But, as a careful reading of the sources will show, psalms were as much "house music" as they were "church music" both for the Jews and for the early Christians. The sources indicate that psalms were an important part of the daily life of Jews and early Christians alike. Jewish households provided many occasions, both formal and informal, for singing.

> The pertinent informal religious assemblies of the family are those intimate occasions when parents discharge their duties as religious instructors of their children. The context of 4 Maccabees xviii.15 suggests that it was not unusual in a devout household for the father to sing psalms to his children on such occasions. Psalm singing may therefore be considered to have been a normal concomitant of the religious life of the family in the home.[9]

Formal occasions that included psalm-singing were weddings, funerals, and, most importantly, Passover.

> The Passover ritual had two consecutive parts. The first was public and took place in the Temple. . . . The second part was private and took place in rooms within the city. This consisted of the Passover meal at which each household, each in its respective room, ate the roasted meat of the lambs that had earlier been sacrificed. During the

9. Smith, "The Ancient Synagogue, the Early Church and Singing," p. 10.

meal . . . blessings and prayers were offered by the head of the household, and explanations of the meaning of the occasion and the symbolism of the foods were given. Also included was the obligatory singing of the *Hallel* [Psalms 113–118]. . . . After the destruction of the Temple the domestic part of the ritual was retained.[10]

It is possible that the "hymn" that Jesus and his disciples sang at the Last Supper was the *Hallel* (Matt. 26:30).

On the basis of surviving evidence, then, it seems that the source of early Christian psalmody was more likely the Jewish household than the Jewish synagogue. Furthermore, though evidence is sparse, it appears that early Christian psalmody was more of a regular feature in Christian households than it was in formal worship. The clearest and most complete surviving description of an early Christian Sunday Eucharist comes from Justin Martyr (died ca. 165), and there is not a word about singing in it.

And on the day called Sunday all who live in the cities or in the country gather together in one place, and the memoirs of the Apostles or the writings of the Prophets are read, as long as time permits. Then when the reader has finished, the Ruler in a discourse instructs and exhorts to the imitation of these good things. Then we all stand up together and offer prayers; and, as we said before, when we have finished the prayer, bread is brought and wine and water, and the Ruler likewise offers up prayers and thanksgivings to the best of his ability, and the people assent, saying Amen; and the distribution and partaking of the Eucharistic elements is to each, and to those who are absent a portion is sent by the deacons. And those who prosper, and so wish, contribute what each thinks fit, and what is collected is deposited with the Ruler, who takes care of the orphans and widows, and those who, on account of sickness or any other cause, are in want, and those who are in bonds, and the strangers who are sojourners among us. . . .[11]

Of course, it is dangerous to make an argument from silence. But Justin's silence is quite convincing because his description is so clear, straightforward, and sequential. Again, as with the synagogue, it would be putting too much weight on skimpy evidence and flying in the face of common sense

10. Smith, "The Ancient Synagogue, the Early Church and Singing," pp. 9-10.
11. *First Apology* 67; p. 71.

to claim that psalm-singing was totally absent from early Christian worship. They may very well have been among "the writings of the Prophets" that were read or, more likely, intoned. And given the positive attitude toward singing that the apostles Paul and James show in their letters, it would seem impossible that singing was totally absent from early Christian worship. But the evidence does not allow us to maintain a picture of early Christian worship in which singing psalms was a fixed and regular liturgical feature.

It is particularly significant that the surviving evidence gives us a much clearer picture of early Christian psalmody in homes, especially at communal meals among which the *agape,* or love feast, is best known. This parallels the Jewish situation and adds support to the theory that it was Jewish daily life rather than the synagogue that was the source of early Christian psalmody. The following passage by St. Cyprian (died 258) is an example of the descriptions of psalmody at meals that we find in early Christian literature.

> [N]ow as the sun is sinking towards evening, let us spend what remains of the day in gladness and not let the hour of repast go untouched by heavenly grace. Let a psalm be heard at the sober banquet, and since your memory is sure and your voice pleasant, undertake this task as is your custom. You will better nurture your friends, if you provide a spiritual recital for us and beguile our ears with sweet religious strains.[12]

In summary, the surviving evidence suggests that early Christian psalmody came into Christian daily life from Jewish daily life. It is difficult to deny that psalmody occurred in formal worship, but it is impossible to prove that it did. In any case, it is clear that psalms were not only — probably not even primarily — songs for formal, public worship among the early Christians any more than they were among the Jews. Wherever Christians sang, psalms were their songs.

Compared to the scarcity of information about psalmody in Christian life during the second and third centuries, the amount of evidence from the fourth century is large. We have already seen examples of the ebullient praise that the fourth-century church fathers lavished on the singing of

---

12. *To Donatus* xvi; quoted from *Music in Early Christian Literature*, p. 49.

psalms. Their enthusiasm for psalm-singing has rarely been matched in the subsequent history of the church, and it certainly helped establish the psalms as the primary texts in the song of the church. During the earlier centuries, newly composed hymns were perhaps as prominent among the church's songs as were the psalms; but that changed in the fourth century: psalmody became overwhelmingly more prominent than hymnody. No doubt one of the reasons for the waning of hymn singing in favor of psalm singing was the threat of heresy. The success with which heretical sects spread their ideas through hymns had made the church wary of noncanonical texts.

Another feature of the fourth century that contributed to the enthusiasm for psalmody was the growth of monasticism. Psalm-singing took place in monastic communities throughout the day and night. According to Palladius, St. Antony "arose and said twelve prayers and chanted twelve psalms. He lay down for his brief first sleep and arose once more in the middle of the night to chant psalms until it was day."[13] Due to St. Antony's influence, as St. Athanasius tells us, "there were monasteries in the mountains . . . filled with saintly choirs reciting psalms. . . ." Antony always instructed the monks to "sing psalms before and after sleep."[14] Initially, the schedule and content of these daily periods of worship varied from place to place. John Cassian noted

> that many throughout different lands . . . have established for themselves various arrangements and regulations in this matter. For some have decided that twenty or thirty psalms ought to be recited each night. . . . Others have sought even to exceed this number, while some use eighteen. And in this way we have observed different rules established in different places, and the arrangements and regulations we have seen adopted are almost equal in number to the monasteries and cells we inspected. There are some also to whom it seemed right that in the daytime prayer offices themselves . . . the number of psalms and prayers should correspond to the number of the hours in which these services are rendered to God; while it pleased some to assign the number six to each of the day time meetings.[15]

---

13. *Lausaic History* xxii; quoted from *Music in Early Christian Literature*, p. 60.

14. *Life of St. Antony* 44 & 55; quoted from *Music in Early Christian Literature*, p. 55.

15. *On the Institutes of the Cenobites* II, 2; quoted from *Music in Early Christian Literature*, p. 146.

Whatever the differences, however, psalmody was always prominent. St. Basil, in his so-called Long Rules *(Regulae fusius tractatae)*, mentions eight times throughout the day and night set aside for prayer and psalmody:

> Daybreak is a set time for prayer so that we dedicate the first stirrings of soul and mind to God, and take up no other consideration until made joyous by the thought of God; as it is written: "I remembered God and was delighted;" and so that the body will busy itself with no work before accomplishing that which was written: "For to you will I pray; O Lord, in the morning you will hear my voice. In the morning I will stand before you, and will see." Again at the third hour the brothers must come together and assist a prayer, even if they each happen to be occupied in different tasks. They must remember the gift of the Spirit, granted to the Apostles at the third hour, and worship all together in one accord. . . . We judge prayer to be necessary at the sixth hour in imitation of those holy ones who said: "Evening and morning and at noon, I will speak and declare; and he shall hear my voice." And so that we might be safe from misfortune and the midday demon, the ninetieth psalm is recited at this time. That we must pray at the ninth hour is related to us by the Apostles themselves in their Acts, where it says that Peter and John went up to the Temple "at the hour of prayer, the ninth." At day's end thanksgiving should be offered for those things given us in its course as well as those things done rightly, and confession should be made of any lapses, deliberately or inadvertent. . . . And again as night begins, we must ask that our rest will be free from sin and evil phantasy; again the ninetieth psalm must be recited at this hour. For the middle of the night Paul and Silas have told us that prayer is necessary, as the account in their Acts narrates: "But about midnight Paul and Silas were singing hymns to God;" and as the Psalmist says: "In the middle of the night I arose to praise you for the judgements of your righteousness." And finally it is necessary to anticipate the dawn and rise for prayer so that one is not caught by the day asleep in bed, according to the saying: "My eyes have awakened before daybreak, that I might meditate on your words."[16]

16. Basil, *Regulae fusius tractatae, Interrogatio xxxvii,* 3-5; quoted from *Music in Early Christian Literature,* pp. 67-68.

By the sixth century, owing to the influence of the order founded by St. Benedict of Nursia, the monastic liturgical day typically consisted of eight periods of worship (not including mass). These periods of worship, collectively known as the Divine Office or the Office Hours, consisted of prayers, Scripture reading, and the chanting of psalms and canticles (biblical poetry of psalmodic style that appears in books outside the book of Psalms). The inhabitants of a monastery followed a strict daily regimen of worship that began at midnight with the office called Matins; before dawn came Lauds, followed at three-hour intervals — from about 6:00 a.m. to 3:00 p.m. — by four brief offices called Prime, Terce, Sext, and None. Vespers occurred in the early evening, and the day ended with Compline, just before retiring.

Most early monastic rules specified some loose ordering and distribution of psalms throughout the day and week. Again, it was St. Benedict who tightened up the practice and whose plan for the weekly chanting of the entire Psalter eventually became the standard in the West. It was not unusual for a monk to have memorized the whole book of Psalms.

Although the singing of psalms was prevalent in worship in the monasteries, psalms were sung in other situations as well. The early church historian Theodoret of Cyrus (ca. 393–ca. 466) tells the story of nuns in Antioch singing psalms to taunt the apostate Emperor Julian.

As the Emperor passed by, they sang together more loudly than usual, since they looked upon this "Destroying angel" as an object of contempt and derision. They sang especially those songs which satirize the impotence of idols, declaiming the words of David that: "The idols of the nations are silver and gold, the work of men's hands." And after this declaration of the idols' insensibility they added: "Let those who make them be like them, and so too all who trust in them." When the Emperor heard these things, he was greatly upset and commanded them to keep silent at the time of his passing by. Publia, however, having little respect for his laws, instilled greater enthusiasm in her chorus, and when he came by again bade them sing: "Let God arise, let his enemies be scattered." Angered by this, he ordered the leader of the chorus to be brought before him, and while recognizing that her advanced age was most worthy of respect, he neither took pity on the grey hairs of her body nor honored the virtue of her soul, but ordered some of his personal guard to box her ears and to redden her cheeks with their blows. But she took this outrage as a great honor, and after returning home, she took up her accustomed assault upon the Emperor in spiritual song, after the manner of that author and teacher of song who quieted the evil spirit which was troubling Saul.[17]

Among the general populace, of course, psalm-singing was not as prevalent as it was in the monasteries. Daily activities prevented most people from full participation in the rigorous schedule of the Divine Office, though it was always available to them. For obvious reasons, they attended the evening offices the most frequently. But even though life outside the monasteries prevented most people from participating in daily, round-the-clock psalm-singing, there seems to have been a relatively short period, the fourth century and perhaps a little beyond, when psalm-singing played a role analogous to — though considerably less extensive than — the role it had in the monasteries. That was the ideal held out by fourth-century church fathers such as St. Ambrose, who urged believers:

At least divide your time between God and the world. When the darkness of night prevents you from performing in public the deeds of this world, then, as you have leisure time for God, give yourself to prayer, and, lest you sleep, sing psalms, thus cheating your sleep by means of a beneficent fraud. In the morning hasten to church and offer the first fruits of your pious devotion, and afterwards, if worldly necessity calls, you are not excluded from saying: "My eyes have anticipated the morning that I might meditate upon thy words." You may now with peace of mind proceed to your duties.[18]

The *Apostolic Constitutions* (ca. 380) told bishops to "order and exhort the people always to assemble in the church, morning and evening of each day." If that was not possible, they should "gather at a house." If that was not possible, each one should "sing psalms, read and pray by himself, or together with two or three."[19]

We cannot say that most Christians lived up to Ambrose's ideal or followed their bishops' orders; but neither can we deny that some tried and

17. *Ecclesiastical History* III, 19; quoted from *Music in Early Christian Literature*, p. 105.

18. *Exposition on Psalm 118* xix, 32; quoted from *Music in Early Christian Literature*, p. 128.

19. *Apostolic Constitutions* II, lix, 1 and VIII, xxxiv, 10; quoted from *Music in Early Christian Literature*, p. 110.

that in some Christian households singing psalms was both regular and frequent. St. John Chrysostom urged men to

> teach your children and wives also to sing such songs, not only while weaving or while engaged in other tasks, but especially at table. For since the devil generally lies in wait at banquets, having as his allies drunkenness and gluttony, along with inordinate laughter and an unbridled spirit, it is necessary especially then, both before and after the meal, to construct a defense against him from the psalms, and to arise from the banquet together with wife and children to sing sacred hymns to God.[20]

St. Jerome wrote to a Roman lady, Demetrias, that she should "always observe [prayer and psalmody] at the third, sixth and ninth hours, at evening, in the middle of the night and at dawn."[21] He told another lady, Laeta, that her daughter Paula "must not comprehend foul words, nor have knowledge of worldly songs, and while still tender her tongue must be imbued with sweet psalms."[22] He gave the same advice to Gaudentius regarding his daughter Pacatula: "Let her learn the Psalter by heart."[23] Macrina, the older sister of Saints Basil and Gregory of Nyssa, was taught the psalms early. Gregory wrote a short biography of his sister, which tells us that, even as a child, Macrina

> was especially well versed in the psalms, going through each part of the Psalter at the proper time; when she got up or did her daily tasks or rested, when she sat down to eat or rose from the table, when she went to bed or rose from it for prayer, she had the Psalter with her at all times, like a good and faithful traveling companion.[24]

People sang psalms at work. The quotation from John Chrysostom above mentions weaving and "other work." Jerome tells of psalms being sung in the fields around Bethlehem:

> As we said above, in the village of Christ all is simple, and aside from psalms there is silence. Wherever you turn, the farmhand grasping

20. *On Psalm xli*, 2; quoted from *Music in Early Christian Literature*, p. 80.
21. Epistle CXXX, 15; quoted from *Music in Early Christian Literature*, p. 144.
22. Epistle CVII, 4; quoted from *Music in Early Christian Literature*, p. 142.
23. Epistle CXXVIII, 4; quoted from *Music in Early Christian Literature*, p. 144.
24. *The Life of Macrina;* p. 165.

the plough handle sings Alleluia, the sweating reaper cheers himself with psalms, and the vine dresser sings something of David as he prunes the vine with his curved knife. These are the lays of this province, these, to put it in common parlance, its love songs. . . .[25]

The writer known as Pseudo-Chrysostom summed it up:

In the churches there are vigils, and David is first and middle and last. In the singing of early morning hymns David is first and middle and last. In the tents at funeral processions David is first and middle and last. In the houses of virgins there is weaving, and David is first and middle and last. What a thing of wonder! Many who have not even made their first attempt at reading know all of David by heart and recite him in order. Yet it is not only in the cities and the churches that he is so prominent on every occasion and with people of all ages; even in the fields and deserts and stretching into uninhabited wasteland, he rouses sacred choirs to God with greater zeal. In the monasteries there is a holy chorus of angelic hosts, and David is first and middle and last. In the convents there are bands of virgins who imitate Mary, and David is first and middle and last. In the deserts men crucified to this world hold converse with God, and David is first and middle and last. And at night all men are dominated by physical sleep and drawn into the depths, and David alone stands by, arousing all the servants of God to angelic vigils, turning earth into heaven and making angels of men.[26]

What did the early Christians sing in addition to psalms? It is probably safe to assume that they sang other biblical poetry — the canticles. Old Testament canticles[27] probably had a status similar to the psalms, and New Testament canticles[28] probably joined them early on. During the earliest years of the church, newly composed hymns seem to have been common.

---

25. Epistle XLVI, 12; quoted from *Music in Early Christian Literature,* pp. 140-141.

26. *On Penitence;* quoted from *Music in Early Christian Literature,* p. 90.

27. Song of Moses (Exod. 15:1-19), Song of Moses (Deut. 2:1-43), Song of Hannah (I Sam. 2:1-10), Song of David (I Chron. 29:10-13), First Song of Isaiah (Isa. 12:1-6), Second Song of Isaiah (Isa. 45:15-25), Song of Hezekiah (Isa. 38:10-20), Song of Jeremiah (Jer. 31:10-14), Song of the Three Children (Dan. 3:52ff.), Song of Habakkuk (Hab. 3:2-19), Song of Tobit (Tob. 13:1-8), Song of Judith (Judith 16:13-17), Song of Sirach (Sir. 1:1-13)

28. Song of Mary (Luke 1:46-55), Song of Zechariah (Luke 1:68-79), Song of Simeon (Luke 2:29-32).

Scholars are in general agreement that quotations from early Christian hymns are embedded in the New Testament. The following texts are a few of the more likely suspects:[29]

> [Christ Jesus,] though he was in the form of God,
> did not count equality with God a thing to be grasped
> but made himself nothing, taking the form of a servant,
> being born in the likeness of men.
> And being found in human form, he humbled himself
> by becoming obedient to the point of death,
> even death on a cross.
> Therefore God has highly exalted him
> and bestowed on him the name which is above every name,
> so that at the name of Jesus every knee should bow,
> in heaven and on earth and under the earth,
> and every tongue confess that Jesus Christ is Lord,
> to the glory of God the Father.
>
> (Philippians 2:6-11)

> He is the image of the invisible God,
> the firstborn of all creation.
> For by him all things were created,
> in heaven and on earth,
> visible and invisible,
> whether thrones or dominions or principalities or authorities —
> all things were created through him and for him.
> And he is before all things,
> and in him all things hold together.
> And he is the head of the body, the church.
> He is the beginning, the firstborn from the dead,
> that in everything he might be preeminent.
> For in him all the fullness of God was pleased to dwell,
> and through him to reconcile to himself all things,
> whether on earth or in heaven,
> making peace by the blood of his cross.
>
> (Colossians 1:15-20)

29. Others are: Eph. 5:14; 1 Tim. 6:15-16; 2 Tim. 2:11-13; Titus 3:4-7; I Pet. 3:18c-19, 22; Rev. 1:4-8; 4:8; 4:11; 5:9-10; 5:12-13; 11:15; 11:17-18; 12:10-12; 15:3-4; 18:1–19:4; 19:6-8; 22:17.

He was manifested in the flesh,
    vindicated in the Spirit,
        seen by angels,
proclaimed among the nations,
    believed on in the world,
        taken up in glory.

(I Timothy 3:16)

Obviously, there is a great deal of uncertainty about any given example; nevertheless, as Paul H. Bradshaw points out,

> [t]hose passages which have been identified by general consensus as hymns and prayers can legitimately be seen as reflecting the sort of liturgical material which early Christians would have used. Even if particular examples are not taken directly from common worship but are the product of the author's creativity, they would inevitably have been influenced to a considerable extent by the liturgical forms with which they were familiar. This conclusion is confirmed by a comparative analysis of the passages in question, which reveals a large number of common stylistic and linguistic features persisting across differences of author, theology, and background, and so suggests that this commonality derives from the similarities within their various liturgical traditions.[30]

Other writings from the first century also seem to contain quotations from Christian hymns. An example is the following from the *Epistle to the Ephesians* by Ignatius of Antioch (ca. 35–ca. 107):

Very flesh, yet Spirit too;
    Uncreated, and yet born;
God-and-Man in One agreed
Very-Life-in-Death indeed,
Fruit of God and Mary's seed;
    At once impassable and torn
By pain and suffering here below:
Jesus Christ, whom as our Lord we know.[31]

---

30. Bradshaw, *The Search for the Origins of Christian Worship*, p. 44.
31. *Epistle to the Ephesians* 7; p. 63.

Another hymn text found in early Christian writing is the one appended at the end of Clement of Alexandria's treatise *The Teacher* (ca. 200). It is the earliest Christian hymn text to survive in its entirety. Written in Greek poetic form, it is a prayer for guidance, especially for youth, and a hymn of praise to Christ that addresses him in metaphors that suggest guidance, leading, steering, and nurturing — for example, a bridle, a shepherd, a rudder, and a husbandman. Clement's hymn is with us to this day in many modern hymnbooks, in rather loose translations that have lost some of the vividness of the original. For example, Clement's first metaphor for Christ is "bridle of untamed steeds." Henry Dexter (1846) translated that as "Shepherd of Tender Youth." F. Bland Tucker originally translated it as "Master of Eager Youth" in 1940, but in a later translation (1982), "Jesus, Our Mighty Lord," he avoided the metaphor altogether. Even if referring to young people as "untamed steeds" is a bit jarring to modern sensibilities, we have to admit that Clement's image is more realistic than "tender (or eager) youth." Whatever the metaphors, the hymn is a most fitting prayer at the end of a treatise on the instruction of young people in the Christian life. Here is Tucker's more recent rendering:

Jesus, our mighty Lord,
our strength in sadness,
the Father's conquering Word,
true source of gladness;
your name we glorify,
O Jesus, throned on high;
you gave yourself to die
for our salvation.

Good shepherd of your sheep,
your own defending,
in love your children keep
to life unending.
You are yourself the Way:
lead us then day by day
in your own steps, we pray,
O Lord most holy.

Glorious their life who sing,
with glad thanksgiving,

true hymns to Christ the King
in all their living:
all who confess his Name,
come then with hearts aflame;
the God of peace acclaim
as Lord and Savior.

The earliest collection of hymn texts is the *Odes of Solomon*, containing forty-one odes (originally forty-two) dating from the late first century. They are in a style called "hymnodic psalmody": lyrical texts constructed in imitation of biblical psalms with irregular meters and accents; their language tends to be mystical, ecstatic, and highly figurative. Wesley W. Isenberg suggests that "recurring themes and metaphors of Baptism . . . recommend their probable origin in the context of the sacrament, perhaps as hymns to be sung by the newly baptized."[32] There may also be some references to Christological themes (incarnation, passion, and so forth), but, unlike the putative hymns embedded in the New Testament and other early Christian literature, the *Odes* are Christologically allusive at best, and they never mention the name Jesus. This has led some to question whether they are Christian or Gnostic. However, Larry W. Hurtado thinks that "there can be no doubt that he is the figure referred to . . . as 'the Beloved,' 'the Son,' 'the Son of God,' 'the Son of the Most High,' 'the Light,' 'the Lord,' 'the Word,' 'Messiah,' and 'our Savior.'"[33] James H. Charlesworth, a leading *Odes* scholar, provides good arguments for the position that they are not Gnostic. But he adds: "It appears probable that the *Odes* are a tributary . . . to the full-blown Gnosticism of the second century."[34]

Regardless of the theological stance of these mysterious *Odes*, it is clear that Gnostic hymnody flourished in the second and third centuries. Bardesanes (154-222) wrote 150 Gnostic hymns, a number suggesting that they were a replacement for the Psalter of the Old Testament. St. Ephraim Syrus (about whom more below) summed up Bardesanes' influence in one of his own anti-Gnostic hymns:

In the resorts of Bardesanes
There are songs and melodies.

32. Isenberg, "Hymnody: Greek," p. 189.
33. Hurtado, *Lord Jesus Christ*, p. 612.
34. Charlesworth, *Critical Reflections on the Odes of Solomon*, p. 190.

For seeing that young persons
Loved sweet music,
By the harmony of his songs
He corrupted their minds.[35]

Harmonios, Bardesanes' son, continued his father's work, apparently with much success. The early church historian Sozomen, during the second quarter of the fifth century, wrote that Harmonios "was not altogether free from the errors of his father, and . . . he introduced some of these sentiments in the lyrical songs which he composed."[36] Likewise, another historian, Theodoret of Cyrus (ca. 393–ca. 466), wrote that "by mixing the sweetness of melody with his impiety [Harmonios] had beguiled his audience and led them to their destruction. . . ."[37]

Gnostic hymns remained effective tools of heresy well into the fourth century. To counteract them, Ephraem Syrus (ca. 306-373) composed a large number of orthodox hymns. According to Sozomen,

> When Ephraem perceived that the Syrians were charmed with the elegant diction and melodious versification of Harmonios, he became apprehensive, lest they should imbibe the same opinions; and therefore, although he was ignorant of Grecian learning, he applied himself to the study of the meters of Harmonios, and composed similar poems in accordance with the doctrines of the church, and sacred hymns in praise of holy men. From that period the Syrians sang the odes of Ephraem, according to the method indicated by Harmonios.[38]

Theodoret adds that, in so doing, Ephraem "presented his listeners with a remedy both exceedingly sweet and beneficial."[39] Ephraem's hymns mark the first peak of orthodox hymnody in the Eastern Church. Their purpose was distinctly didactic and apologetic. They may have served their immediate purpose well, but they were too time-bound to achieve a lasting place in the church's hymnody.

35. Quoted from Julian, *A Dictionary of Hymnology*, p. 1110.

36. *A History of the Church* III, 16; p. 133.

37. *Ecclesiastical History* IV, 29, 1-3; quoted from *Music in Early Christian Literature*, p. 105.

38. *A History of the Church* III, 16; p. 133.

39. *Ecclesiastical History* IV, 29, 1-3; quoted from *Music in Early Christian Literature*, p. 105.

Two separate hymns of the second and third centuries deserve special mention. One is the so-called Oxyrhynchus Hymn: found on an Egyptian papyrus, it has the distinction of being the only Christian hymn with musical notation until several centuries later. Only three lines survive, and though we can decipher the pitches, other aspects of the music — including the rhythm — remain unknown. Thus, as tantalizing as it is, we can learn little about what it sounded like. But the surviving text clearly shows three New Testament characteristics of Christian song: it is a hymn of thanksgiving, sung with all creation, to the Triune God.

> . . . all splendid creations of God . . . must not keep silent, nor shall the light-bearing stars remain behind. . . . All waves of thundering streams shall praise our Father and Son, and Holy Ghost, all powers shall join in: Amen, Amen! Rule and Praise (and Glory) to the sole Giver of all Good, Amen, Amen.[40]

The other hymn is *Phos hilarion,* the "lamp-lighting hymn." Its origin is unknown, but in the fourth century St. Basil referred to it as having been in widespread use for some time.

> Now, to our forefathers it was likewise evident that they should not withhold their praise from the grace of the evening lamp light, so that at the appointed time every day when the evening light appeared they would offer praise for it. We do not know, however, who the author of this praise for the lamp is, but the entire people which is in the churches of Christ retains, and has over a long period of years, this praise. . . .[41]

It is possible that *Phos hilarion* is the evening prayer that Basil's sister, Macrina, sang silently on her deathbed, of which her other famous brother, St. Gregory of Nyssa, wrote in his *Life of St. Macrina*:

> As she said [a prayer], she made the sign of the cross upon her eyes and mouth and heart, and little by little, as the fever dried up her lips, she was no longer able to speak clearly; her voice gave out and only from the trembling of her lips and the motion of her hands did we know that she was continuing to pray.

40. Quoted from Werner, *The Sacred Bridge,* p. 210.
41. *Concerning the Holy Spirit;* p. 114.

Then, evening came on and the lamp was brought in. Macrina directed her eye toward the beam of light and made it clear that she was eager to say the nocturnal prayer and, although her voice failed her, with her heart and the movement of her hands, she fulfilled her desire and moved her lips in keeping with the impulse within her. When she had completed the thanksgiving and indicated that the prayer was over by making the sign of the cross, she breathed a deep breath and with the prayer her life came to an end.[42]

The hymn is still in use today in the evening service and the liturgy of the Presanctified of the Greek Orthodox Church. There are numerous English translations, dating back as far as the seventeenth century. The following translation by F. Bland Tucker can be sung to several familiar hymn tunes, including the Tallis Canon and *Conditor alme siderum*.

O gracious Light, Lord Jesus Christ,
in you the Father's glory shone.
Immortal, holy, blest is he,
and blest are you, his holy Son.

Now sunset comes, but light shines forth,
the lamps are lit to pierce the night.
Praise Father, Son, and Spirit: God
who dwells in the eternal light.

Worthy are you of endless praise,
O Son of God, Lifegiving Lord;
wherefore you are through all the earth
and in the highest heaven adored.

Hymns in Latin originated somewhat later than the Greek hymns. St. Hilary of Poitiers (ca. 315-367) is generally regarded as the first hymn writer in the Latin West. He wrote a *Liber hymnorum*, but his hymns never took hold; all but three fragments have been lost. St. Ambrose of Milan (339-397) is the true "father of Western hymnody." In 386, Justina, mother of the fifteen-year-old King Valentinus II, issued an edict of toleration for Arianism and demanded that Ambrose turn over the churches for Arian

42. *Life of Macrina;* p. 181.

worship. Ambrose organized vigils to prevent Justina from taking the churches by military force. St. Augustine described this situation in his *Confessions:*

> The devout congregation kept continual guard in the Church, ready to die with their bishop, your servant. There my mother, your hand-maid, was a leader in keeping anxious watch and lived in prayer. We were still cold, untouched by the warmth of your Spirit, but were ex-cited by the tension and disturbed atmosphere in the city. That was the time when the decision was taken to introduce hymns and psalms sung after the custom of the eastern Churches, to prevent the people from succumbing to depression and exhaustion. From that time to this day the practice has been retained and many, indeed almost all your flocks, in other parts of the world, have imitated it.[43]

Four hymns can be ascribed to Ambrose with some certainty, because they are mentioned in the writings of Augustine: *Aeterna rerum Conditor, Deus Creator omnium, Iam surgit hora tertia,* and *Intende qui Regis Israel.* There is also a fairly strong scholarly consensus that at least ten others can be ascribed to Ambrose. But the popularity of Ambrose's hymns also gave rise to hundreds of imitations, many of which have been falsely ascribed to him.

Ambrosian hymns have a simple structure that contributes to making them easy to sing and memorize. Each strophe of the hymn consists of four lines of four iambic feet. According to James J. Wilhelm, this was "the underlying beat for the marching songs of the Roman legions."[44] Whatever the source, this simple, sturdy meter certainly gives these hymns a strong and assured character that served the church well, not only in the tense sit-uation Augustine described but in all kinds of situations through the cen-turies. Like the metrical structure, the language of Ambrose's hymns is also simple and direct; but that doesn't mean it is simplistic or devoid of liter-ary quality. As Robert Wilken points out, Ambrose realized that, "if Latin hymns were to take hold in the minds and hearts of the faithful, they had to be genuinely poetic in the classical sense, yet thoroughly biblical and Christian in vocabulary and sentiment." As the following example shows, Ambrose succeeded remarkably well. "The line is short, the meter simple,

---

43. *Confessions* IX, vii, 15; p. 165.
44. Wilhelm, *Medieval Song,* p. 31.

and the hymn is easily memorized. Yet the language is dignified. It is also biblical and bears distinct Christian overtones."[45]

Aeterna rerum conditor,	Eternal maker of all,
Noctem diemque qui regis	you rule day and night
Et temporum das tempora,	and changes of time and season
Ut alleves fastidium,	to relieve monotony,
Praeco diei iam sonat,	The herald now sounds the day,
Noctis profundae pervigil,	having kept vigil through deep darkness,
Nocturna lux viantibus,	a lamp at night for travelers,
A nocte noctem segregans.	Marking off the night-watches.
Hoc excitatus lucifer	At this the morning star awakes
Solvit polum caligine;	and frees the skies from darkness;
Hoc omnis erronum chorus	and all the band of evil spirits
Viam nocendi deserit.	leave the pathways of night.
Hoc nauta vires colligit,	At this the sailor finds courage,
Pontique mitescunt freta;	and the angry seas grow calm;
Hoc ipse Petra ecclesiae	at this the Rock of the Church himself
Canente culpam diluit.	washed away his sin.
Surgamus ergo strenue;	Let us then rise promptly;
Gallus iacentes excitat	the rooster awakens the one lying down
Et somnolentos increpat;	and rebukes the sleeper;
Gallus negantes arguit.	the rooster convicts those who deny.
Gallo canente spes redit;	At the crowing of the rooster hope returns;
Aegris salus refunditur;	health comes back to the sick;
Mucro latronis conditur;	the robber sheaths his sword;
Lapsis fides revertitur.	and faith returns to the lapsed.
Jesu, labantes respice	Jesus, look on us when we waver
Et nos videndo corrige;	and with your glance correct us;
Si respicis, lapsus cadunt,	if you look on us, our lapses fall away,
Fletuque culpa solvitur.	and our tears wash away our guilt.

45. Wilken, *The Spirit of Early Christian Thought*, pp. 219-220.

Tu lux refulge sensibus	Be a shining light to our minds
Mentisque somnum discute;	and drive away sloth from our souls;
Te nostra vox primum sonet,	may our voices first sound praise to you,
Et vota solvamus tibi.	and thus pay our vows to you.

For this morning hymn, Ambrose seized upon the simple, everyday image of a rooster crowing to announce the coming of day. Joseph Connelly relates the opening to God's words to Job.

> Who is it, asks God of Job, that has "put wisdom in the heart of man? Or who gave the cock understanding?" (Job 38:36). St. Ambrose, following this idea, sees a manifestation of God's wisdom and power in the division of day and night and in the God-given instinct of the cock to announce this division.[46]

This, in turn, works well with biblical symbolism of day/night, light/darkness, and sleep/wakefulness (watchfulness). There is strong resonance throughout the hymn with passages such as Romans 13:11-12, 1 Thessalonians 5:4-8, and Ephesians 5:8-14.

> Besides this you know the time, that the hour has come for you to wake from sleep. For salvation is nearer to us now than when we first believed. The night is far gone; the day is at hand. So then let us cast off the works of darkness and put on the armor of light.

> But you are not in darkness, brothers, for that day to surprise you like a thief. For you are all children of the light, children of the day. We are not of the night or of the darkness. So then let us not sleep, as others do, but let us keep awake and be sober. For those who sleep, sleep at night, and those who get drunk, are drunk at night. But since we belong to the day, let us be sober, having put on the breastplate of faith and love, and for a helmet the hope of salvation.

> . . . for at one time you were darkness, but now you are light in the Lord. Walk as children of the light. . . . Take no part in the unfruitful works of darkness. . . . Therefore it says,

---

46. Connelly, *Hymns of the Roman Liturgy,* p. 15.

> "Awake, O sleeper,
> and arise from the dead
> and Christ will shine on you."

Stanza four of the hymn refers directly to the biblical incident that the crowing of the rooster most readily brings to our minds — Peter's denial of Jesus. The reference returns in stanza five, this time applying it more broadly to all who deny their Lord; stanza seven continues the broad application and includes penitence and forgiveness. Stanza seven focuses, particularly, on a detail in the story that only Luke, among the four evangelists, reports: "And Jesus turned and looked at Peter" (Luke 22:61). Thus the repeated emphasis on Jesus' looking at us — *respice, videndo, respicis* — in the first three lines. Stanza seven's final line refers to Peter's response: "And he went out and wept bitterly" (Luke 22:62). In concluding, the final lines of stanza eight make clear reference to Psalm 65:1: "Praise is due to you, O God, in Zion, and to you shall vows be performed."

Joseph Connelly's high appraisal of this hymn is certainly warranted: "On a simple fact [a rooster crow] joined with the story of St. Peter's denial [Ambrose] builds up one of the most beautiful hymns of the Breviary. For simplicity and sublimity it has few rivals."[47]

Ambrose may be the greatest hymnodist of the early Christian era, but the prize for the greatest poet surely goes to Prudentius (348–ca. 413), his younger contemporary. Prudentius wrote long poetic works that he intended for private reading, not for public, communal singing, as were the hymns of Ambrose. Thus it would be out of place to mention him here, except that a hymn extracted from one of his larger works has found a permanent place in Christian hymnody: the great Christmas hymn known in English translation as "Of the Father's Love Begotten."

Finally, this chapter would not be complete without referring to one of the greatest of all Christian hymns, the *Te Deum*. Although it probably dates from the fourth century, it harks back to an older hymn style — before Ambrose made regular-metered, strophic structure the norm. Its line lengths and accentuation are irregular, and it has a good deal of parallelism.

> We praise you, O God,
> we acclaim you as Lord;

---

47. Connelly, *Hymns of the Roman Liturgy*, p. 15.

all creation worships you,
the Father everlasting.
To you all angels, all the powers of heaven,
the cherubim and seraphim, sing in endless praise:
    Holy, holy, holy Lord, God of power and might,
    heaven and earth are full of your glory.

The glorious company of apostles praise you.
The noble fellowship of prophets praise you.
The white-robed army of martyrs praise you.
Throughout the world the holy Church acclaims you:
    Father, of majesty unbounded,
    your true and only Son, worthy of all praise,
    the Holy Spirit, advocate and guide.

You, Christ, are the king of glory,
the eternal Son of the Father.
When you took our flesh to set us free
you humbly chose the virgin's womb.
You overcame the sting of death,
and opened the kingdom of heaven to all believers.
You are seated at God's right hand in glory.
We believe that you will come to be our judge.
    Come, then, Lord, and help your people,
    bought with the price of your own blood,
    and bring us with your saints to glory everlasting.[48]

A metrical, strophic translation into English by Clarence A. Walworth loses some of the richness of the original, but it does provide English-speaking congregations with the opportunity to sing this venerable hymn.

Holy God, we praise your name;
Lord of all, we bow before you.
Saints on earth your rule acclaim;
all in heaven above adore you.
Infinite your vast domain;
everlasting is your reign.

48. Trans. English Language Liturgical Commission, 1988.

Hark, the glad celestial hymn
angel choirs above are raising;
cherubim and seraphim,
in unceasing chorus praising,
fill the heavens with sweet accord:
"Holy, holy, holy Lord!"

Lo, the apostolic train
joins your sacred name to hallow;
prophets swell the glad refrain,
and the white-robed martyrs follow;
and from morn to set of sun,
through the church the song goes on.

Holy Father, holy Son,
Holy Spirit, three we name you,
though in essence only one;
undivided God, we claim you,
and, adoring, bend the knee
while we own the mystery.

Since about the ninth century, legend has it that the *Te Deum* was improvised antiphonally by Ambrose and Augustine at Augustine's baptism. According to Landulf, an eleventh-century successor to Ambrose as bishop of Milan,

> By the will of God, at the springs called St. John's, Augustine was finally baptized and confirmed by Ambrose, with God aiding him, in the name of the holy and indivisible Trinity. All the believers of the city stood by and watched, just as formerly many had watched him in his errors and agreed with him. And at these springs the Holy Spirit granted them eloquence and inspiration; and so, with all who were there hearing and seeing and marveling, they sang together the *Te Deum laudamus,* and so brought forth what is now approved of by the whole church, and sung devoutly everywhere. Rejoicing together in God, like men just granted riches and pearls of great price, they ate together and were very glad; they rejoiced with great joy, and took comfort in God.[49]

49. Quoted from *Music in the Western World,* p. 31.

As much as we might like to believe this attractive story, there is little to give it historical credence. We do not know who wrote the *Te Deum*. Several names have been suggested over the centuries, but in the late nineteenth century a fairly strong scholarly consensus developed that the author was Niceta (died after 414), bishop of Remesiana (now Bela Palenka, in former Yugoslavia). He is known to have written hymns, and the name (or word) "Nicetas" appears in some manuscripts. More recent scholarship has cast doubts on attributing the *Te Deum* to Niceta, though it has offered no alternative. Whether or not Niceta was the author of the *Te Deum*, he is an interesting figure in the history of hymnody. He is mentioned in several letters and poems by his friend, St. Paulinus of Nola, and also by St. Jerome. Jerome says that Niceta wrote hymns, but any hymns he may have written are now lost, unless he is indeed the author of the *Te Deum*. What has survived from Niceta, however, is a sermon entitled *On the Usefulness of Hymns*. Particularly interesting is a passage in which he advocates congregational singing that is well regulated, that is, harmonious in the broad sense of that term.

> Thus, beloved, let us sing with alert senses and a wakeful mind, as the psalmist exhorts: "Because God is king of all the earth," he says, "sing ye wisely," so that a psalm is sung not only with the spirit, that is, the sound of the voice, but with the mind also, and so that we think of what we sing rather than allow our mind, seized by extraneous thoughts as is often the case, to lose the fruit of labor. One must sing with a manner and melody befitting holy religion; it must not proclaim theatrical distress but rather exhibit Christian simplicity in its very musical movement; it must not remind one of anything theatrical, but rather create compunction in the listeners.
>
> Further, our voice ought not to be dissonant but consonant. One ought not to drag out the singing while another cuts it short, and one ought not to sing too low while another raises his voice. Rather each should strive to integrate his voice within the sound of the harmonious chorus and not project it outwardly in the manner of a cithara as if to make an immodest display. . . . And for him who is not able to blend and fit himself in with the others, it is better to sing in a subdued voice than to make a great noise, for thus he performs both his liturgical function and avoids disturbing the singing brotherhood.[50]

50. Quoted from *Source Readings in Music History*, p. 21.

It has often been said that the Reformation spread more as the result of Luther's hymns than of all his theological tracts and treatises. A similar claim could be made for the spread of the church in the early centuries of its existence. Niceta's hymns are an example. Both Paulinus and Jerome speak highly of Niceta's missionary activity among the Scythian tribes in the cold north. Paulinus says that he melted their icy hearts with the warmth of the gospel, and Jerome says that he Christianized barbarians with the sweetness of his hymns. As much as anything else, the singing of psalms and hymns proclaimed Jesus as Savior and Lord, taught and solidified true doctrine, and expressed the joy and thanksgiving of those who "once were not a people, but now . . . are God's people" (1 Pet. 2:10). Further, in the words of the great patristic scholar Johannes Quasten, "the hymn played an important role not only in developing the Christian liturgy but also in suffusing the surrounding culture with Christian ideas."[51]

51. Quasten, *Patrology* I, p. 160.

CHAPTER 11

St. Augustine: The Problems of Eloquence and Inordinate Love

. . . the eye is not satisfied with seeing,
nor the ear filled with hearing.

Ecclesiastes 1:8

If any should say, "Let us now hear you talk of your doctrine, you
speak so beautifully," may I be struck dumb ere I speak beautifully.

Hasidic proverb

[The cult of art as religion] can only fall into a worship of the instru-
ment — idolatry. And to say idolatry is to say failure, for what is
wrong with idolatry is that it is a dead stop along the way to the tran-
scendent.

Jacques Barzun

After hearing the vehement and uniform polemic of the church fathers against what must have been a big part of the musical life in the late Roman Empire, we will undoubtedly hear with relief their enthusiasm for psalmody and hymnody. Though that enthusiasm probably strikes most of us as far too narrowly directed, we are at least relieved that their denunciation of music was not total. And we may be especially heartened when we discover how deeply the greatest of the church fathers, St. Augustine, was moved by music. In his *Confessions* he exclaims,

> How I wept during your hymns and songs! I was deeply moved by the music of the sweet chants of your Church. The sounds flowed into my ears and the truth was distilled into my heart. This caused the feeling of devotion to overflow. Tears ran, and it was good for me to have that experience.[1]

These words come from a lover of music, one who is profoundly affected by its charms. And here, finally, we seem to have found in the great St. Augustine a church father whose appreciation of music might lead to a broader affirmation of the music of his culture than we find in the other church fathers. Here, at last, we may think, is someone "of like passion" with us.

But that is simply not the case. However extensively one reads Augustine, one will not find him countering the vehemence of the early Christian polemic against pagan music. On the contrary, one finds him contributing to the uniformity of the polemic. In *On Christian Doctrine,* for example, he says that Christians "should not turn to their [the pagans'] theatrical frivolities to discover whether anything valuable for spiritual purposes is to be gathered from their harps and other instruments."[2] In *The City of God* he frequently points out the moral degeneracy of the entertainments of the Roman Empire and points to that as a cause of its downfall. He abhors the "female singers . . . and other licentious abominations," which were introduced at banquets,[3] and the "thefts of Mercury, the wantonness of Venus, and the base and flagitious deeds of the rest of them, which . . . are daily sung and danced in the theaters."[4]

If Augustine's voice against pagan musical practices and in praise of psalmody and hymnody were just one more voice in the unison chorus, it would not be necessary to devote a separate chapter to him. But his voice did add something distinctive — though it was clearly in harmony with the others. As his enthusiasm for the moving power of music soars above that of the others, so does his sensitivity to the dangers of its charms run deeper. It is precisely in his scrupulous sensitivity to the dangers of music that Augustine

---

1. *Confessions* IX, vi, 14; p. 164.
2. *On Christian Doctrine* II, xviii, 28; p. 54.
3. *The City of God* III, xxi; p. 99.
4. *The City of God* VII, xxvi; p. 233.

disturbs our comfort. If we take him seriously, Augustine will not allow us to relax even when we are singing wholesome psalms and hymns because, though he recognizes their value, he also sees them as occasions for sin. He recorded his wrestling with that dilemma in Book X of his *Confessions*:

> The pleasures of the ear had a more tenacious hold on me, and had subjugated me; but you set me free and liberated me. As things now stand, I confess that I have some sense of restful contentment in sounds whose soul is your words, when they are sung by a pleasant and well-trained voice. Not that I am riveted by them, for I can rise up and go when I wish. Nevertheless, on being combined with your thoughts which give them life, they demand in my heart some position of honour, and I have difficulty in finding what is appropriate to offer them. Sometimes I seem to myself to give them more honour than is fitting. I feel that when the sacred words are chanted well, our souls are moved and are more religiously and with a warmer devotion kindled to piety than if they are not so sung. All the diverse emotions of our spirit have their various modes in voice and chant appropriate in each case, and are stirred by a mysterious inner kinship. But my physical delight, which has to be checked from enervating the mind, often deceives me when the perception of the senses is unaccompanied by reason, and is not patiently content to be in a subordinate place. It tries to be first and to be in a leading role, though it deserves to be allowed only as secondary to reason. So in these matters I sin unawares, and only afterwards become aware of it.
>
> Sometimes, however, by taking excessive safeguards against being led astray, I err on the side of too much severity. I have sometimes gone so far as to wish to banish all the melodies and sweet chants commonly used for David's psalter from my ears and from the Church as well. But I think a safer course one which I remember being often told of bishop Athanasius of Alexandria. He used to make the Reader of the psalm chant with so flexible a speech-rhythm that he was nearer to reciting than to singing. Nevertheless, when I remember the tears which I poured out at the time when I was first recovering my faith, and that now I am moved not by the chant but by the words being sung, when they are sung with a clear voice and entirely appropriate modulation, then again I recognize the great utility of music in worship.
>
> Thus I fluctuate between the danger of pleasure and the experi-

ence of the beneficent effort, and I am more led to put forward the opinion (not as an irrevocable view) that the custom of singing in Church is to be approved, so that through the delights of the ear the weaker mind may rise up towards the devotion of worship. Yet when it happens to me that the music moves me more than the subject of the song, I confess myself to commit a sin deserving of punishment, and then I would prefer not to have heard the singer.

See my condition! Weep with me and weep for me, you who have within yourselves a concern for the good, the springs from which good actions proceed. Those who do not share this concern will not be moved by these considerations. But you "Lord my God, hear, look and see" and "have mercy and help me." In your eyes I have become a problem to myself, and that is my sickness.[5]

This passage occurs in the part of the *Confessions* that follows Augustine's conversion. Here he is examining his conscience and scrupulously analyzing the temptations offered to the senses by food and drink, smells, music, and visually beautiful objects.

Regarding food he says: "You have taught me that I should come to take food in the way I take medicines. But while I pass from the discomfort of need to the tranquility of satisfaction, the very transition contains for me an insidious trap of uncontrolled desire." So although "health is the reason for eating and drinking, a dangerous pleasantness joins itself to the process like a companion" and "the quest for pleasure is obscured by a pretext of health." The problem, he makes clear, is not with the food itself: "It is not the impurity of the food I fear but that of uncontrolled desire." So every day he has to struggle "against uncontrolled desire in eating and drinking."

> It is not something I could give up once and for all and decide never to touch it again, as I was able to do with sexual intercourse. And so a rein has to be held upon my throat, moderated between laxity and austerity. Who is the person, Lord, who is never carried a little beyond the limits of necessity?[6]

Augustine spends little time with the temptations of smell because he says the "allurement of perfumes is not a matter of great concern" to him.

5. *Confessions* X, xxxiii, 49-50; pp. 207-208.
6. *Confessions* X, xxxi, 44-47; pp. 204-207.

Nevertheless, he does admit that he might be deceived; and thus he warns: "No one should be complacent in this life which is called a 'total temptation.' Anyone who could change from the worse to the better can also change from the better to the worse."[7]

Following the passage on music quoted above, Augustine turns to visual beauty. Beautiful objects, he confesses, are a problem for him. Although he recognizes God as the source of their beauty and understands the principle of their "right use," they still cause him to fall.

> [T]he beautiful objects designed by artists' souls and realized by skilled hands come from that beauty which is higher than souls; after that beauty my soul sighs day and night. From this higher beauty the artists and connoisseurs of external beauty draw their criterion of judgment, but they do not draw from there a principle for the right use of beautiful things. The principle is there but they do not see it, namely that they should not go to excess, but "should guard their strength for you" and not dissipate it in delights that produce mental fatigue. But, although I am the person saying this and making the distinction, I also entangle my steps in beautiful externals. However, you rescue me, Lord, you rescue me. "For your mercy is before my eyes." I am pitifully captured by them, and in your pity you rescue me. . . .[8]

To Augustine, this life is an "immense jungle full of traps and dangers," and he rejoices that by God's grace he has been able to "cut out and expel" many of them from his heart. "Nevertheless," he asks, "when so many things of this kind surround our daily life on every side with a buzz of distraction, when may I be so bold as to say . . . that . . . I am not caught by any vain concern?" Among the "vain concerns" that distract him "from thinking out some weighty matter" are "a dog chasing a rabbit," "a lizard catching flies," and "a spider entrapping them as they rush into its web."[9]

By this time many readers are probably ready to agree with Fr. Robert O'Connell, who says that this passage

> makes, surely, some of the most depressing reading in all of Christian literature. There is something profoundly saddening about the por-

7. *Confessions* X, xxxii, 48; p. 207.
8. *Confessions* X, xxxiv, 53; p. 210.
9. *Confessions* X, xxxv, 57; pp. 21-213.

trait it presents: the great Bishop of Hippo tormenting himself about the pleasure he cannot avoid while eating or listening to psalmody; berating himself that the spectacle of a dog chasing a hare, or of a lizard snaring a fly, can still distract his interest.[10]

But not all readers respond in this way. Kenneth Burke finds the Augustine passage, as a personal portrait, "the most appealing section in the book." He enjoys the irony of watching Augustine apologize "for traits that many people today would be quite proud of." Augustine's temptations, he says, "they'd doubtless think of as 'vitality' or 'sensitivity.'"[11]

I am not interested in discussing here the irony that Burke sees; and, though I understand — and, to a certain extent, share — O'Connell's response, I am not ready to dismiss this whole passage as a sad and unfortunate picture of an overly zealous puritan. On the contrary, I think Augustine's scrupulous conscience is a much-needed guide in our sensation-hungry society. Augustine's problem with music has its source in two important aspects of his thought. The first is his great concern with the problem of rhetoric, the problem that people are often moved more by eloquence than by truth; the second is his great concern about the ordering of loves. These two aspects of his thought can be found throughout the *Confessions,* and they come together in this famous dilemma in Book X.

Marcia Colish, in her excellent chapter on Augustine in *The Mirror of Language,* says the following about the *Confessions:* "From the very beginning Augustine interprets his moral and intellectual failings in terms of the misuse of his linguistic faculties."[12] Sweeping as it is, this statement is hardly an exaggeration. Augustine observes that, already in infancy, attempts at communication are self-centered; even before babies speak, their cries, gestures, and facial expressions reveal selfishness. Augustine tells us that he has "personally watched and studied a jealous baby. He could not yet speak and, pale with jealousy and bitterness, glared at his brother sharing his mother's milk."[13] When the child is a little older, he uses speech as a form of power to get his way. Assuming he was no better than the children he later observed, Augustine says:

10. O'Connell, *St Augustine's Confessions,* p. 133.
11. Burke, *The Rhetoric of Religion,* p. 135.
12. Colish, *The Mirror of Language,* p. 19.
13. *Confessions* I, vii, 11; p. 9.

I was no longer a baby incapable of speech but already a boy with the power to talk. This I remember. But how I learned to talk I discovered only later. It was not that grown-up people instructed me by presenting me with words in a certain order by formal teaching, as later I was to learn the letters of the alphabet. I myself acquired this power of speech with the intelligence which you gave me, my God. By groans and various sounds and various movements of parts of my body I would endeavour to express the intentions of my heart to persuade people to bow to my will.[14]

Even his early attempts at prayer were selfish attempts to manipulate God: "I pleaded with you that I might not be caned at school."[15]

Given Augustine's hardheaded realism and lack of sentimentality about the depraved nature of "innocent" babies and children, it will not be difficult to understand that he could also be hardheadedly realistic about the potential for sinning that he saw in such seemingly innocent pleasures as eating, listening to music, or watching a dog chase a rabbit. As he looked back on his early education, Augustine found more misuse of words. His education, typical of his time, was dominated by an emphasis on rhetoric as practiced by the so-called Second Sophistic school, which emphasized means of expression over meaning, persuasive eloquence over truth. Thus his education aimed more at teaching eloquence than morality, as he shows in this quotation:

[Those men held up as models] would be covered with embarrassment if, in describing their own actions in which they had not behaved badly, they were caught using a barbarism or a solecism in speech. But if they described their lusts in a rich rewarding vocabulary of well constructed prose with a copious and ornate style, they received praise and congratulated themselves.[16]

As a result, he became "more afraid of committing a barbarism" than he was on guard against "feeling envy towards those who did not,"[17] and his goal in achieving eloquence was "to gain access to human honours and to

14. *Confessions* I, viii, 13; p. 10.
15. *Confessions* I, ix, 14; p. 11.
16. *Confessions* I, xviii, 28; p. 20.
17. *Confessions* I, xix, 30; p. 21.

acquire deceitful riches."[18] The more advanced education he later received was no better: it "had the objective of leading me to distinction as an advocate in the law courts, where one's reputation is high in proportion to one's success in deceiving people."[19] It enabled him "to please men, not to impart to them any instruction, but merely to purvey pleasure."[20]

Not surprisingly, Augustine has no more good to say about his profession as an orator and teacher of rhetoric than he does about his education. He confesses that as a teacher he sold "eloquence that would overcome an opponent," and he taught his students the "tricks" of rhetoric.[21] As an orator he "sought arrogant success by telling lies"[22] in a panegyric on the emperor. He speaks of the purveyors of Manichaeism (a heresy that had seduced him for a while) as "deceived deceivers" and "word-spinners with nothing to say."[23] One of their leaders was a man named Faustus, a "great trap of the devil" who captured many with his "smooth talk." Augustine had gone to him "interested not in the decoration of the vessel in which his discourse was served up but in the knowledge put before me to eat."[24] Behind the eloquence of Faustus, however, Augustine found no answers to his questions, only "the things they usually say." He expresses his frustration in a rhetorical question: "What could the most presentable waiter do for my thirst by offering precious cups?"[25]

Eloquence is the precious cup, but a precious cup does not necessarily contain water; as was the case with Faustus, eloquence does not necessarily convey truth. On the other hand, something eloquently said is not necessarily false, that is, eloquence is neither a sign of truth nor a sign of its absence. And the same can be said for a crude style. In his thoroughness, Augustine considers all the possibilities:

> [N]othing is true merely because it is eloquently said, nor false because the signs coming from the lips make sounds deficient in a sense of style. Again, a statement is not true because it is enunciated in an

---

18. *Confessions* I, ix, 14; p. 11.

19. *Confessions* III, iii, 6; p. 38.

20. *Confessions* VI, vi, 9; p. 98.

21. *Confessions* IV, ii, 2; p. 53.

22. *Confessions* VI, vi, 10; p. 98.

23. *Confessions* VII, ii, 3; p. 112.

24. *Confessions* V, iii, 3; p. 73.

25. *Confessions* V, vi, 10; p. 77.

unpolished idiom, nor false because the words are splendid. Wisdom and foolishness are like food that is nourishing or useless. Whether the words are ornate or not does not decide the issue.[26]

The dilemma occurs, of course, in relation to the eloquent style. Faustus's eloquence masked the emptiness of his teaching; worse, it seduced the unsuspecting into error. But Augustine's experience with St. Ambrose, which he relates in the same book of the *Confessions* as his encounter with Faustus, was the opposite. Ambrose's eloquence drew Augustine to the truth. At first Augustine was only interested in Ambrose's rhetorical technique; yet, in spite of that, the subject matter seeped in.

> I used enthusiastically to listen to him preaching to the people, not with the intention which I ought to have had, but as if testing out his oratorical skill to see whether it merited the reputation it enjoyed or whether his fluency was better or inferior than it was reported to be. I hung on his diction in rapt attention, but remained bored and contemptuous of the subject-matter. My pleasure was in the charm of his language. . . . Nevertheless, gradually, though I did not realize it, I was drawing closer.
>
> I was not interested in learning what he was talking about. My ears were only for his rhetorical technique. . . . Nevertheless together with the words which I was enjoying, the subject matter, in which I was unconcerned, came to make an entry into my mind. I could not separate them. While I opened my heart in noting the eloquence with which he spoke, there also entered no less the truth which he affirmed, though only gradually.[27]

What does all of this have to do with Augustine's problem with music? Simply this: music is a form of rhetoric, and its power of attraction is like that of eloquence. The eloquence of Faustus and the melodies of a figure such as Bardasian attracted people to their heresies. The eloquence of Ambrose and the melodies of his hymns attracted people to orthodoxy. Augustine himself is a witness to the potential of Ambrose's hymns for good: "I feel that when the sacred words are chanted well, our souls are

26. *Confessions* V, vi, 10; p. 78.
27. *Confessions* V, xiii-xiv, 23-24; p. 88.

moved and are more religiously and with a warmer devotion kindled to piety than if they are not so sung."[28]

James Winn has pointed out the similarity between Augustine's description of the moving power of music and eloquence — or, as he calls it here, "figurative speech." The language in the passage from the *Confession* just quoted

> is exactly parallel to a passage on scriptural interpretation in one of Augustine's letters, where "things expressed figuratively" are described as "feeding and blowing upon the fire of love" more effectively than "naked" or literal expression. By consistently using the same set of metaphors to describe figurative language in the Bible and vocal music in the church, Augustine reveals a . . . fundamental similarity: sung music, like such sensual scriptural texts as the Song of Songs, has a potential for proper use if correctly understood, and a danger for earthly enjoyment if the senses are allowed to take over.[29]

For the senses to take over is exactly the sin Augustine is confessing in the passage we are considering. The problem is that it is difficult to assign the senses their proper place: they are "not content to be in a subordinate place. [They] try to be first and to be in a leading role. . . . So in these matters," he confesses, "I sin unawares. . . ."[30] The problem with the earthly enjoyment that the senses offer, which Augustine fears, is that it so easily turns into an inordinate love of lower things over higher things and ultimately over the highest thing, God. He expresses this in many ways and in many different contexts throughout the *Confessions*. For example:

> [As a boy] I hated to be deceived, I developed a good memory, I acquired the armoury of being skilled with words, friendship softened me, I avoided pain, despondency, ignorance. In such a person what was not worthy of admiration and praise? But every one of these qualities are gifts of my God: I did not give them to myself. They are good qualities, and their totality is my self. Therefore he who made me is good, and he is my good, and I exult to him, for all the good things that I was even as a boy. My sin consisted in this, that I sought

28. *Confessions* X, xxxiii, 49; p. 207.
29. Winn, *Unsuspected Eloquence*, p. 47.
30. *Confessions* X, xxxiii, 49; p. 208.

pleasure, sublimity, and truth not in God but in his creatures, in myself, and in other created beings.[31]

The life we live in this world has its attractiveness because of a certain measure in its beauty and its harmony with all these inferior objects that are beautiful. Human friendship is also a nest of love and gentleness because of the unity it brings about between many souls. Yet sin is committed for the sake of all these things and others of this kind when, in consequence of an immoderate urge towards those things which are at the bottom end of the scale of good, we abandon the higher and supreme goods, that is you, Lord God, and your truth and your law. These inferior goods have their delights, but not comparable to my God who has made them all. It is in him that the just person takes delight; he is the joy of those who are true of heart.[32]

Let these transient things be the ground on which my soul praises you, "God creator of all." But let it not become stuck in them and glued to them with love through the physical senses. For these things pass along the path of things that move towards non-existence. They rend the soul with pestilential desires; for the soul loves to be in them and take its repose among the objects of its love. But in these things there is no point of rest: they lack permanence.[33]

I was astonished to find that already I loved you, not a phantom surrogate for you. But I was not stable in the enjoyment of my God. I was caught up to you by your beauty and quickly torn away from you by my weight. With a groan I crashed into inferior things. This weight was my sexual habit.[34]

Behind all of these passages is Augustine's distinction between enjoying *(frui)* and using *(uti)*, which he explains in Book I of *On Christian Doctrine:* "To enjoy something is to cling to it with love for its own sake. To use something, however, is to employ it in obtaining that which you love."[35]

---

31. *Confessions* I, xx, 31; pp. 22-23.
32. *Confessions* II, v, 10; pp. 29-30.
33. *Confessions* IV, x, 15; p. 62.
34. *Confessions* VII, xvii, 23; p. 127.
35. *On Christian Doctrine* I, iv, 4; p. 9.

Some things are to be enjoyed, others to be used, and there are others which are to be enjoyed and used. Those things which are to be enjoyed make us blessed. Those things which are to be used help and, as it were, sustain us as we move toward blessedness in order that we may gain and cling to those things which make us blessed. If we who enjoy and use things, being placed in the midst of things of both kinds, wish to enjoy those things which should be used, our course will be impeded and sometimes deflected, so that we are retarded in obtaining those things which are to be enjoyed, or even prevented altogether, shackled by an inferior love.[36]

As an illustration, he invites us to imagine that we are pilgrims trying to find our way home, the place of our blessedness.

We would need vehicles for land and sea which could be used to help us to reach our homeland, which is to be enjoyed. But if the amenities of the journey and the motion of the vehicles itself delighted us, and we were led to enjoy those things which we should use, we should not wish to end our journey quickly, and entangled in a perverse sweetness, we should be alienated from our country, whose sweetness would make us blessed. Thus is our mortal life, wandering from God; if we wish to return to our native country where we can be blessed we should use this world and not enjoy it, so that the "invisible things" of God "being understood by the things that are made" may be seen, that is, so that by means of corporal and temporal things we may comprehend the eternal and spiritual.[37]

The problem, it should be noted, is not the badness of the things we enjoy. The "vehicles for land and sea" and the "amenities of the journey" in this illustration are good. The problem is that we quickly fall in love with the good things of this life as if they were ultimate goods, so they "retard" or even "prevent" our love of God, the ultimate good, the maker and giver of all other goods. Whenever it is relevant in his writings, Augustine summons the full powers of his very considerable eloquence to make this point. Here are two examples:

36. *On Christian Doctrine* I, iii, 3; p. 9.
37. *On Christian Doctrine* I, iii, 4; pp. 9-10.

191

But let us not love the world nor the things that are in the world. For these are the things in the world: "there is the desire of the flesh and the desire of the eyes and the ambition of this age." These are the three, in case anyone should say, "The things which are in the world God made, that is, the sky and the earth, the sea, the sun, the moon, the stars, all the adornments of the heavens. What are the adornments of the sea? All creeping things. What [are those] of the land? Animals, trees, flying creatures. These are in the world, God made them. Why therefore should I not love what God has made?" Let the Spirit of God be in you so that you may see that all these things are good, but woe to you if you have loved the creatures and abandoned the Creator! They are beautiful to you. But how much more beautiful is he who formed them! Pay attention, my beloved people. For you can be instructed by similitudes, so that Satan not stealthily creep up on you, saying what he usually says: "Be happy in God's creatures. Why did he make these things except for you to be happy?" And they are intoxicated and perish and forget their Creator; while they use created things not temperately but wantonly, the Creator is despised. About such men the Apostle says, "They worshipped and served the creature rather than the Creator who is blessed forever." God does not forbid you to love these things, but not to devote your love [to them] for the attainment of happiness, but to approve and praise [them] in order that you may love the Creator.[38]

Behold again, and see if you can. You certainly do not love anything except what is good, since good is the earth, with the loftiness of its mountains, and the due measure of its hills, and the level surface of its plains; and good is an estate that is pleasant and fertile; and good is a house that is arranged in due proportions, and is spacious and bright; and good are animals and inanimate bodies; and good is air that is temperate and salubrious; and good is food that is agreeable and fit for health; and good is health, without pains or lassitude; and good is the countenance of man that is disposed in fit proportions, and is cheerful in look, and bright in color; and good is the mind of a friend, with the sweetness of agreement, and with the confidence of love; and good is a righteous man; and good are riches, since they are readily useful; and good is the heaven, with its sun, and moon, and stars; and

38. *Tractate 2 on I John* 11.1; pp. 153-154.

good are the angels, by their holy obedience; and good is discourse that sweetly teaches and suitably admonishes the hearer; and good is a song that is harmonious in its numbers and weighty in its sense. And why yet add more and more? This thing is good and that good, but take this and that, and regard good itself if you can; so you will see God, not good by a good that is other than Himself, but the good of all good. For in all these good things, whether those which I have mentioned, or any else that are to be discerned or thought, we could not say that one was better than another, when we judge truly, unless a conception of the good itself had impressed upon us, such that according to it we might both approve some things as good, and prefer one good thing to another. So God is to be loved, not this or that good, but the good itself. For the good that must be sought for the soul is not one above which it is to fly by judging, but to which it is to cleave with loving; and what can this be except God?[39]

To bring this back to our particular issue: it is not wrong to delight in the beauties of sound, whether in eloquent speech or harmonious music. The problem comes when we stop there, when we do not go beyond the beautifully turned phrase or the elegantly shaped melody. Delight in eloquence and music should never be an end in itself. Rather, as Carol Harrison puts it, "Desire in the artistry of the preacher, or the literary form of Scripture, [or, we can add, the beauty of the melody] is meant to inspire love that points beyond them, to their inspiration and source, that is, to love of God."[40]

At the end of a passage in the *City of God* that is similar to — but not as prolix as — the ones quoted above, Augustine sums it all up by quoting a short poem:

These are yours, they are good,
because you are good who created them.
There is in them nothing of ours,
unless the sin we commit
when we forget the order of things,
and instead of you we love what you made.

And so he prays, "Order love within me."[41]

---

39. *On the Trinity* VIII, iii, 4; p. 117.
40. Harrison, "Rhetoric of Scripture and Preaching," p. 226.
41. *The City of God* XV, xxii; pp. 510-511.

CHAPTER 12

Postlude: What Can the Early Church Teach Us about Music?

Do not remove the ancient landmark
that your fathers have set.

Proverbs 22:28

They shall build up the ancient ruins;
they shall raise up the former devastations;
they shall repair the ruined cities,
the devastations of many generations.

Isaiah 61:4

Much of what we can learn from the early Christians we can learn from their example. We would do well to heed their praise of the psalms and follow their example of making them central to our music — not just snippets and a few favorites, but complete psalms, indeed the whole Psalter with its full-orbed expression. We could also enrich our singing with the best of their hymns. Their value is enduring, and they can serve our hymn-writers as models of texts that address God communally in language that is simple yet dignified, poetically excellent, and redolent with scriptural vocabulary, stories, sentiments, and imagery. We would also do well to follow their example of making psalms and hymns a part of our daily life. We must teach them to our children and find ways and occasions to use them regularly. In the scattered lives we live to the beat of whatever is on our individual Ipods, it will not be easy to find the time and place to sing together; but any success will be spiritually enriching. And if we cannot find communal occasions, at least we can make the singing of psalms and hymns a part of our individual devotions (remembering that God can hear us even if we sing silently).

The church fathers' affirmation of psalmody and hymnody is evidence that they held a high view of music, which they also showed in their rejection of much of the music of the pagan Roman society in which they lived. Their high view of music was echoed by John Calvin, whose musical thought was heavily indebted to the church fathers. He considered music to be "either the first or one of the principal" gifts of God "to recreate man and give him pleasure." "Wherefore," he concluded, "we must be the more diligent in ruling it in such a manner that it may be useful to us and in no way pernicious."[1] The church fathers would have endorsed Calvin's view. Because music is such a great gift, it needs to be taken seriously — ruled diligently, as Calvin put it. If the church fathers had not taken music so seriously, they would not have affirmed its proper uses so strongly; nor would they have been so uniform and vehement in their rejection of its abuses. Following the sentence quoted above, Calvin gives the church fathers' uncompromising rejection of some of the music of pagan Rome as an example of diligent ruling: "For this reason the early doctors of the Church often complain that the people of their times are addicted to dishonest and shameless songs, which not without reason they call mortal and Satanic poison for the corruption of the world."

We live in a society that has often been likened in its decadence to the late Roman Empire in which the early Christians lived. Thomas Merton says that our society is an example of "the same old story of greed and lust and selfishness, of the three concupiscences bred in rich, rotted undergrowth of what is technically called 'the world.' . . ." Our materialistic society, he continues,

> has produced what seems to be the ultimate limit of this worldliness. And nowhere, except perhaps in the analogous society of pagan Rome, has there ever been such a flowering of cheap and petty and disgusting lusts and vanities. . . . We live in a society whose whole

---

1. *The Geneva Psalter,* Epistle to the Reader; quoted from *Source Readings in Music History,* Vol. 3, p. 88.

policy is to excite every nerve in the human body and keep it at the highest pitch of artificial tension, to strain every human desire to the limit and to create as many new desires and synthetic passions as possible, in order to cater to them with the products of our factories and printing presses and movie studios and all the rest.[2]

In our sensation-hungry, pleasure-mad society, we should be no less courageous than were the church fathers in holding and promoting counter-cultural views and practices. They did not hesitate to denounce the music of their society that they saw as pernicious, no matter how popular it was. We should be as ready to denounce what is pernicious in our own society.

Three arguments, however, inhibit us from believing that music can be pernicious. First, there is the argument that "it's just a song," which is dismissive of the age-old and virtually universal belief that a song is not *just* a song. It has been recognized for many centuries and across many cultures that song has great rhetorical power. Plato would have forbidden certain kinds of music in his ideal republic. "Let me make the songs of a nation and I won't care who makes its laws," he or one of his followers said. Aristotle was convinced that the character of music had an influence on the character of people. Clement of Alexandria championed music that promoted "composed manners." Augustine recognized the mysterious relationship between certain modes in song and various human emotions — and so on, through the medieval philosophers, the Reformers, and well beyond.

What I find just as telling as the long line of historical witnesses to music's power to shape human character is that most of those who say "it's just a song" do not actually act as if that were true. Most of those who use that argument bring it into the discussion only when they feel threatened by criticism. They argue that a song is just a song when they feel — quite illogically in a society where we have "rights" to just about anything — that something they treasure might be taken away; or, perhaps, when they feel that the criticism has a ring of truth that will spoil their pleasure. So they argue: "It's just a song. It gives me pleasure. What can be the harm?" People in Tertullian's day (and, I suspect, just about any day) made the same argument. Tertullian correctly recognized the lure of pleasure as its source. "Such is the force of pleasure," he says, "that

2. Merton, *Seven Storey Mountain*, p. 133.

it can prolong ignorance to give it its chance, and pervert knowledge to cloak itself."[3]

Making pleasure, often of the titillating kind, the primary goal of art, literature, and music has fostered the "flowering of cheap and petty and disgusting lusts and vanities" that Merton has observed in our society. That flowering has been aided and abetted by a recent phase in the history of art criticism that has rejected ethical criticism. "It's just a song" is dismissive of music and of the necessity of any kind of criticism. At the opposite extreme, this phase of art criticism views art as so important, subtle, and sophisticated in its own right that ethical concerns become trivial. What matters are "purely artistic" concerns — whatever those are.

Although the academic rejection of ethical criticism has provided what purports to be an intellectually credible theory to those who wish to deflect any particular bit of that criticism from themselves or their work, Wayne C. Booth points out, in *The Company We Keep: An Ethics of Fiction*, that "no one seems able to resist ethical criticism for long."[4] Whatever their theoretical stance, "even those critics who work hard to purge themselves of all but the most abstract formal interests turn out to have an ethical program in mind."[5] Ethical criticism is almost inevitable and it should be taken seriously. "[I]f the powerful stories we tell each other really matter to us — and even the most skeptical theorists imply by their *practice* that stories do matter — then a criticism that takes their 'mattering' seriously cannot be ignored."[6] And lest we think this is relevant only for literature, Booth adds that a "complete ethical criticism of 'narrative' would obviously also include most music, perhaps even, as Plato insisted, all music."[7] Because the church fathers knew this, music mattered in their thought. Therefore, they took ethical criticism seriously: they realized that the musical company we keep matters, and that if we think otherwise, we do so to our own detriment.

A second argument that would remove music from the purview of ethical criticism begins with an important theological fact: all things were created by God; therefore, all things, being the work of a good Creator, are good. So far, so good. But then, in claiming that music is one of the good

3. *On Spectacles* I; p. 231.
4. Booth, *The Company We Keep*, p. 6.
5. Booth, *The Company We Keep*, p. 5.
6. Booth, *The Company We Keep*, p. 4.
7. Booth, *The Company We Keep*, p. 14.

things God created, the argument comes to the erroneous conclusion that music is thus removed from the purview of ethical criticism. Tertullian, as we have seen, encountered this line of thought and pointed out its error (see pp. 68-69 above); but it is still with us today. Few declare it as bluntly as did the student who wrote, "God created rock music just as he created everything on earth." But no matter how bluntly or subtly it is advanced, the argument keeps returning, and we need to point out its error. God did not create music — at least not what we normally mean by music — and thus music cannot be subsumed under "all things" that God created. *Sound* is part of God's creation, and it is one of God's good gifts. So are musical talents such as aural skills, rhythmic sense, memory, imagination, and the like. Music itself is one of God's good gifts if by music we mean something akin to what the ancients meant by *musica mundana* — order, balance, harmony, and proportion. These are characteristics of creation, and thus they are also good when they are present in the sonic arrangements humans make. But here is where the problem comes: humans have fallen from their originally created, perfect state, so now all their products are tainted. Sound, talent, and music (in its ancient sense) are God's good gifts, but God did not make any "pieces" of music. They have all been made by human creatures, all of them depraved, all of them potential vessels of common grace, and some of them redeemed. Therefore, their works make up a mixed bag that needs careful and critical scrutiny.

Tertullian saw through the "all-things-in-God's-creation-are-good" argument to its root cause. People resort to this argument, he said, when they fear "losing some delight or enjoyment of the world."[8] Again, it is the magnetism of pleasure that brings out specious arguments to protect the sources of one's pleasure.

Third, there is the argument from church growth: if we wish to see the church grow, we must adopt the music of the ambient culture. In a well-balanced discussion of cultural adaptation in worship (which the church fathers would extend to all of life), Cornelius Plantinga, Jr., and Sue A. Rozeboom point out that it is not only inevitable but also desirable. Cultural adaptation is desirable for evangelism and for enrichment that helps worship more fully to "reflect the glory of God [and] display the very complexion of God's creation."[9] But they point out that it is also risky: adapta-

8. *On Spectacles* II; p. 233.
9. Plantinga and Rozeboom, *Discerning the Spirits,* p. 68.

tion, or "translation," can mislead us. It can even use "cultural forms that might clash with the gospel, or with a reverent attitude toward God, or with a respectful approach to God's people."[10] So there are difficult questions and challenging issues.

> How do we translate or embody or "inculturate" our worship of God in cultural forms that will reach our neighbors but will not distort the gospel? . . . [A]re we upholding the integrity of the gospel and of Christian worship even as we translate them into fresh cultural idioms?
>
> Translation, of course, is always hazardous. Every translation is itself an interpretation. As a result, a translation opens hearers not only to the possibility of new understandings but also to the possibility of new misunderstandings. . . . Then, too, every message is affected by its medium. . . . And so our central question returns: Once the gospel has been translated . . . do we still have the gospel according to Jesus Christ, or have we fashioned a gospel according to contemporary culture?[11]

The church fathers did not always agree in their answers to the tough questions about cultural adaptation. Recall, for example, the differences between Clement and Tertullian. But they took the questions seriously, and they were all wary of the danger of mistranslating the gospel and of mistaking "the Lord's song [for] just another rendition of the Babylonian national anthem."[12] And although they all certainly had a zeal for expanding the church, they never sacrificed their essential countercultural stance in order to entice people into the faith.

Richard A. Muller, in "Tertullian and Church Growth," notes that "the progress of Christianity from the time of the calling of the first disciples (ca. 30 CE) to the beginning of Roman toleration of Christianity (311 CE) was one of virtually unparalleled church growth." Although some "accommodation to the ways of the Greeks, of Romans, and eventually, of Germanic tribes" accounts in part for the remarkable growth, he points out that an "equally important aspect of the growth of the church was its intransigent opposition to the social and intellectual currents of the Greco-Roman world." He points to Tertullian in particular as one whose

10. Plantinga and Rozeboom, *Discerning the Spirits*, p. 48.
11. Plantinga and Rozeboom, *Discerning the Spirits*, pp. 50-51.
12. Plantinga and Rozeboom, *Discerning the Spirits*, p. 74.

eloquent but often strident polemic offers a lesson: culture is never neutral to Christianity. Culture always embodies its own spiritual dynamic. As we make changes in the style of Christianity in order to draw people to the gospel, we need to be aware of the dynamic of the culture. And we must learn where to draw the line.[13]

Tertullian is just one of many early Christians who qualify as particularly good teachers of this lesson. They can teach us that ethical criticism is necessary, especially in a society like ours, which, like theirs, has lost its moral and ethical moorings. They can teach us that what T. S. Eliot said about literary criticism is equally valid for musical criticism.

Literary criticism should be completed by criticism from a definite ethical and theological standpoint. In so far as in any age there is common agreement on ethical and theological matters, so far can literary criticism be substantive. In ages like our own, in which there is no such common agreement, it is the more necessary for Christian readers to scrutinize their reading, especially of works of imagination, with explicit ethical and theological standards.[14]

In addition to teaching us this important lesson, the early Christians can inspire and encourage us by their courageous and unwavering posture against the corrupt and very popular culture of their day. They can teach us that we need to draw a line, and they can encourage us to stand bravely behind that line. But can they show us *where* to draw the line?

The answer, of course, is that they cannot. At least that's the answer if we are looking for watertight lists of what is on each side of the line. We have no concrete examples from their own time from which we might be able to learn, nor do we have specific lists of principles from them that could help us know where to draw the line. And it is doubtful, in any case, that they all agreed where the line should be drawn. From what has survived of their writings, we can learn that they drew two lines about which there was widespread agreement: they agreed that some very specific — and prevalent — areas of music fell below one of the lines, and that psalms and hymns — if their texts were not heretical — rose above the other line. We will never know what they thought about everything in between. But

13. Muller, "Tertullian and Church Growth," p. 8.
14. Eliot, "Religion and Literature," p. 21.

they have left us something more valuable than lines and lists: they left us imagery, and with their musical imagery as our guide, we can make responsible choices.

The musical imagery found in early Christian writings derives from the Bible, which should come as no surprise. In *The Spirit of Early Christian Thought*, Robert Wilken notes "the omnipresence of the Bible in early Christian writings. Early Christian thought is biblical. . . ."[15] The church's mission

> was to win the hearts and minds of men and women and to change their lives. . . . In this endeavor the Bible was a central factor. It narrated a history that reached back into antiquity even to the beginning of the world . . . and it poured forth a thesaurus of words that created a new religious vocabulary and a cornucopia of scenes and images that stirred literary and artistic imagination as well as theological thought.[16]

The musical imagery in early Christian writing, though multifaceted, can be subsumed under the image of the "new song." At the end of chapter 2, I summed up the features of the "new song" as described in the New Testament as follows: it is "a joyful response to the works of God, stimulated by the Word and the Spirit; it is sung to God and to each other, with the saints and angels and all creation."

Few will quarrel with the idea that the song of the church should be joyful. Indeed, that idea may be too readily and superficially embraced. Our problem is that the darker countermelody ("ashes and tears")[17] is so severely muted, even silenced, that the joy expressed is empty and trivial — merely "upbeat" without being truly joyful. Too many Christians wish to have Christmas without Advent, Easter without Lent, trumpets without tears and ashes, a crown without a cross. Too many are eager to give an affirmative answer to George Herbert's question:

> Shall I then sing, skipping thy doleful story,
> And side with thy triumphal glory?[18]

15. Wilken, *The Spirit of Early Christian Thought*, p. xviii.
16. Wilken, *The Spirit of Early Christian Thought*, pp. xiv-xv.
17. See Wolterstorff, "Trumpets, Ashes, and Tears."
18. "The Thanksgiving," ll. 11-12.

There is an additional problem. While suppressing the "doleful" countermelody leads to a trivialization of the joy theme, a tendency toward a pagan kind of *epiclesis* leads to a perversion of it. Those misled by this kind of *epiclesis* think — or at least act as though — "we convene ourselves [for worship] and then wait for God to show up because we have said the magic words or cranked up enough volume in our praise."[19] They also inevitably blame the music when they feel worship to be joyless and spiritless. They see music as a stimulus to rather than a vehicle for the expression of joy, an enticement for the Spirit's presence rather than a grateful response for it, as though the Spirit were at the beck and call of our music. Granted, the border between a response and a stimulant is obscure. In addition, as Augustine and other church fathers attest, music can be a legitimate stimulant for "inflaming" our piety and devotion. Nevertheless, it is as important for us as it was for the church fathers to keep the distinction clear, and to remember (1) that response, not stimulation, is the fundamental role of worship music; (2) that "inflaming" can easily degenerate into manipulation; and (3) that not all that is called "spiritual" is of the Spirit, or, as Plantinga and Rozeboom put it, "not all that moves us is of God."[20] I am convinced that there would be a marked and salutary difference in the church's music and worship if we would maintain the central focus of our "new song" to be a joyful *response,* offered in humble gratitude, not a *stimulant* "to excite every nerve . . . and to create as many . . . synthetic passions as possible" (to quote Thomas Merton again).

Similarly, I believe that there would be a marked difference in the church's music if Christians truly recognized to whom and with whom they are singing. Would there be so much insistence on having one's own musical taste satisfied if there were a strong awareness that God is the primary audience? Would we be so ready to demand our personal favorites if we really acknowledged that we are part of the great church choir of saints and angels and galaxies? We sing:

Hark, the glad celestial hymn
Angel choirs above are raising,
Cherubim and seraphim
In unceasing chorus praising

19. Plantinga and Rozeboom, *Discerning the Spirits,* p. 124.
20. Plantinga and Rozeboom, *Discerning the Spirits,* p. 74.

Fill the heavens with sweet accord,
Holy, holy, holy Lord!

Lo, the apostolic train
Joins the sacred name to hallow.
Prophets swell the glad refrain
And the white-robed martyrs follow,
And adoring bend the knee
While we own the mystery.

We also sing, "All creatures of our God and King, lift up your voice and with us sing," and among the "creatures" we invite to sing with us are "burning sun," "shining moon," rushing wind," "fierce fire," and "all fruits and flowers." It is a struggle to take those words seriously in a world that has been working for a long time to make us think that the idea of singing to God in the cosmic choir is nothing but a fantasy concocted by pre-scientific minds. But struggle we must if we are to keep our singing in harmony with this fundamental biblical feature of the "new song." To preserve this feature from being blown away by a cynical scientism, we need to sing such texts with a firm conviction that they are not mere poetic conceits.

A related "pre-scientific fantasy" that the church fathers believed is Boethius's threefold division of music derived from Plato — *musica mundana, musica humana,* and *musica instrumentalis* (see p. 53). We have seen in Clement and Ambrose that this idea lends itself quite readily to Christianization. Another early Christian who picked up on this belief is Gregory of Nyssa, who, in his commentary *On the Inscriptions of the Psalms,* says that the universe is "a diverse and variegated musical harmony."

> For just as when the plectrum skillfully plucks the strings and produces a melody in the variety of the notes . . . so too the composition of the universe in the diversity of the things which are observed individually in the cosmos plucks itself by means of some structured and unchanging rhythm, producing the harmony of the parts in relation to the whole, and sings this polyphonic tune in everything. It is this tune which the mind hears without the use of our sense of hearing. It listens to the singing of the heavens by transcending and being above the faculties of sense-perception that belong to our flesh. This, it seems to me, is also how the great David was listening when he heard

the heavens describing the glory of the God who effects these things in them. . . .

The "concord of all creation" *(musica mundana)*, he goes on to say, "is truly a hymn of the glory of the inaccessible and inexpressible God."[21]

There is also *musica humana* in his thought. The musical harmony of the whole is also found in human nature, which is "a miniature cosmos . . . made in the image of the one who composed the cosmos" and in which "the music perceived in the universe is seen."[22] This belief had a long life in Christian thought. No one has given more beautiful Christian expression to the idea than John Milton in "At a Solemn Musick":

> Blest pair of Sirens, pledges of Heav'ns joy,
> Sphear-born harmonious Sisters, Voice, and Vers,
> Wed your divine sounds, and mixt power employ,
> Dead things with inbreath'd sense able to pierce,
> And to our high-rais'd phantasie present,
> That undisturbed Song of pure concent,
> Ay sung before the sapphire-colour'd throne
> To him who sits thereon
> With Saintly shout, and solemn Jubily,
> Where the bright Seraphim in burning row
> Their loud up-lifted trumpets blow,
> And the Cherubick host in thousand quires
> Touch their immortal Harps of golden whires,
> With those just Spirits that wear victorious Palms,
> Hymns devout and holy Psalms
> Singing everlastingly;
> That we on Earth with undiscording voice
> Might rightly answer that melodious noise;
> As once we did, till disproportion's sin
> Jarr'd against natures chime, and with harsh din
> Broke the fair music that all creatures made
> To their great Lord, whose love their motion sway'd
> In perfect Diapason, whilst they stood
> In first obedience, and their state of good.

21. *Treatise on the Inscriptions of the Psalms* I, 19-20; p. 89.
22. *Treatise on the Inscriptions of the Psalms* I, 22; pp. 90-91.

O may we soon again renew that Song,
And keep in tune with Heav'n, till God ere long
To his celestial consort us unite,
To live with him, and sing in endless morn of light.

The Platonic idea of *musica mundana,* which was Christianized in the early Christian era and remained in wide currency until the Enlightenment, deserves to remain in our image of the "new song" because it expresses a basic truth most beautifully: God is a God of order and harmony. It speaks to our imaginations of the Creator as an artist, the Creator who made the universe not only useful and mechanically efficient, but who also made it beautiful. At each word from the Creator, order emerged from chaos, and it was good — a kind of goodness that was not limited to, but certainly included, beauty. As Orthodox theologian David Bentley Hart says,

> There are abundant biblical reasons, quite apart from the influences of pagan philosophy, for Christians to speak of the *harmonia mundi:* in Scripture creation rejoices in God, proclaims his glory, sings before him; the pleasing conceits of pagan cosmology aside, theology has all the warrant it needs for speaking of creation as a divine composition, a magnificent music, whose measures and refrains rise up to the pleasure and the glory of God.[23]

But we live in a culture that believes it lives in a universe that has long since been "untuned." The "music of the spheres" is part of what C. S. Lewis calls "the discarded image,"[24] the discarding of which is traced by John Hollander in *The Untuning of the Sky.* Thomas Howard says that, when given the choice of "chance or the dance," our culture has opted for chance.[25] We live in a world in which "the mechanization of the world picture"[26] has long since taken place. Few look at the cosmos and see a dance or hear a symphony; most see, at best, a machine or, at worst, chaos. Regarding this mental shift, the historian of science E. J. Dijksterhuis says:

> That the adoption of the mechanistic view has had profound and far-reaching consequences for the whole of society is an historical fact

---

23. Hart, *The Beauty of the Infinite,* p. 275.
24. See Lewis's book so titled.
25. See Howard, *An Antique Drum* (later editions bear the title *Chance or the Dance*).
26. See E. J. Dijksterhuis's book so titled.

which gives rise to the most divergent opinions. Some commend it as a symptom of the gradual clarification of human thought, of the growing application of the only method that is capable of producing reliable results in every sphere of knowledge. . . . Others, though recognizing the outstanding importance it has had for the progress of our theoretical understanding and our practical control of nature, regard it as nothing short of disastrous in its general influence. . . . [T]hey are inclined to look upon the domination of the mind by the mechanistic conception as one of the main causes of the spiritual chaos into which the twentieth-century world has, in spite of all its technological progress, fallen.[27]

To argue that the mechanistic view is "one of the main causes of [our] spiritual chaos" would lead this discussion too far afield and turn this into quite a different chapter. Others have argued knowledgeably and eloquently for that position, and I recommend them to my readers.[28] I mention all of this here simply to suggest that we should not let our cultural conditioning cause us to reject out of hand the idea that, as Clement put it, the "new song" "composed the universe into melodious order, and tuned the discord of the elements to harmonious arrangement, so that the whole world might become harmony."[29] It makes a difference whether we think of the universe as a symphony or a machine, and I am suggesting that the shift in our cosmic imagery from *musica mundana* to *musica machina*[30] did not deepen our understanding of either the cosmos or of music.

One of the places our image of the cosmos makes a difference is in our practical music-making, because cosmic imagery is not as divorced from practical music-making as is often thought. In the ancient way of "looking at the cosmos musically, and at music cosmically,"[31] audible melodies and harmonies *(musica instrumentalis)* are meant to reflect, in Clement of Alexandria's words, the "melodious order" and "harmonious arrangement" of the cosmos *(musica mundana)*. In more modern terms, Jeremy Begbie puts

27. Dijksterhuis, *The Mechanization of the World Picture*, pp. 3-4.

28. See, for example, Thomas Howard, *An Antique Drum*.

29. *Exhortation to the Heathen*, p. 13.

30. This, I'm sorry to say, is John Calvin's term for the cosmos. See *Institutes of the Christian Religion*, ed. John T. McNeill, trans. Ford Lewis Battles (Philadelphia: The Westminster Press, 1960), Vol. I, p. 96, n. 2.

31. This succinct description is from Godwin, "The Revival of Speculative Music," p. 373.

it this way: "[N]ature is pervaded with a God-given order. Whatever else we say about music, if it is to honour God the Creator, then to some degree it should reflect and bear witness to this basic order permeating all things."[32] I realize how fanciful it sounds to say with Gregory of Nyssa that David listened for and heard the cosmic hymn, but isn't that, in a sense, something composers need to do to be good stewards of God's gift of sound? Shouldn't a composer be cognizant of the "God-given order . . . permeating all things" rather than being in touch with no "reality beyond [his or her] own inventive mind"[33] or, worse, his or her sentimental feelings?

With one of the truly seminal works of our civilization, *The City of God*, St. Augustine impressed deeply on Christian thought the imagery of two cities — the heavenly city and the earthly city, Jerusalem and Babylon. Love of God creates Jerusalem; love of self or the world creates Babylon. Jerusalem signifies peace; Babylon signifies confusion. Babylon is the city by which we are enslaved. Jerusalem is the city to which we long to return. The histories of the two cities have been inextricably mingled since the Fall and will remain so until the end of time. Each city has a song, and those two songs are also inextricably mingled for the duration of time.

But the outer bookends of the Bible, Genesis and Revelation, show the origin and destiny of both songs. "In the beginning God created. . . ." At each word from God, chaos gave way to order and harmony, and the song of the City of God, the "new song," came to earth when "the morning stars sang together" (Job 38:7). But the earthly song, the "old song," soon made its appearance as well. After the Fall had untuned creation, Genesis 4 tells us about the musical accomplishments of Cain's line by recording Lamech's boasting, taunting song:

> Adah and Zillah, hear my voice;
>> you wives of Lamech, listen to what I say:
> I have killed a man for wounding me,
>> a young man for striking me.
> If Cain's revenge is sevenfold,
>> then Lamech's is seventy-sevenfold.

(vv. 23-24)

---

32. Begbie, *Music in God's Purposes*, p. 11.
33. Begbie, *Music in God's Purposes*, p. 12.

Genesis 4 also informs us that Lamech's son Jubal "was the father of all who play the harp and flute." By pointing to the origin of the "old song" in the line of Cain, this passage warns us to be on guard. The "old song" is a counterfeit; it is not really a song at all. Dante knew this. As he takes us through the circles of the *Inferno,* we hear much noise but no music, a cacophony of sound but no song. In *Purgatorio,* music makes its appearance in the form of penitential psalms. *Paradiso* is bursting with music, the "new song."

The destiny of the two songs is told in Revelation: chapter 18 describes the doom of Babylon. A mighty angel tells her that "the sound of harpers and minstrels, of flute players and trumpeters, shall be heard in you no more." But the "new song," the song of the City of God, goes on forever. The four living creatures around the throne never stop singing:

> Holy, holy, holy is the Lord God Almighty,
>   who was, and is, and is to come.

They are joined by the twenty-four elders:

> Worthy are you, our Lord and God,
>   to receive glory and honor and power,
> for you created all things
>   and by your will they existed and were created.

These, in turn, are joined in ever-expanding circles by "the voice of many angels numbering myriads of myriads and thousands upon thousands," and by "every creature in heaven and on earth and under the earth and in the sea, and all that is in them," saying:

> To him who sits on the throne and to the Lamb
> be praise and honor and glory and power,
>   forever and ever!

The vision of the ultimate demise of the earthly counterfeit song and the eternal resonance of the heavenly song is a source of great hope. St. Augustine likens our hope for Jerusalem to an anchor "to safeguard us from shipwreck when the weather here is rough."

> When a ship is riding at anchor we rightly consider her to have made landfall already, for although she is still tossed by the waves she has in

a real sense been led out of the force of the winds and storms by her grip on the earth. In the same way our hope is fastened in the city of Jerusalem, safeguarding us against the perils of our voyage, and preventing us from being dashed on the rocks.

And even though we are still bodily in Babylon, we sing in Zion, for

anyone who sings in this hope is singing there, in Zion. . . . But you are in Babylon at present, surely? "Yes," replies this person, this lover, this citizen of Jerusalem. "Yes, I am in Babylon as to my body, but not in my heart. Both these things are true of me: that I am here in Babylon bodily, but not in heart, and that I am not in the place whence my song springs; for I sing not from my flesh, but from my heart." . . . With this in mind the apostle exhorted Jerusalem's citizens to sing canticles of love and to arouse their longing to return to that most fair city, to that vision of peace: *Sing hymns and psalms in your hearts to the Lord,* he tells them (Eph. 5:19). What does he mean by *sing in your hearts?* Do not let your songs be inspired by the place where you are now, by Babylon; but sing from where your hearts are, sing as from your habitation on high.[34]

Sing the "new song" to the Lord among the nations; sing the "new song" in this old world, which so desperately needs to hear it.

34. *Expositions of the Psalms* 64.3; p. 628.

Early Christian Hymns in Devotional Context

You make the going out of the morning and the evening
to shout for joy.

Psalm 65:8

From the rising of the sun to its setting
the name of the Lord is to be praised!

Psalm 113:3

The following collection of texts is meant to provide devotional context for early Christian hymns. The hymns can, of course, stand alone, as when sung by an individual in the course of a day's work or private prayer. But they reflect deeper nuances of meaning within the contexts of time, place, company, circumstances, and surrounding texts. Obviously, I can only supply the textual context here, but imaginative readers can re-create some of the rest in their minds.

Since morning and evening were the most common devotional times (and still are), I have chosen texts fitting (and often even specified) for those times of day. In each case the hymn is surrounded by three other types of text in early Christian devotion and worship — psalms, canticles, and prayers.

Morning Prayer

"Daybreak is a time set for prayer so that we dedicate the first stirrings of soul and mind to God, and take up no other consideration until made joyous by the thought of God."

St. Basil

Psalm: O God, you are my God, earnestly I seek you,
    my soul thirsts for you;
  my flesh faints for you,
    as in a dry and weary land where no water is.
  So I have looked upon you in the sanctuary,
    beholding your power and glory.
  Because your steadfast love is better than life,
    my lips will praise you.
  So I will bless you as long as I live;
    In your name I will lift up my hands. (63:1-4)

Hymn: O splendor of God's glory bright,
  the one who brings the light from light,
  O Light of Light, light's Living Spring,
  O Day, all days illumining.

  True Sun, let fall on us your glance
  in all its royal radiance,
  the Spirit's sanctifying beam
  upon our earthly senses stream.

  The Father too our prayers implore,
  Father of glory evermore,
  the Father of all grace and might,
  to banish sin from our delight:

  To guide whate'er we nobly do,
  with love all envy to subdue,
  to make ill-fortune turn to fair,
  and give us grace our wrongs to bear.

Our mind be in His keeping placed,
our body true to Him and chaste,
where only faith her fire shall feed
to burn the tares of Satan's seed.

And Christ to us for food shall be,
from Him our drink that springs up free,
the Spirit's wine, that makes us whole,
and mocking not, exalts the soul.

Rejoicing may this day go hence,
like virgin dawn our innocence,
like fiery noon our faith appear,
nor know the gloom of twilight drear.

St. Ambrose (tr. Robert Bridges [alt.])

Prayer: Benefactor of all who turn to you, you who make your light shine in every darkness, who gives growth to every seed, who makes spiritual grace blossom and grow, have pity on me, Lord. Build me as a priceless temple, look not upon my sinfulness, for if you take account of my iniquities, I cannot stand before your face. But in accordance with your great compassion, and with the fullness of your mercies, remove my sins through Jesus Christ, our Lord, your only-begotten, most holy Son, the physician of our souls. Through him, glory to you and power and all greatness and magnificence forever and ever, ceaselessly and always! Amen. (Tr. Lucien Deiss, p. 253)

Canticle: Glory be to God on high,
and on earth peace, to all goodwill.
We praise you, we bless you, we worship you, we glorify you,
we give thanks to you for your great glory.
O Lord God, heavenly King, God the Father Almighty.
O Lord, the only begotten Son, Jesus Christ,
O Lord God, Lamb of God, Son of the Father,
who takes away the sins of the world, have mercy on us;
who takes away the sins of the world, receive our prayer;
who sits at the right hand of God the Father, have mercy

on us.
For you alone are holy, you alone are the Lord;
you alone, O Christ, with the Holy Spirit, are most high
in the glory of God the Father. Amen.

*   *   *

Evening Prayer

"But I wish also that even in your bedchamber you weave together psalms with the Lord's prayer in frequent interchange, both so you stand vigil and before drowsiness suffuses your body; so that at the beginning of rest sleep finds you free from anxiety over secular affairs and meditating upon those of heaven."

St. Ambrose

Psalm: O Lord, I call upon you; hasten to me!
Give ear to my voice when I call to you!
Let my prayer be counted as incense before you,
and the lifting up of my hands as an evening sacrifice!

(141:1-2)

Prayer: Our Father in heaven, hallowed be your name.
Your kingdom come, your will be done, on earth as it
is in heaven.
Give us today our daily bread,
and forgive us our debts as we forgive our debtors.
And lead us not into temptation, but deliver us from evil,
For yours is the kingdom, and the power, and the glory
forever. Amen.

Hymn: Our God who did all things create,
and still the heavens does regulate,
who clothes each day with splendid light,
and decks with gracious sleep the night;

Day sinks; we thank you for your gift,
night comes; to you again we lift

213

our prayers and vows and hymns, that we
against all ills defended be.

That so, when shadows round us creep
and all is hid in darkness deep,
faith may not feel the gloom; and night
borrow from faith's clear gleam new light.

From snares of sense, Lord, keep us free;
on you alone let our dreams be.
Let not the envious foe draw near
to vex our quiet rest with fear.

Hail we the Father and the Son
and Son's and Father's Spirit, one
blest Trinity who all obey;
O guard the souls that to you pray. Amen.

from the *Liturgia Horarum*. tr. F. A. Wright (alt.)

Prayer: We give you thanks, O God, through your Son, Jesus Christ, our Lord, for having enlightened us by revealing to us the incorruptible light. Having ended the course of this day and reached the edge of night, having been filled by the light of day which you create for our joy, we now possess, through your kindness, the evening light. Therefore do we praise you and glorify you through your Son, Jesus Christ, our Lord. Through him be glory yours, power and honor, with the Holy Spirit, now and always and for ever and ever. Amen. (Tr. Lucien Deiss, p. 147)

Canticle: Lord, now you are letting your servant depart in peace, according to your word;
for my eyes have seen your salvation
that you prepared in the presence of all peoples,
a light for revelation to the Gentiles,
and for the glory of your people Israel.

The World of Early Christianity

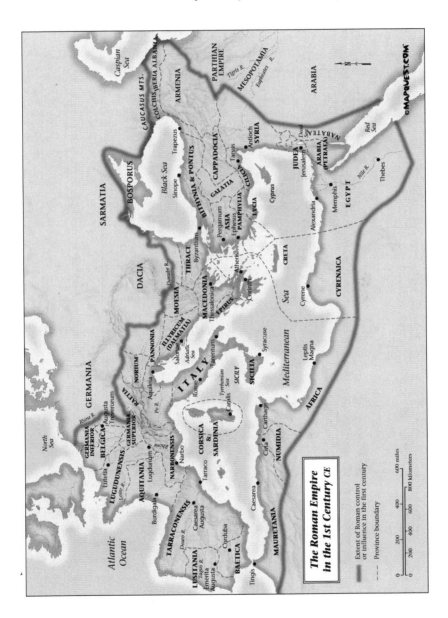

The Roman Empire
in the 1st Century CE

Extent of Roman control
or influence in the first century

Province boundary

Timeline

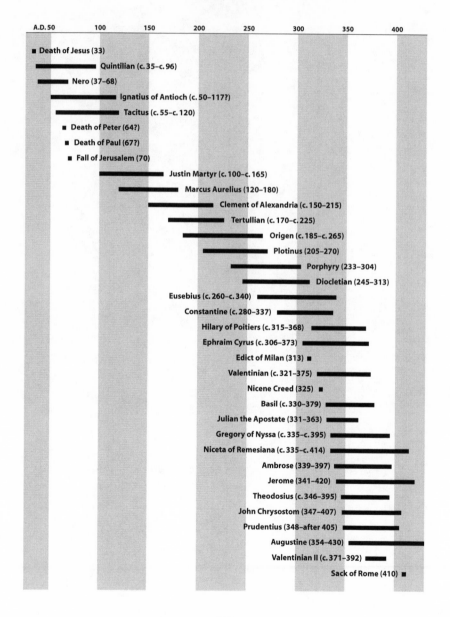

For Further Reading

The following books contain brief, engagingly written biographies of some of the major early church fathers.

Payne, Robert. *The Fathers of the Western Church* and *The Fathers of the Eastern Church* (New York: Dorset Press, 1989). *The Fathers of the Eastern Church* was originally titled *Holy Fire*.

von Campenhausen, Hans. *The Fathers of the Church* (Peabody, Mass.: Hendrickson Publishers, 1998). This is a combined edition of *The Fathers of the Greek Church* and *The Fathers of the Latin Church*.

Two invaluable introductions to early Christian writings are:

Ramsey, Boniface. *Beginning to Read the Fathers.* New York: Paulist Press, 1985.

Wilken, Robert Louis. *The Spirit of Early Christian Thought: Seeking the Face of God.* New Haven: Yale University Press, 2003.

For a detailed account of the development of doctrine during the early Christian era, see Jaroslav Pelikan, *The Emergence of the Catholic Tradition (100-600)* (Chicago: The University of Chicago Press, 1971). This is the first volume of Pelikan's magisterial *The Christian Tradition: A History of the Development of Doctrine.*

For a basic introduction to worship in the early church, see Paul Bradshaw, *Early Christian Worship: A Basic Introduction to Ideas and Practice* (Collegeville, Minnesota: Liturgical Press, 1996), and Kenneth Stevenson, *The First Rites: Worship in the Early Church* (Collegeville, Minnesota: Liturgical Press,

1989). For the scholarly study of worship in the early church, begin with Paul Bradshaw, *The Search for the Origins of Christian Worship: Sources and Methods for the Study of Early Liturgy* (New York: Oxford University Press, 1992).

Books dealing principally with music in the early Christian church are rare. Johann Quasten's *Music and Worship in Pagan and Christian Antiquity* has been a standard in the field since it first appeared in German in 1929. It remains a valuable resource and is available in an English translation by Boniface Ramsey (Washington, D.C.: National Association of Pastoral Musicians, 1983). Edward Foley's *Foundations of Christian Music* (Collegeville, Minn.: Liturgical Press, 1996) is an interesting recent study that focuses on the auditory environment of liturgical music before Constantine.

Works Cited

Primary Sources: Anthologies

A Classical Storybook. Edited by Morris Bishop. Ithaca: Cornell University Press, 1970.

Medieval Latin Lyrics. Translated by Helen Waddell. Harmondsworth, UK: Penguin Books, 1952.

Music in Early Christian Literature. Edited by James McKinnon. Cambridge Readings in the Literature of Music. John Stevens and Peter le Huray, gen. eds. Cambridge, UK: Cambridge University Press, 1987.

Music in the Western World: A History in Documents. Selected and annotated by Piero Weiss and Richard Taruskin. New York: Schirmer Books, 1983.

Prayers of the Eucharist: Early and Reformed. Translated and edited by R. C. D. Jasper and G. J. Cuming. Collegeville, MN: The Liturgical Press, 1990.

Source Readings in Music History. Revised and enlarged edition. Edited by Oliver Strunk. Leo Treitler, gen. ed. Vol. 2: *The Early Christian Period and the Latin Middle Ages,* ed. James McKinnon. Vol. 3: *The Renaissance,* ed. Gary Tomlinson. New York: W. W. Norton and Co., 1998.

The Springtime of the Liturgy. Edited by Lucien Deiss. Trans. Matthew J. O'Connell. Collegeville, MN: Liturgical Press, 1979.

Primary Sources in English Translation

Ambrose of Milan. *Hexameron.* Trans. John J. Savage. The Fathers of the Church, Vol. 42. Washington, DC: The Catholic University of America Press, 1985.

———. *Letters.* Trans. Sister Mary Melchoir Beyenka. The Fathers of the Church, Vol. 26. Washington, DC: The Catholic University of America Press, 1967.

Ammianus Marcellinus. *Books of History.* Trans. John C. Rolfe. Loeb Classical Library. Cambridge, MA: Harvard University Press, 1935-1939.

Arnobius of Sicca. *Against the Pagans.* Trans. George E. McCracken. Ancient Christian Writers, No. 8. Westminster, MD: The Newman Press, 1949.

Augustine of Hippo. *The City of God.* Trans. Marcus Dods. New York: The Modern Library, 1950.

———. *Confessions.* Trans. Henry Chadwick. Oxford: Oxford University Press, 1981.

———. *Expositions of the Psalms.* Six vols. Trans. Maria Boulding. Hyde Park, NY: New City Press, 2000-2004.

———. *On Christian Doctrine.* Trans. D. W. Robertson, Jr. New York: Macmillan Publishing Co., 1958.

———. *On the Trinity.* Trans. Arthur West Haddan. A Select Library of the Nicene and Post-Nicene Fathers. Ed. Philip Schaff. Grand Rapids, MI: Wm. B. Eerdmans Publishing Co., 1956.

———. *Tractates on the First Epistle of John.* Trans. John W. Rettig. The Fathers of the Church, Vol. 92. Washington, DC: The Catholic University of America Press, 1995.

Basil of Caesarea. *Concerning the Holy Spirit.* Trans. David G. K. Taylor. The Syriac Versions of *De Spirito Sancto.* Louvain: Peeters, 1999.

Chrysostom, John. *Address on Vainglory and the Right Way for Parents to Bring Up Their Children.* Trans. M. L. W. Laistner. In *Christianity and Pagan Culture in the Later Roman Empire.* Ithaca, NY: Cornell University Press, 1951.

———. *Homilies on Colossians.* Trans. Gross Alexander. A Select Library of the Nicene and Post-Nicene Fathers, Vol. 13. Ed. Philip Schaff. Grand Rapids: Eerdmans, 1956.

———. *Homilies on the Epistles of Paul to the Corinthians.* Trans. Talbot W. Chambers. A Select Library of the Nicene and Post-Nicene Fathers, Vol. 12. Ed. Philip Schaff. Grand Rapids: Eerdmans, 1956.

———. *Homilies on the Gospel of St. Matthew.* Trans. M. B. Riddle. A Select Library of the Nicene and Post-Nicene Fathers, Vol. 9. Ed. Philip Schaff. Grand Rapids: Eerdmans, 1956.

————. *On the Priesthood*. Trans. W. R. W. Stephens and T. P. Brandram. A Select Library of theNicene and Post-Nicene Fathers, Vol. 9. Ed. Philip Schaff. Grand Rapids: Eerdmans, 1956.

Cicero. *In Defense of Sextus Roscius of Ameria*. Trans. John Henry Freese. Loeb Classical Library. New York: G. P. Putnam's Sons, 1930.

————. *Laws*. Trans. Clinton Walker Keyes. Loeb Classical Library. New York: G. P. Putnam's Sons, 1928.

Clement of Alexandria. *Exhortation to the Heathen*. Ante-Nicene Fathers, Vol. 2. Grand Rapids: Eerdmans, 1986.

————. *The Instructor*. Ante-Nicene Fathers, Vol. 2. Grand Rapids: Eerdmans, 1986.

————. *Miscellanies*. Ante-Nicene Fathers, Vol. 2. Grand Rapids: Eerdmans, 1986.

Clement of Rome. *The First Epistle to the Corinthians*. Trans. Maxwell Staniforth. Revised by Andrew Louth. Early Christian Writings: The Apostolic Fathers. New York: Penguin Books, 1988.

Cyril of Alexandria. *Mystagogical Lectures*. Trans. Leo P. McCauley. The Fathers of the Church, Vol. 2. Washington, DC: The Catholic University of America Press, 1970.

The Epistle to Diognetus. Trans. Maxwell Staniforth. Revised by Andrew Louth. Early Christian Writings: The Apostolic Fathers. New York: Penguin Books, 1988.

Eusebius. *The History of the Church*. Trans. G. A. Williamson. Baltimore: Penguin Books, 1967.

Gregory of Nyssa. *The Life of Macrina*. The Fathers of the Church, Vol. 58. Ascetical Works. Trans. Virginia Woods Cullahan. Washington, DC: The Catholic University of America Press, 1967.

————. *Treatise on the Inscriptions of the Psalms*. Trans. Ronald E. Heine. Oxford: The Clarendon Press, 1995.

Ignatius of Antioch. *Epistle to the Ephesians*. Trans. Maxwell Staniforth. Revised by Andrew Louth. Early Christian Writings: The Apostolic Fathers. New York: Penguin Books, 1988.

Justin Martyr. *Dialogue with Trypho*. Trans. Thomas B. Falls. Revised by Thomas P. Halton. Selections from the Fathers of the Church, Vol. 3. Washington, DC: The Catholic University of America Press, 2003.

————. *The First and Second Apologies*. Trans. Leslie William Barnard. Ancient Christian Writers, No. 56. New York: Paulist Press, 1997.

Martial. *Epigrams*. Volume II. Trans. D. R. Shackelton Bailey. Loeb Classical Library. Cambridge, MA: Harvard University Press, 1993.

Minucius Felix. *Octavius*. Trans. Gerald H Rendall. Loeb Classical Library. Cambridge, MA: Harvard University Press, 1984.

Palladius. *Dialogue on the Life of St. John Chrysostom*. Trans. Robert T. Meyer. Ancient Christian Writers, No. 45. Ed. Johannes Quasten, et al. New York: The Newman Press, 1985.

Plato. *Timaeus*. Trans. H. D. P. Lee. Baltimore: Penguin Books, 1965.

Pliny the Younger. *Letters*. Trans. Betty Radice. Loeb Classical Library. Cambridge, MA: Harvard University Press, 1969.

Quintilian. *On the Instruction of an Orator*. Volume 1. Trans. H. E. Butler. Loeb Classical Library. Cambridge, MA: Harvard University Press, 1963.

Seneca. *Moral Letters to Lucius*. Trans. Richard M. Gummere. Loeb Classical Library. New York: G. P. Putnam's Sons, 1917.

Sozomen. *A History of the Church*. London: Samuel Bagster and Sons, 1846.

Suetonius. *Lives of the Caesars*. Trans. J. C. Rolfe. Loeb Classical Library. New York: The Macmillan Co., 1914.

Tacitus. *The Histories and the Annals*. 4 volumes. Trans. Clifford H. Moore and John Jackson. The Loeb Classical Library. Cambridge, MA: Harvard University Press, 1937.

Tertullian. *Against Praxeas*. Ante-Nicene Fathers, Vol. 3. Grand Rapids: Eerdmans Publishing Co., 1951.

———. *Apology*. Trans. T. R. Glover. The Loeb Classical Library. New York: G. P. Putnam's Sons, 1931.

———. *On Prayer*. Trans. Sister Emily Joseph Daly. The Fathers of the Church, Vol. 40. Washington, DC: The Catholic University of America Press, 1959.

———. *On Repentance*. Ante-Nicene Fathers, Vol. 3. Grand Rapids: Eerdmans, 1951.

———. *On Spectacles*. Trans. T. R. Glover. The Loeb Classical Library. New York: G. P. Putnam's Sons, 1931.

———. *On the Flesh of Christ*. Ante-Nicene Fathers, Vol. 3. Grand Rapids: Eerdmans, 1951.

———. *The Prescription Against Heretics*. Ante-Nicene Fathers, Vol. 3. Grand Rapids: Eerdmans, 1951.

———. *To His Wife*. Trans. William P. Le Saint. Ancient Christian Writers, No. 13. Ed. Johannes Quasten, et al. New York: The Newman Press, 1956.

———. *To Scapula*. Ante-Nicene Fathers, Vol. 3. Grand Rapids: Eerdmans, 1951.

Secondary Sources

Balsdon, J. P. V. D. *Life and Leisure in Ancient Rome.* London: The Bodley Head, 1969.

Barnes, Timothy David. *Tertullian: A Historical and Literary Study.* Oxford: Clarendon Press, 1971.

Begbie, Jeremy. *Music in God's Purposes.* Edinburgh: The Handsel Press Ltd., 1989.

Blaiklock, E. M. *The Christian in Pagan Society.* London: The Tyndale Press, 1951.

Bobrinskoy, Boris. "The Holy Spirit in the Liturgy." *The Indian Journal of Theology* 12 (1963): 123-132.

Bondi, Roberta C. *To Love as God Loves: Conversations with the Early Church.* Philadelphia: Fortress Press, 1987.

Booth, Wayne C. *The Company We Keep: An Ethics of Fiction.* Berkeley: University of California Press, 1988.

Bradshaw, Paul F. *The Search for the Origins of Christian Worship.* New York: Oxford University Press, 1992.

Brown, Peter. *The Body and Society: Men, Women, and Sexual Renunciation in Early Christianity.* New York: Columbia University Press, 1988.

Bruce, F. F. *The Spreading Flame.* Grand Rapids: Eerdmans, 1958.

Burke, Kenneth. *The Rhetoric of Religion: Studies in Logology.* Berkeley: University of California Press, 1970.

Butterfield, Herbert. *Christianity and History.* New York: Charles Scribner's Sons, 1949.

Chambers, E. K. *The Medieval Stage,* Vol. 1. Oxford: Oxford University Press, 1903.

Charlesworth, James H. *Critical Reflections on the Odes of Solomon,* Vol. 1. Sheffield, England: Sheffield Academic Press, 1998.

Colish, Marcia. *The Mirror of Language.* Lincoln, NE: University of Nebraska Press, 1983.

Connelly, Joseph. *Hymns of the Roman Liturgy.* London: Longmans, Green and Co., 1957.

Davies, J. G. *The Early Christian Church.* Grand Rapids, MI: Baker Book House, 1980.

Dijksterhuis, E. J. *The Mechanization of the World Picture.* London: Oxford University Press, 1969.

Dill, Samuel. *Roman Society from Nero to Marcus Aurelius.* Reprint of 2nd ed., 1905. New York: Gordon Press, 1973.

Dix, Dom Gregory. *The Shape of the Liturgy.* 2nd ed. London: Dacre Press, 1945.

Dodds, E. R. *Pagan and Christian in an Age of Anxiety.* New York: W. W. Norton and Co., 1970.

Dronke, Peter. *The Medieval Lyric.* New York: Harper and Row, 1968.

Dudden, F. Hommes. *The Life and Times of St. Ambrose.* 2 vols. Oxford: Oxford University Press, 1935.

Eliot, T. S. "Religion and Literature." In *Religion and Modern Literature: Essays in Theory and Criticism,* edited by G. B. Tennyson and Edward E. Erickson, Jr., pp. 21-30. Grand Rapids: Eerdmans, 1975.

Ferguson, John. *Clement of Alexandria.* New York: Twayne Publishers, Inc., 1974.

Foley, Edward. *Foundations of Christian Music: The Music of Pre-Constantinian Christianity.* Collegeville, MN: Liturgical Press, 1996.

Frend, W. H. C. *The Early Church.* Philadelphia: Fortress Press, 1982.

———. *The Rise of Christianity.* Philadelphia: Fortress Press, 1984.

Gallagher, Susan, and Roger Lundin. *Literature Through the Eyes of Faith.* San Francisco: Harper and Row Publishers, 1989.

Gelineau, Joseph. *Voices and Instruments in Christian Worship.* Collegeville, MN: Liturgical Press, 1964.

Gilbert, Katharine Everett, and Helmut Kuhn. *A History of Esthetics.* New York: The Macmillan Co., 1939.

Godwin, Joscelyn. "The Revival of Speculative Music." *The Musical Quarterly* 68 (1982): 373-389.

Harrison, Carol. "Rhetoric of Scripture and Preaching." In *Augustine and His Critics,* edited by Robert Dodaro and George Lawless, pp. 214-230. New York: Routledge, 2000.

Hart, David Bentley. *The Beauty of the Infinite: The Aesthetics of Christian Faith.* Grand Rapids: Eerdmans, 2003.

Hollander, John. *The Untuning of the Sky.* New York: W. W. Norton and Co., 1970.

Hoppin, Richard. *Medieval Music.* New York: W. W. Norton and Co., 1978.

Howard, Thomas. *An Antique Drum.* Philadelphia: J. B. Lippincott Co., 1969.

Hurtado, Larry W. *Lord Jesus Christ: Devotion to Jesus in Earliest Christianity.* Grand Rapids: Eerdmans, 2003.

Isenberg, Wesley W. "Hymnody: Greek." In *Key Words in Church Music,* edited by Carl Schalk, pp. 185-192. St. Louis: Concordia Publishing House, 1978.

Julian, John. *A Dictionary of Hymnology.* New York: Dover Publications, 1957.

Kelly, J. N. D. *Golden Mouth: The Story of John Chrysostom — Ascetic, Preacher, Bishop.* Grand Rapids: Baker, 1995.

Kuyper, Abraham. *Lectures on Calvinsim.* Grand Rapids: Eerdmans, 1931.

Laistner, M. L. W. *Christianity and Pagan Culture in the Later Roman Empire.* Ithaca, NY: Cornell University Press, 1951.

L'Engle, Madeleine. *Walking on Water.* New York: Bantam Books, 1980.

Lewis, C. S. *The Discarded Image: An Introduction to Medieval and Renaissance Literature.* Cambridge, UK: Cambridge University Press, 1964.

————. Introduction to *St. Athanasius on the Incarnation.* London: A. R. Mowbray and Co., 1963.

————. *Reflections on the Psalms.* New York: Harcourt, Brace and World, Inc., 1958.

Macdonald, A. B. *Christian Worship in the Primitive Church.* Edinburgh: T&T Clark, 1935.

Martin, Ralph. *Worship in the Early Church.* Westwood, New Jersey: Fleming H. Revell Co., 1964.

Marty, Martin. *A Short History of Christianity.* Philadelphia: Fortress Press, 1987.

McKinnon, James. "The Church Fathers and Musical Instruments." Unpublished Ph.D. dissertation. Columbia University, 1965.

————. "The Question of Psalmody in the Ancient Synagogue." *Early Music History* 6 (1986): 159-191.

Meeks, Wayne A. *The Moral World of the First Christians.* Philadelphia: The Westminster Press, 1986.

Merton, Thomas. *The Seven Storey Mountain.* New York: Harcourt Brace Jovanovich, 1976.

Muller, Richard A. "Tertullian and Church Growth." *Calvin Seminary Forum* 1 (Fall 1994): 8.

O'Connell, Robert. *St. Augustine's Confessions: The Odyssey of Soul.* New York: Fordham University Press, 1989.

Paredi, Angelo. *Saint Ambrose: His Life and Times.* Trans. M. Joseph Costelloe. Notre Dame, IN: University of Notre Dame Press, 1964.

Pelikan, Jaroslav. *The Christian Tradition: A History of the Development of Doctrine.* Vol. 1: *The Emergence of the Catholic Tradition (100-600).* Chicago: The University of Chicago Press, 1971.

Piper, Otto. "The Apocalypse of John and the Liturgy of the Ancient Church." *Church History* 20 (1951): 10-22.

Plantinga, Cornelius, Jr., and Sue A. Rozeboom. *Discerning the Spirits: A Guide to Thinking about Christian Worship Today.* Grand Rapids: Eerdmans, 2003.

Quasten, Johannes. *Music and Worship in Pagan and Christian Antiquity.* Trans. Boniface Ramsey. Washington, DC: National Association of Pastoral Musicians, 1983.

————. *Patrology.* 4 vols. Utrecht: Spectrum Publishers, 1950-1960. Vol. 4, edited by Angelo di Berardino. Westminster, MD: The Newman Press, 1960.

Rand, E. K. *The Founders of the Middle Ages.* New York: Dover Publications, Inc., 1957.

Smith, J. A. "The Ancient Synagogue, the Early Church and Singing." *Music and Letters* 65 (1984): 1-16.

Smith, William S. *Musical Aspects of the New Testament.* Amsterdam: W. Ten Have, 1962.

Spence, Sarah. *Rhetorics of Reason and Desire: Vergil, Augustine, and the Troubadours.* Ithaca, NY: Cornell University Press, 1988.

Spitzer, Leo. *Classical and Christian Ideas of World Harmony.* Baltimore: The Johns Hopkins Press, 1963.

Stewart, James S. *A Man in Christ.* New York: Harper and Brothers, n.d.

Tollington, R. B. *Clement of Alexandria: A Study in Christian Liberalism.* London: Williams and Norgate, 1914.

Van Dyk, John. "Church and World in Early Christianity." *Pro Rege* 8 (1979): 2-8.

Webber, Robert E. *Common Roots.* Grand Rapids: Zondervan Publishing House, 1978.

Wellesz, Egon. *A History of Byzantine Music and Hymnography.* 2nd ed., revised and enlarged. Oxford: Oxford University Press, 1962.

Wells, Ronald A. *History Through the Eyes of Faith.* San Francisco: Harper and Row Publishers, 1989.

Werner, Eric. *The Sacred Bridge.* New York: Columbia University Press, 1959.

Wilhelm, James J. *Medieval Song.* New York: E. P. Dutton and Co., Inc., 1971.

Wilken, Robert Louis. *John Chrysostom and the Jews: Rhetoric and Reality in the Late Fourth Century.* Berkeley: University of California Press, 1983.

————. *The Spirit of Early Christian Thought.* New Haven: Yale University Press, 2003.

Williams, Charles. *The Descent of the Dove.* Grand Rapids: Eerdmans, 1939.

Williams, Daniel D. "The Significance of St. Augustine Today." In *A Companion to the Study of St. Augustine,* edited by Roy W. Battenhouse. London: Oxford University Press, 1950.

Williams, D. H. *Retrieving the Tradition and Renewing Evangelicalism.* Grand Rapids: Eerdmans, 1999.

Winn, James. *Unsuspected Eloquence: A History of the Relations Between Poetry and Music.* New Haven: Yale University Press, 1981.

Wolterstorff, Nicholas. "Trumpets, Ashes, and Tears." *Reformed Journal* 36, No. 2 (1986): 19-22.

Permissions

The author and publisher gratefully acknowledge permission to reprint material from the following sources:

Excerpts from Augustine, *The Confessions*, edited and translated by H. Chadwick. By permission of Oxford University Press.

Excerpts from Augustine, *Tractates on the First Epistle of John*, translated by John W. Rettig, The Fathers of the Church, volume 92 (1995). Used with permission: The Catholic University of America Press, Washington DC.

Excerpts from *Source Readings in Music History*, Leo Treitler, general editor, volume 2 (Norton, 1998). Reprinted by permission.

Excerpts from Suetonius: Reprinted by permission of the publishers and the Trustees of the Loeb Classical Library from *Suetonius: Volume II*, Loeb Classical Library® volume 38, translated by J. C. Rolfe, Cambridge, Mass.: Harvard University Press, 1914. The Loeb Classical Library® is a registered trademark of the President and Fellows of Harvard College.

Excerpts from Tertullian, *On Prayer*, translated by Sister Emily Joseph Daly, The Fathers of the Church, volume 40 (1959). Used with permission: The Catholic University of America Press, Washington DC.

Index

Made in the USA
Columbia, SC
19 October 2024

44723071R00148